Praise for Heidi Julavits's

THE FOLDED CLOCK

"A profound meditation on the passing of time."
                        —*Entertainment Weekly*

"Cleverly crafted [and] thoughtfully entertaining. . . . Julavits's best book yet."   —*O, The Oprah Magazine*

"Julavits's do-over, an adult account that she begins in order to reclaim the solitary day as a unit of time—and it would appear, to reclaim the 'genre,' too."
                        —*The Los Angeles Review of Books*

"[Julavits] has a native's eye for the small, sometimes indiscernible quirks that define local behavior. . . . There is glorious slippage, just enough to see [the] author in the various stages of her life, adhering to the truth as she sees it."   —*Minneapolis Star Tribune*

"[Julavits] takes moments in time and blows them up with thought and introspection and tangential relations. She condenses them down into polished nuggets. . . . Her mind is so smart and delightful and open."
                        —*The Rumpus*

"I was utterly compelled by the big-hearted engine of rigor and wonder that drives [Julavits's meditations]: her live electric mind."   —Leslie Jamison,
                        author of *The Empathy Exams*

"Hilarious. . . . The thrill is where Julavits takes us."

—*New York Post*

"Daring and inquisitive. . . . By probing deeply her interior and exterior environments, Julavits shows us our potential for expansion in all areas of our lives, even the most mundane."

—*Bustle*

"Blur[s] the lines between contemplation and revelation, fact and fiction. . . . Julavits reveals a whole lot, in often-flawless prose, about motherhood, time, petty jealousies, grand debates, and the irresistible attractions of *The Bachelorette*."

—*Vulture*

"Irresistible and, at times, transcendent. . . . [Julavits is] like a mash-up of Lena Dunham and Kierkegaard. Which is to say, the book is at once raunchy, outrageous and funny, wistful, contemplative and smart." —*Portland Press Herald*

"A joy to read. It's a treasure house of revealing stories, and a thought-provoking illustration of the way that everyday encounters . . . provoke kaleidoscopic and dramatic memories to unfold within us. . . . This is a book worth reading and rereading." —Rebecca Curtis, author of *Twenty Grand: And Other Tales of Love and Money*

"Intricate and delicately worked. . . . Julavits transforms her diary into an exceptional work of art." —*BookPage*

"*The Folded Clock* is evidence of Julavits at her finest—an incisive and penetrating thinker, as exacting as she is forgiving in her observations about the self and the world."

—*Electric Literature*

Heidi Julavits

THE FOLDED CLOCK

Heidi Julavits is also the author of four critically acclaimed novels (*The Vanishers*, *The Uses of Enchantment*, *The Effect of Living Backwards*, and *The Mineral Palace*) and coeditor, with Sheila Heti and Leanne Shapton, of the *New York Times* bestseller *Women in Clothes*. Her fiction has appeared in *Harper's Magazine*, *McSweeney's*, and *The Best American Short Stories*, among other places. She's a founding editor of *The Believer* magazine and the recipient of a Guggenheim Fellowship. She lives in Manhattan, where she teaches at Columbia University. She was born and raised in Portland, Maine.

thefoldedclock.tumblr.com

THE FOLDED CLOCK

A Diary

HEIDI JULAVITS

Anchor Books
A Division of Penguin Random House LLC
New York

FIRST ANCHOR BOOKS EDITION, MARCH 2016

Copyright © 2015 by Heidi Julavits

All rights reserved. Published in the United States by Anchor Books, a division of Penguin Random House LLC, New York, and distributed in Canada by Random House of Canada, a division of Penguin Random House Canada Ltd., Toronto. Originally published in hardcover in the United States by Doubleday, a division of Penguin Random House LLC, New York, in 2015.

Anchor Books and colophon are registered trademarks of Penguin Random House LLC.

The Library of Congress has cataloged the Doubleday edition as follows:
Julavits, Heidi.
The folded clock : a diary / Heidi Julavits. — First edition.
pages cm
1. Julavits, Heidi—Diaries.
2. Authors, American—21st century—Diaries.
3. Women authors, American—21st century—Diaries.
4. Women—United States—Diaries.   5. Wives—United States—Diaries.
6. Mothers—United States—Diaries.   I. Title.
PS3560.U522Z46 2015   818'.603—dc23   2014031562

Anchor Books Trade Paperback ISBN: 978-0-8041-7144-1
eBook ISBN: 978-0-385-53899-2

Book design by Maria Carella

www.anchorbooks.com

Printed in the United States of America
10 9 8 7 6 5 4 3 2

FOR BEN

This book is an accounting of two years of my life. I have altered identifying characteristics to protect people's privacy.

THE FOLDED CLOCK

Today I wondered *What is the worth of a day?* Once, a day was long. It was bright and then it wasn't, meals happened, and school happened, and sports practice, maybe, happened, and two days from this day there would be a test, or an English paper would be due, or there would be a party for which I'd been waiting, it would seem, for years. Days were ages. Love bloomed and died in a day. Rages flared and were forgotten and replaced by new rages, also forgotten. Within a day there were discernible hours, and clocks with hands that ticked out each new minute. I would think, *Will this day never end?* By nightfall, I'd feel like a war had been fought. I was wounded; sleep was not enough to heal me. Days would linger in my nerves, aftershocks registered on the electrical plain. Days made a physical impact. Days could hurt.

Not anymore. The "day" no longer exists. The smallest unit of time I experience is the week. But in recent years the week, like the penny, has also become a uselessly small currency. The month is, more typically, the smallest unit of time I experience. But truthfully months are not so noticeable either. Months happen when things are, with increasing rapidity, due. Tuitions are due, and rent is due, and the health insurance is due. A month is marked, not by a sense that time has passed, but by a series of automated withdrawals. I look at my bank account, near zero, and realize, *It must be March.*

Since I am suddenly ten years older than I was, it seems, one year ago, I decided to keep a diary. Like many people I kept a diary when I was young. Starting at age eight I wrote in this diary every day, and every day I began my entry with "Today I." Today I went to school. Today I went to Andrea's house. Today I played in the cemetery. Today I did nothing.

Recently I cited this childhood diary-keeping as the reason I became a writer. I needed to explain to a roomful of people, most of them over seventy years old, *why.* I could have answered the question in a variety of ways. But I try to anticipate the needs of my audience. I desire to give them an anecdote customized to resonate with their life situation. This desire guides my answers more strongly than truth. What did these people want or need to hear? If I were, like them, nearing the end of my life, I imagine I'd be impatient with equivocation and uncertainty. I imagine I would desire clear stories because soon I'd be in a grave where my life would be condensed to a name, a date, some commas, a category ("Wife").

So I told a clean story. A *why* story. I said that I became a writer because on one March day, when I was ten, during the interminable gray-scale finale of a typical Maine winter, my father took me to the mall because we'd long ago run out of ways to kill time before spring. At the mall, he bought a color TV. On certain practical and emotional levels, his expenditure made sense. Our old TV was black-and-white. We switched between the two and a half available channels by using a pair of pliers to rotate a metal stub, once connected to a dial (now lost). The original antenna (also lost) had been replaced by a clothes hanger. The whole contraption was so pathetic and downtrodden, who could blame a man for trying to bring literal color into the lives of his wife and children, emotionally slogging their way through another mud season?

Unfortunately, my father did not have permission to buy a color TV. At an earlier point in time, he'd bought something else without permission, and before that something else, and now he was deeply in permissions debt. He would never get permission to buy anything ever again. Every acquisition was unauthorized. This did not prevent him from buying the TV.

My father also bought me, if I promised to write in it, a diary.

I started the diary the next day. I wrote:

Today I woke up and watched TV.

I found and reread these diaries about ten years ago. Before I found and reread them, I was proud of what the fact of my rigorous diary keeping predicted about me. I'd been fated to be a writer! I had proof of my doggedness—many volumes of it. I imagined the diaries published at some future date, when my literary fame might bestow upon them an artistic and biographical value. I believed I was born to posthumous greatness. I often imagined myself more famous when dead than when alive.

The actual diaries, however, fail to corroborate the myth I'd concocted for myself. They reveal me to possess the mind, not of a future writer, but of a future paranoid tax auditor. I exhibited no imagination, no trace of a style, no wit, no personality. Each entry is an accounting of (or an expressed anxiety about) my school performance.

> *Today at school I got a 100 on my math test and I finished my science assignment. I am all set for my literature report but I'm really scared!*
> *Today I gave my report and I got an A.*
> *Today I didn't finish my worksheet and I am in trouble.*
> *Today I really flubbed up in my math test because we have to get 5 100s in a row and I had 2 100s but then today I got a 99!*

Later, when I turn ten, the tone starts to change. I stop worrying and start fretfully wishing.

> *I want to have a thin lovely figure, very pretty and smart and Alec and I love each other, never sick, happy life, my family isn't killed, I am a great ATHLETE, popular, lots of friends, no pimples, a nicer nose.*

Virginia Woolf wrote, "I do not know how far I differ from other people." I tend to think, based on the above evidence, that I don't differ much. Admirable, I guess, is my absence of guile or pretense. I was clearly not prepping very well for my posthumous fame, as certain people I know prep and have been prepping practically since birth for theirs. Everything written by these people—even an online exchange with a computer repair technician—is treated as archival evidence to be scoured by future scholars. If the future scholars come to care at all about me, I wish them to know this: with certain variations (substitute *my husband* for *Alec*), the desires of my ten-year-old self have more or less held steady for the past thirty-odd years.

So I told the seventy-year-olds a story that stressed the continuity (the immortality!) of self. What I failed to mention, however, was my recent worry: As a writer, I have mistaken how to use words. I write too much. I write like some people talk to fill silence. When I write, I am trying through the movement of my fingers to reach my head. I'm trying to build a word ladder up to my brain. Eventually these words help me come to an idea, and then I rewrite and rewrite and rewrite what I'd already written (when I had no idea what I was writing about) until the path of thinking, in retrospect, feels immediate. What's on the page appears to have busted out of my head and traveled down my arms and through my fingers and my keyboard and coalesced on the screen. But it didn't happen like that; it never happens like that.

MARCH 3

Today my friend asked me, "Am I crazy?" She is convinced that her husband is having an affair. We were in her apartment drinking beer. She seemed oddly energized by the prospect of this affair, as if we were gossiping about the maybe-infidelity of a person not married to her.

Her husband, she said, had become friendly with the single woman who used to live in the neighboring apartment. The woman had since moved to San Francisco; however, she called her husband regularly to check on her mail. Was there a package for her in their lobby? According to my friend, her husband always left the room so he could speak to the woman in private.

"I don't know," she said. "Am I crazy?"

I considered the evidence. Was this all she had? I asked. If so, I was sorry to disappoint her—she really was so excited that her husband might be cheating on her—but I did not think her husband was having an affair. She was, perhaps, being a little crazy. At the worst, it sounded as though her husband had a crush on their former neighbor, and if he did, she should continue to rejoice. I'd recently heard of a study that concluded: the marriages that last are the ones in which the two members regularly develop (but do not act upon) extramarital infatuations. Here was proof of her marriage's durability. Her husband wanted to sleep with a woman who was not his wife.

Then she told me more. A few weeks ago, her family had gone on vacation to Lake Tahoe. On the morning of their departure, her husband claimed he needed to stay in New York to deal with a work emergency. She flew ahead with their son; he flew to San Francisco a day later and spent a night in the city before meeting his family at the lake. Less than a week into the vacation, he claimed he needed to return home earlier than expected (another work emergency). He drove to San Francisco, ostensibly to catch a plane. Ostensibly, he missed it. Again, he spent the night in the city. He'd told his wife he'd stayed on a friend's couch, but she later learned, by finding a receipt in his pocket, that he'd checked into a hotel. When asked why he'd decided against staying with the friend (she did not ask him why he had lied), he said, "I'm too old to sleep on couches."

Now I told her: I didn't think she was crazy. If my husband behaved that way, I'd know he was having an affair.

But their relationship wasn't our relationship. A couch, a crush, a hotel. What might appear suspicious in my husband might not appear suspicious in hers.

I tried to interpret her husband's behavior using their relationship template.

I still thought he was having an affair.

"I don't think you're crazy," I repeated.

We wondered if she should break into his e-mail account. We were less concerned about the ethics of this breach than we were about its uselessness in court, so to speak. Reading her husband's e-mail was the equivalent of an illegal phone tap. She wouldn't be able to confront him with evidence procured in this manner. If she admitted that she'd read his e-mail, the marital wrongdoing could be shifted to her. She'd read his e-mail! What a trespass, what a violation! No wonder he'd needed to have an affair! Etc.

Let's say, I said, that she read his e-mail and confirmed he was having an affair. How might she "stumble" upon further proof she could actually use? We talked about credit card receipts and whether or not a big charge at a hotel bar might signal that he hadn't been drinking alone. I wondered if she might accidentally discover a suspicious text string. A chain of acronyms exchanged with their former neighbor that might suggest—they were speaking in code to avoid detection.

"But," she said, returning to the possibility of reading his e-mail, "do I really want to find what I might find?"

She quoted something I'd apparently said to her last winter—that if my husband read my e-mail, he deserved to learn whatever he discovered. I didn't remember saying this. On reflection, however, it seemed exactly the type of thing I would say. I stood by it.

"Maybe you don't want to know," I observed of her husband's possible infidelity. What would knowing get her? Her husband had slipped up once before they were married and evaded conviction despite compelling testimony against him—a statement from the woman he'd slept with, for example. He did not confess nor deny when presented with this testimony. He simply refused to admit the evidence to the court. (He refused to accept that there *was* a court.)

My friend returned to the original evidence, such as it existed. "I don't know," she said. "Am I just crazy?" We'd entered a loop. Each time we found ourselves at a potential course of action, we'd shy away from the exit and the loop would reboot. *Am I just crazy?*

Our loop reminded me of a recent interaction with a different friend. She's an artist; I am not. She'd tried as an artist (as opposed to a psychologist or, I don't know, a dentist) to demystify for me my obsession with certain objects. One of these objects is a hot-water tap handle I found in my house in Maine where, when I'm not teaching in New York, I live. The tap handle is enamel; it is cracked. I carry it with me everywhere. Once purely functional, it now serves no other purpose than to weigh down my bag. Every day, before I start writing, I draw this tap handle. The artist diagnosed my attraction to it as *l'amour fou*. André Breton, she told me, identified the affliction in his book *Mad Love*. He and Alberto Giacometti—depressed at the time—were walking through a Paris flea market in the spring of 1934; Breton feared that Giacometti might fall in love with a girl and, as a consequence of his sudden happiness or his brighter outlook on life, ruin a statue on which he was working and to which Breton felt obsessively

attached. Breton worried in particular about the placement
of the statue's arms, which were raised in a way to suggest
they were holding or protecting something.

He was right to worry. Due to precisely the sort of
fleeting "feminine intervention" Breton feared, Giacometti
fell in love with a girl and lowered the statue's arms. (Once
this feminine intervention concluded, Breton reports of
the arms, "with some modifications, they were reestab-
lished the next day in their proper place.") What bothered
Breton was not the loss of modesty implied by the lowered
arms. What bothered him was the "disappearance of the
invisible but present object."

My tap handle—according to my artist friend, and also
to Breton—was the invisible but present object, invisible
in that I could not perceive its use or meaning, but I always
needed it around. My friend's husband's maybe-infidelity
was also the invisible but present object. My friend did not
want her suspicion—which sustained the possibility that
her husband both was and was not having an affair—to
disappear by exposing it. She feared the lowering of hands.
Still, I said to her as we drank beer, You are not crazy. You
are not crazy. This is what she needs from me, I guess—
the opportunity to perpetually wonder about her husband
without the threat of ever knowing what, in a marriage, is
or is not there.

.
.

JULY 29

.

.

Today I was reading *The Men's Club* by a California
writer, now dead, named Leonard Michaels. (When I told

a friend in the grocery store parking lot that I was reading Michaels, she said, "Talk about dead men in Berkeley we don't like!" I can't remember who the other dead man in Berkeley was we didn't like.) Leonard writes, "Everybody has a doppelganger. You may sometimes catch a glimpse of him in the mirror, or in a storefront window. He is the one you fear, the other you." For decades I never saw anything but my doppelganger when I looked in the mirror. In the house where I grew up, a huge mirror hung at the bottom of our staircase, where there was also a small landing. This landing functioned as a stage from which I would audition for my future role as a person. I kept waiting for the girl in the mirror to look like me. She never did. Starting in my late thirties, however, I no longer felt the same disconnect when I looked in a mirror. That's *your* face! I would think. I mean, *my* face! This face was leaner and sharper, and suggested that when I was an old woman I'd resemble a kindly witch. At around this same time, men stopped checking me out on the street. This was fine by me, but it also made me confused. I was so beautiful now. Was I the only person who thought so?

I wanted to ask one of my real-life doppelgangers what she thought about how we looked. Apparently there are many I could ask. I am always meeting people who say, "You look exactly like my cousin!" This has happened frequently enough that I've decided I am a generic type. I am everywhere. This explains why strangers are always asking me for directions. During the school year, when I live in New York, I am asked for directions almost every day. I've witnessed so many lost people in New York scan the pedestrian horizon and settle on me. They looked relieved. *There. There is a familiar face.* I've been lost in cities where I don't live, and even then I'm asked for directions. I say, "I don't live here. I'm lost too!" These pedestrians think I'm lying. They turn from me, disappointed. How small and ungenerous I am, pretending I'm a tourist in my own city, pretending not to speak German or Croatian, just to avoid helping them out.

The other possibility: I am trusted by strangers because I am a teacher. I was informed by the psychic I saw for research purposes, *You are a teacher.* (She also told me that my three-year-old son would grow up to run a bed-and-breakfast.) In fact I *am* a teacher, but I think she meant it metaphorically. I am a person who guides other people. I share and impart knowledge. I can tell people where the nearest subway is located. I did not take the psychic seriously until I was stricken by a weird illness this past spring. When my friend advised me to see my affliction as an opportunity to become a new person, I decided that I'd give up writing fiction and become a different kind of teacher. A life teacher. I'd give directions to the nearest life subway. I'd say things like, "There is nowhere to be, only everywhere to go." I'd become a guru. I honestly had a moment when I thought, *This is why I got sick, because the world needs me.*

Then I got better.

Once I met one of my doppelgangers. She was not some abstracted cousin; she was the good friend of one of my good friends. We spent a weekend together celebrating our mutual friend's wedding engagement. Looking at her was like looking in the mirror when I was a kid—*Is that really me?* She thought I was her. She said, "It's so weird! We really do look so much alike!" I wasn't seeing it beyond the hair and eye color. It's true that we emitted a similar vibe; at the onset, we presented as energy twins. But she is never self-deprecating (I am always self-deprecating), and always confident (I am confident, but not outwardly). As the weekend progressed, we looked less and less alike to me, then not alike at all. Which didn't mean I didn't *like* her. I really liked her. I politely agreed with her pronouncements that we resembled one another. *I know, it's so weird!* It seemed impossible to deny our similarity without inadvertently insulting her (*You? God no, I look nothing like you*) or sounding bizarrely defensive, like a woman who has only recently come to resemble herself.

JULY 18

Today, or rather tonight, my husband and I will be watching "The Men Tell All." This is the penultimate show of *The Bachelorette,* Season Eight. On "The Men Tell All," the men whom the bachelorette, Emily Maynard, has rejected over the course of the season are interviewed by Chris, the host of what my husband and I call "The Franchise." The Franchise comprises three shows: *The Bachelor, The Bachelorette,* and *Bachelor Pad.* It is my husband's contention that everyone on the planet will eventually be part of The Franchise. We dream of this happening.

On "The Men Tell All," the guys don't dish on Emily; they dish on the other guys. They dish about inter-guy relations. The guys live in a house called "the house," and "the house" remains the name for their communal living situation, even if "the house" is a hotel suite in Dubrovnik. In the house there are assholes, there are sweetly misunderstood wallflowers, there are asshole wallflowers, and, on "The Men Tell All," everyone accuses everyone of being exactly what they are, and a studio audience boos when jerky guys refuse the mantel of jerkhood, and applaud when the jerks are called out by the narcs, who would probably be jerks themselves if the bigger jerks hadn't been around to fill the role.

I am asked by apparently more sensible people why I watch this show. It's so fake, the sensible people say; it's totally rigged. The contestants are actors. They just want to become famous. To enjoy the show, to these people, is to fail to remember this, and to be swept up by a fiction you think is not one.

But I believe there are a few more floors to the house of fiction/reality than these people, and maybe even the contestants, realize. I honestly believe that people fall in love on these shows. I do. Here is why: Crushes thrive in small spaces. Humans must be programmed to respond positively when faced with a small sampling of other humans in, say, caves. You're stuck in a cave with three other people—all mankind, presumably, was hidden away in such tiny groups during the winters until the thaw—and so, in order for the species to thrive, you must biologically be compelled to fuck at least one person in your cave, despite the fact that, when surrounded by a plenitude of Neanderthals at the Neanderthal summer barbecue, none of them struck your fancy. Without the element of choice, and in conjunction with captivity, you find love, or at least you find lust.

This has happened to me many times. It happened to me on a canoe trip; the minute we returned to civilization, I recanted my crush on the guy I'd angled to sit next to at the nightly campfires. I have been so cognizant of this phenomenon, and its inevitability, that I got nervous in college while waiting to hear where in France I was to spend my semester abroad, because I knew that a guy my friend was dating, someone I'd always found abstractly cute, was also going to

France. Fortunately we were sent to different cities. Had we been in the same city, I am certain we would have fallen in love, or the sort of love that occurs in those situations, call it what you will, probably a mistake. This is also why I get nervous about going to art colonies, especially now that I am happily married to a man I met at an art colony. I don't want to fall for anyone else—I am pointedly *not* looking to fall for anyone—but these situations conspire against our best intentions. Art colonies, often located in remote woods or on beautiful estates, are communities in which all the residents sever ties to the real world within hours of arrival; they are like singles mixers for the married or otherwise spoken for. (I was married when I met my now-husband, who was otherwise spoken for.) When I arrive at a colony these days, I take a measure of the room, I identify the potential problems, I reinforce my weak spots, and then I relax.

Even the larger world can conspire to trick its inhabitants with caves of a sort. A few summers ago I developed a crush on a guy working on the barn outside my studio in Maine. For many hours a day we worked in the same approximate space. I've known him for years; he and his partner are good friends of ours. My point is that this crush had no basis in reality or in my imagination; it had so little basis in either realm that I couldn't even fantasize about a next move. He was just a fun reason to go to work each day, and he reminded me how, during the eighteen months that I had a real job, i.e., an office job and not a waitressing or teaching job, I had to develop a crush in order to want to go to work. My office crush was a very capable and married Norwegian. He once joined a rescue mission in the Sierra Nevada Mountains to find our lost coworker. He later told me he'd spent two grim days stabbing his ski poles into snowdrifts, looking for a body.

Also my crush on this guy working on my barn explained much that I'd formerly failed to understand about the social workings of our Maine town—how, over the course of a long Maine winter, husbands and wives manage to fall in love with other husbands and wives they've known forever.

However, as a believer in The Franchise, and as a believer in my own marriage, I feel the need to defend the attractions that can arise in deceptive environments. My husband, for example, is not the sort of man I would have been smart enough to date and marry until many more years of dating and marrying the wrong kind of man. Had it not been for the art colony and the intense exposure I had to my husband, who was so different from the husband I had at the time, I may never have fallen in love with him. And yet he is the perfect human for me. Had it not been for my own personal version of The Franchise, I'd have suffered many more years of mistakes.

Which does not explain much about the actual Franchise—for example, why the bachelors and bachelorettes always select to marry the hottest person, even if that person's hotness is massively iced by their personality. I got really excited, for example, when I thought that Brad, the man-boy with abandonment issues from Season Fifteen, might reject the obvious, beautiful girl and choose the cute-enough girl with the cool father. I was really touched by the idea that Brad might marry a woman because he wanted her dad to be his dad too. Of course Brad chose the obvious, beautiful girl. Does that mean Brad didn't love her, because she was obvious? I think he did love her, and I think she loved him. Sometimes we love obvious people. I also think that all of the rejected women who claimed to love Brad really did love him. Most of the men who claim tonight that they love Emily really do love her, even if they've barely spoken to her. Is this normal? No. But that doesn't mean it's dismissible as acting. Fakeness gives rise to realness that, granted, given The Franchise's dismal marriage record (many of the engaged couples experience ugly breakups within a year), may not survive when the fakeness ends. But the contestants do, or did, experience real feelings as a result of fiction. The readers of novels experience real feelings as a result of fiction. And what about the characters? They don't not fall in love just because a writer orchestrated it.

AUGUST 2

Today I was stung by a wasp. A wasp nest hangs over the door to my studio. The wasps fly in and out. I walk in and out. Thus far, our patterns of cohabitation have meshed peaceably. I'd been accepted as one of them. Once I found a wasp crawling on my shoulder and I didn't kill it. I tricked it onto a piece of paper and freed it on the grass.

But today our nonaggression pact was proven to be a bit of sham faith on my part, generated to protect my cowardice (I do not want to deal with that nest). I was sitting at my desk. My phone rang. It was a painter inviting me to her gallery opening. I exited my studio. I climbed up the porch and back down it. I always pace when I talk on the phone. One night I paced my parents' unlit living room for an hour, not knowing that I had a bleeding gash on the bottom of my foot. I turned on the lights when my call ended to discover thousands of stains on the rug, like a hiking trail dashed across a map. After my parents yelled at me, we marveled at the shape of my talking travels, the places in the living room I visited time and again, and the outlier areas to which I made only one or two forays, because the topography was more challenging, or the view less spectacular. We understood our living room differently after that.

Suddenly, I felt a sharp burn behind my knee. A wasp dropped from the bottom of my shorts. I continued to walk and talk to the artist about her opening. "I'll be there!" I said. "What time?" I limped into the house. I waved to get my husband's attention and mouthed the word "alcohol." Meaning *rubbing*. I mimed what had happened. I said, "And where is it?" My husband returned with rubbing alcohol, but then understood why I needed it. "You need bleach, not alcohol," he corrected. "On Main Street," I said, "got it." My husband returned with the bleach. The artist gave me the sort of micro-directions that are confusing in their micro-ness. I finally cut her off. I said, "Don't worry, I'll find you!" and hung up the phone.

"Why didn't you just tell her you were stung by a wasp and had to get off?" my husband asked me.

I don't know why. Or I kind of know. This woman is inundated by motherhood. Her career has been interrupted by people who need her. I didn't want to interrupt her with my need. My behavior makes perfect sense to me. Just as my behavior on an airplane this past spring made sense to me. I was traveling on a red-eye from L.A. to New York. I always ask for an aisle seat because I am claustrophobic. Also, when a task becomes difficult, my body develops an urgent need to regularly do it. It needs to regularly pee, especially when I'm in a window seat.

On this flight, I had a window seat.

I drank no liquids for hours before the flight. I peed just before boarding. My neighbor in the middle seat spoke

Russian and wore a white tracksuit. He fell asleep before takeoff, his head whiplashing up and down. He'd clearly taken a sleeping pill in the waiting area. Nothing would wake him. In the aisle seat was a woman about my age, wearing chic black workout clothes and neon sneakers. She was unrumpled, with a pre-moisturized sleep face and neatly stored long hair. She arranged her space as though she were an organized temp secretary, placing on her desk a few personal items she'd brought to work in her purse.

I tried to make eye-friends with the woman in the aisle seat. I wanted her to acknowledge me, and for us both to recognize, and express surprise over, the man sleeping so soundly between us. Should I, in a few hours, need to use the lavatory, I'd be able to ask her with a glance. But she was not making eye-friends on this plane. We took off. I listened to music and counted the number of songs it took for the lights of L.A. to completely disappear behind us.

The woman in the aisle seat put on her eye mask.

Less than an hour into the flight, I needed to pee. I shifted positions; I took a Xanax. The urge grew worse. I started to panic; I took another Xanax.

I became more awake than ever.

I tried to override my body with meditation. I failed. I thought I'd distract myself with a movie, but the backseat monitor was broken. Reading was too interior an activity; it only brought me closer to the irritation site.

I tried to outsmart the situation. How could I pee without leaving my seat? My options were limited. Really there was but one option: to pee in the airsickness bag. This seemed a very sound plan. It was so sound I was surprised it wasn't usual practice. Airsickness bags are water resistant. An airsickness bag could be folded neatly and stored under the seat until I could get to the lavatory to dispose of it (I would never hand it to an air steward).

I was not wearing the ideal clothing for this maneuver, the ideal being no clothing. I was wearing jeans. Fortunately, I had a big sweater—I draped this over me, performed a shimmy, and then rested, naked to the knees under my sweater, while I planned the next move. I needed to crouch between my seat and the seat in front of me, but there was not enough room for this. I turned sideways, which meant my face was basically pressed into the lap of the white tracksuit guy. But he was so totally asleep! This incipient blow-job position would embarrass no one but me.

I hunched between the seats. I put my face inches from the Russian guy's crotch. I opened the airsickness bag. I waited for relief. None came. I sat back in my seat. I rested, I refocused on the task, I tried again to practice my version of meditation, also known as self-bullying. Who cares about all of these people? They are asleep! No one is looking at you! *You can do this!* The situation was quickly becoming less about peeing into a bag to avoid disturbing strangers; now I wanted bragging rights. I wanted the accomplishment high.

I tried again. Again I failed. Everything I know about my body I learned from a book written by a home-birth midwife. I channeled her wisdom. Of particular use is her Sphincter Law, which is applicable to all muscles, even those belonging to nonpregnant people.

> Sphincter muscles open more easily in an
> atmosphere where the woman feels safe.
> The muscles are more likely to open if the
> woman feels positive about herself.

The muscles may close if the woman feels threatened.

But I didn't feel threatened! And I did feel positive about myself! I was actually feeling incredibly positive about myself that I'd (a) come up with this solution and (b) dared to implement it. I tried a third time, and a fourth. I failed. I failed to pee into an airsickness bag while eight strangers slept within a two-foot radius of me.

Whenever I've told this story to friends, I lose the sympathies of certain reasonable people. "I would have just woken them up," these people will say. "Fuck them, you had to pee." I've defended myself as I define myself: I am a person who never wants to put another person out. I did not know these people, but I did know how terrible it is to be woken from a hard-won sleep, especially one that permits you to endure an awkward experience without experiencing it, like flying with total strangers through the night.

.

.

NOVEMBER 5

.

.

Today I spoke with a person about a book we'd both read. The book had been billed to him as "original" and he was complaining about how not-original this book was. I personally thought the book was original enough; besides, what does it mean to be original anymore? Hasn't originality obsolesced? Worrying about originality is like worrying about the best place to hang your wall phone.

This person said, of the book's unoriginality, "I mean, we all read *Walden* in college."

I did not read *Walden* in college. I did not read *Walden*

ever, though I recently pretended to a Spanish translator of *Walden* that I had read it. I *have* been to Walden Pond; I've toured Thoreau's cabin where he wrote *Walden*. As a result of that visit (and after reading a few online excerpts), I've felt okay occasionally describing my diary as a "contemporary take on *Walden*." Like Thoreau, I am pretending that I wrote this diary over the course of a year, when in fact I wrote it over the course of two years, two months, and two days (give or take). Like Thoreau, I wanted to "live deliberately" and was worried that if I did not I might, "when I came to die, discover that I had not lived." Like Thoreau, I wanted to "live deep and suck out all the marrow of life."

Unlike Thoreau, I have no fondness for sparse living. I do not covet hardship. I liked the *idea* of *Walden,* however, because it was written in a cabin in the woods. It's a sort-of nature book that took place (at least the writing did) inside. Interiors are where I do my exploring. Interiors are my nature. I am an outdoorsman of the indoors. In the summer, when the teaching is done and I'm in Maine, I work in a studio that was once a chicken shack and is now scarcely better than one, that is unheated not by design but because it's too catawumpus to support much modern infrastructure. When I am there I am happiest. In my outbuilding I am sucking out optimum marrow.

New York, however, is not so full of marrow-sucking places, not for me. I am the one being sucked empty in New York; I am harried, I grow thin, I develop face rashes. I persist in staying there for nostalgic reasons; I always dreamed of living in New York, and I am intent on realizing (and realizing and realizing, to the point of total body dissolution) this dream. At a certain point, you ask yourself, "Is this where I am going to die?" and the answer is *yes.* You have, without realizing it, committed your body to a plot.

But I have found one place in New York that calms me. Café Sabarsky is in the Neue Galerie, itself in an old mansion on Fifth Avenue. Café Sabarsky invokes the '20s intellectual and artistic Austro-Hungarian wildness before all the real hell broke loose. My great-grandfather was from Austro-Hungary, anecdotally, "the Hungarian part." His wife came from Vienna. This great-grandfather, once he relocated to America, ran the employee cafeteria at the Royal Typewriter factory in Hartford, Connecticut. He wasn't an intellectual, but he fed people who made the typewriters on which intellectuals (maybe? a handful?) worked. He was a gourmand; he preached, via his food, the fatty, pickled gospel of the old empire. He made my father, when he was a child, for lunch, green tomato and pork sandwiches. He used an old meat grinder—I own it now—to grind dill pickles and bologna before mixing them with mayonnaise.

The connection, I realize, is super slim, but it's enough to permit me to visit Café Sabarsky and believe that I am entitled to sit in an Adolf Loos chair beneath the Josef Hoffmann ceiling lights and eat a *weisswurst mit brezen.* These are *my people,* people. My fondness for cured meats and sauerkraut (in college, broke, I ate it with my fingers from a can), my object lust for Vienna Secessionist/ Bauhaus anything, these are not superficially nostalgic graspings for the debauched and brainy scene we (as in We of Café Sabarsky) wish we'd experienced. This is my true heritage speaking through my hunger.

Only very recently—like last month—did I learn that my great-grandfather was not of Hungarian origin. A Croatian set me to rights when he asked about my name, and I told him it was Hungarian. Julavits is not a Hungarian surname, he told me. Julavits is likely Bosnian, this Croatian concluded after some research. Here, more thoroughly, is what he found.

> *That -its is a Hungarian way how to write the end of the south Slavic surnames*
> *So your grand-grandfather was (or his father etc.) emigrant also in Hungary. . . . Maybe his identity was in some way unclear also to him. I would say that your surname probably originally was Đulabić (read: Julabich)*
> *Đul means rose and*
> *Đulab (Julab) is, some said, red sweet apple (Turkish-Persian word).*
> *I found small willage in Bosnia near Tuzla called Đulabići, from where seems the surname coming.*

The Croatian also discovered this, written by the wife of my grandfather's brother, and posted on a lineage website I had never visited:

> *My father-in-law came from "Vezprem" (all he ever told us) in 1905 at the age of 17. Came to Ellis Island, then Hartford, where he catered the Colt Firearm Factory restaurant. He said he left a mother, who borrowed money to send him to the States, because he was going to have to serve in the German army. His father, a jaeger (woodsman) was killed in 1894 when a tree fell on him.*

Does this mean my great-grandfather didn't work at the Royal Typewriter factory but at a gun factory? (This would explain why his old typewriter—also in my possession—is a Corona.) Does this mean he maybe was more Hungarian than not (Veszprém is in Hungary)? Does this mean he was Jewish? ("Joseph Julavits" does not appear on any of the Ellis Island ship manifests; the closest match is a person named Harry Judovitz, arrived in 1905 from Budapest, denoted as "Hungarian; Hebrew.") Who knows. The Croatian speaks the truth: *Maybe his identity was in some way unclear also to him.* In the midst of such uncertainty, I cling not to what I know, but what I feel. I feel I belong in Café Sabarsky. An inexcusable nostalgia drives me there, I confess it; I have no nobler claim. I went there for lunch a few years ago when I suspected I was pregnant. I told myself, "If I am pregnant, and if it is a son, I will give him the middle name of Sabarsky." I was not pregnant. When I did eventually have a son, I gave him the middle name Dabelstein, the maiden name of my maternal grandmother. His full name is now basically that of a law firm, but fuck it. Mine is now maybe the name of a Bosnian. I recently asked my other grandmother about her mother-in-law, my *Viennese* great-grandmother who made strudel and remains, despite the meddlings of the Croatian, 100 percent Viennese. What was her maiden name? Where in Vienna did she live? "Her maiden name was Korny," my grandmother said. "Her family was so poor, they lived seven days in a ditch."

OCTOBER 13

Today I spun tops with my son. We did this for six straight hours. So much of the pleasure of hanging out with children is successfully losing yourself, if only for a minute or two, in the activity with which you're both engaged.

Suddenly, I am drawing a shoe that makes us both happy. The cogs of the day smoothly and quickly turn. Once I've finished the shoe, however, I am back to wondering—how can this day not mostly involve my waiting for it to be over? Yet when this day has ended my child will be older and I will be nearer to dead. Why should I wish for this to happen any sooner than it already will?

But I genuinely had fun spinning tops with my son. I did not have to concentrate so hard in order to effortlessly enjoy myself, and to forget the admittedly stupid things that otherwise preoccupied me. I wondered what it was about tops, and why they were so engrossing, and why spinning them so relaxed me. After I put my son to bed, I decided to watch a documentary about famed modern designer couple Charles and Ray Eames. I thought theirs would be the story of a happy marriage (it wasn't entirely). I thought a movie about their lives would be like watching *The Bachelorette* finale but with better furniture. In this documentary, a short film made by Charles is mentioned, a film called—I couldn't believe it—*Tops*. The film is all about tops and the eternal appeal of tops. I found the film on YouTube, but I didn't watch it. It was late and I was tired. Besides, I knew what I needed to know about tops, i.e., that one of the most respected design minds of the twentieth century had validated, on film, my experience. The Eameses were into the complex beauty of the everyday object. ("The Eameses saw beauty in everyday objects, like the tumbleweed they hung from their living room ceiling.") A day, like a top, can be an everyday object. A day, like a top, can be a time-skewing device. A day can also move downward, not only across, as it spins.

September 5

Today I went to the Columbia library for the first time in four months. Despite my regular absences, I have two spots I consider permanently mine. Both are located in a catwalk; both are desks separated from other desks by tall bookshelves. In the bookshelves of the first spot (where I am today) is a series of large bronze volumes called *Germanstik*. Best I can tell (I do not speak German) this is a Who's Who in Germany, scanning the years 1960–2007, after which the library's subscription ran out, or nobody was anybody in Germany anymore. There is a book called *Shadows in the Attic*, which I thought might be a V. C. Andrews title. I would have so much respect for the Columbia University library if it could count V. C. Andrews among its holdings. But *Shadows in the Attic* is "A Guide to British Supernatural Fiction" from 1820 to 1950. According to this book, one of the enduring themes of supernatural fiction is "the little people," which I did not know, but which explains Murakami's *1Q84* to me a bit better (there are characters in the novel called "the little people"). *Shadows in the Attic* is useful for other reasons as well. It is highly recommended (by me) as a source for character names and story titles. The following is a list of real authors who, depending on their spiritual disposition, may haunt you from beyond the grave if you repurpose their names for use on fictional characters:

Oliver Onions
Harrington Hext (pseudonym for Eden Phillpotts)
Ernest R. Suffling

Nina Toye
Allen Upward
Weatherby Chesney (pseudonym for C. J. Cutliffe
    Hynde)
John Gloag
W. P. Drury

Here are some excellent book and story titles that, if appropriated for reuse, may come with the same risk:

"The Persecution Chalice"
"A Carnation for an Old Man"
"In the Cliff Land of the Dane"
"Another Little Heath-Hound"
"Uncle Phil on TV"
"A Blue Pantomime"
"The House Which Was Rent Free"
"The Weirdale Assize"
"A Strange Christmas Game"
The Carpet with a Hundred Eyes
"The Haunted Physician"
"The Case of the Thing That Whimpered"
Jorkens Borrows Another Whiskey

I have stolen names and I have stolen titles, two at this point; I intend to steal more. (I will, at a future point, steal the title of this book from my daughter. We will be at lunch following a visit to an Egyptian museum in Berlin; we will have bought a book on hieroglyphics. We will be trying to learn the picture letters, one of which is based on a drawing of folded cloth. "Folded *clock*?" my daughter will ask. "Folded cloth," I'll correct. And then I'll pickpocket her accident.)

Once I stole the name of a fetus. I was at a baby shower for a friend, and the table talk came around to names. My friend wasn't disclosing the names she and her husband were considering; she revealed only that they'd winnowed the choices to two, and each of them had a favorite. She was trying to convince her husband to back her top name candidate. He was trying to do the same to her. I wondered what sort of campaigning was involved. And then I didn't. In most couples there is the person who wins and the person who doesn't. The winner isn't necessarily stronger or smarter or righter. The winner is the person who won't give up, and the non-winner ("loser" is not the correct word for the person who does not win), at a certain point, realizes the battle is a silly one, and the spoils are not worth the extended warfare. I am the winner in my relationship, which is why I have so much respect for the non-winner. The non-winner, i.e., my husband, doesn't give a shit whether or not he's going to win the fight over the new dishwasher's load capacity, or how to best teach children to calculate military time. I wish I were not always the winner. But this is like wishing I were not a girl.

The pregnant woman at the shower was the winner in her relationship. Whatever name she wanted, such would be the baby's name. This did happen. At the shower, however, since she wasn't disclosing either name candidate, we talked about the names other people she knew were considering for their babies. One of her friends, whose last name was Sheidegger, wanted to name her daughter Violet.

Violet Sheidegger was the best name I'd ever heard. I urged her to tell her friend (whom I did not know) to name her daughter Violet. The name Violet Sheidegger inspired me to write the short story that gave me my first big publishing break, and which subsequently inspired a person in publishing to pay me a stunning sum of money for my partially finished (actually scarcely begun), and really not very good, first novel. Since I didn't know this Sheidegger woman, and would likely never meet her, and lived 3,000 miles from her, I didn't consider it stealing to use a name she hadn't committed to using, and which, in fact, she did not use.

I later heard that my friend disapproved of what she considered my "theft." She believed I'd invaded this stranger's privacy; I'd stolen what was hers to use or not, as she chose.

Four years later I also had a daughter. I found her name on a tombstone near our Maine house. I stole it, I guess. This name is not in my family. I have no rights to it or to the story that accompanies it (the woman on the tombstone died unmarried; she was, according to my neighbor, a bootlegger). I thought using her name was an interesting way for my family to take part in the history of our town, but not everyone agreed. My neighbor didn't accuse me of stealing. He didn't get mad at me. He just found the whole thing strange.

Not long after my daughter was born, my husband and I disseminated not only the fact of her birth but other relevant statistics, such as what we intended to call her. My disapproving friend's husband, the non-winner in the battle to name his daughter, wrote me a congratulation note. He revealed, somewhat mournfully, that his first choice had been the same name I'd chosen for my daughter. He did not accuse me of stealing the name. And I hadn't, of course, at least not from him. Given his wife's discretion, I'd had no idea what he'd failed to name his daughter four years ago. But I worried, though this time I was mostly innocent, that I still somehow qualified as a thief.

JULY 4

Today we marched in our town's Fourth of July parade. Our float was by far the best—a team of ten (mostly under eight years old) doctors performed a rescue on a sick dolphin, played by a boat builder whom we'd sewn inside a few sheets of sound insulation. The sound insulation had the hand-feel of blubber. It was very realistic to the touch and helped us take our roles seriously. Unfortunately our dolphin became enamored of the crowd and swam very far ahead of our "ambulance," and did headstands in the middle of the street, and did not appear in need of rescue. Tired of cartwheeling, the dolphin would finally drop to the ground. We'd blow our whistles, run to him with stethoscopes, roll him onto a pair of canvas firewood carriers, and heft him into the back of the ambulance. Then he'd swim off, ready to do cartwheels again. We were the crowd favorite. We were definitely winning first prize in the float contest.

The judge did not agree. The judge awarded us a second place tie. (Our prize—a $20 bill—was handed to us without pomp at the post-parade BBQ.) Who won first place? We asked the judge. First place, he said, went to the farmers market float.

The farmers market float consisted of three old men driving three old tractors.

"I was impressed that they got those old tractors running," said the judge.

We shared our second place distinction with the Girl Scout float. The Girl Scouts did nothing but ride in a truck until it was parked and the parade was over, at which point they danced atop the flatbed to "Funky Cold Medina."

We smelled a rat. Two of the judge's daughters were on the Girl Scout float! Coincidence? The farmers market takes place on the judge's front lawn! Coincidence? No and no. We drank beer out of rubber work gloves and bitched about the judge. Oh, the corruption! This judge must be deposed! I spent the rest of the day polling everyone I saw, including the woman who works in the general store about the float situation. She's a native Mainer who doesn't speak much, or at least she doesn't speak much to me. When I arrive each summer, I've decided that the most respectful way to greet her is to fail to greet her at all. But I solicited her opinion on the parade outcome. She seemed to agree that we'd been screwed. "Yeah," she said. "Who cares about a bunch of tractors?"

I felt vindicated—there is no higher word in our land than that of the woman at the general store—until I remembered: The judge is a controversial figure in our town. Her desire for us to win might more accurately be described as her commitment to never, ever side with the judge. The judge had arrived from a big city with big ideas about how to fix everything that was wrong here, in his opinion. He was going to install a ferry system to bring tourists from the national park that was eleven miles away by boat (sixty by land). He wanted to build low-income housing on his back property. (Not even the low-income people in town liked this idea.) I believe at one point he talked about starting a university here. Then he almost burned his barn down by leaving a bag of live stove ashes on the floor. This gave everyone permission to officially discredit him, and then to ease up on him a bit. Now that he's been proven incompetent, he is tolerated.

JULY 16

Today I started reading a book called *How to Navigate Today*. *How to Navigate Today* is not a spiritual guide but a book about actual nautical navigation written in the '40s by a woman named Marion Rice Hart. Marion Rice Hart was born in 1891 and was a chemical engineer, a geologist, a research physicist, a miner, a surveyor, a sculptor, a painter, a photographer, a sailboat skipper, an aviator, an author, and a radio operator. According to the preface of *How to Navigate Today*, Rice Hart navigated her day by keeping a low profile. "She has never been a noisy rebel flouting the conventions for women of her generation; she has just quietly done what she felt like doing."

I am navigating today by drawing the tap handle I found in my dining room wall. What continues to confound me is why I cannot simply own, as in possess in a manner that is satisfying, this tap handle. My inability to enjoyably accomplish this calls into question how I've managed, in the past, to own anything successfully. What does it mean to own this wooden table, this pottery bowl, this random ancestor painting (not my ancestor)? Owning is revealed as a doubly passive business. One just sits around owning these things one already owns. My doubt in my overall owning abilities, however, remains focused on the tap handle. I frequently experience the urge to flailingly, like with my mind or my heart or my body, fuck the thing.

Given the *l'amour fou* diagnosis I received from my artist friend, I clearly require treatment. I have decided, as previously stated, to draw the tap handle each morning even though I do not draw (unless I'm hanging out with children). I've never seen a still life of spice jars or a sunset or a person and thought, *I want to draw that.* My capturing impulses are not visual. In the past, if I wanted to capture an object, I owned it.

Yet I do not know how to own the tap handle, perhaps because it has been in a state of dis-ownership for so many years. It was found between the wall studs of my house by a guy who demo-ed our dining room. Who knows how a tap handle ended up in a wall. There are plenty of objects in our walls that make sense—the old newspapers added insulation, the old razor blades were too sharp to throw in the trash heaps hidden like Abenaki middens in the back woods—and others that don't, like the vertebra of a cow. I, too, have been frustrated by objects that you cannot file anywhere in your life, but neither can you throw them away. They drift around a house transiently, in a death row limbo, first on the dining room table, then on a bookshelf. Suddenly there's a hole in the wall, and an opportunity presents itself. I can get rid of this object while still keeping it. This is what I imagine the person who put the tap handle in the wall thought at the time.

So I decided that the only way to treat my affliction was to draw the tap handle, because the act of drawing would be frustrating enough to possibly distract me from the inherent frustration of the object. I would draw it every day. (It would become my "everyday object," like the tumbleweed the Eames hung from their ceiling.) I started work each morning by drawing the tap handle; afterward I would draw, in words, the day. The poet Mary Ruefle wrote, "an ordinary life was an obscure life, if we can extend the meaning of *obscure* to mean covered up by dailiness, glorious dailiness, shameful dailiness, dailiness that is difficult to figure out, that is not always clear until a long time afterward." If an object is relegated to dailiness it becomes a part of you. It is ingested by habit. It is stored between the studs of the walls of your self. When I'm autopsied they will find inside—this tap handle, a child too scared to go to matinees, a song I once loved, maybe also a cow bone and some old news. Who knows what else I've hidden in there because I could make no sense of it at the time, and found nowhere else to put it.

OCTOBER 18

Today I sat on the steps to the library and wrote e-mail replies on my computer. I was replying to replies to replies. Where is the question that began all of these replies? Was there *ever* a question?

A tourist approached me. She was Japanese. She wore a white business suit; she held an iPhone. A lot of tourists visit this campus. What are they here to see? Often they ask my permission to take pictures of my children playing on the wheelchair ramp, which suggests even they may not know why they're here. A famous university in theory might sound exciting, but in reality it's just a bunch of buildings, and often some droopy balloons hanging from an iron banister, and a loose gathering of people that might be a poorly attended Falun Gong liberation protest, or some students playing Assassin.

The Japanese woman, I assumed, wanted me to take her picture in front of a statue. I checked the direction of the sun. I considered telling her to pose in front of a smaller library, because I had taken a lot of successful pictures of tourists there.

Instead the woman asked me, "Do you imagine God as a woman?"

I took her question seriously. I didn't want to be dismissive or rude and thus reflect badly on my city or my country. I always feel a keen responsibility to be a good host. Her question better explained, too, why she was on campus. Maybe she thought she'd strike up a more interesting conversation with a stranger she found at a university rather than one she found in, say, Carnegie Deli. What is the place of man in the universe? What determines the fate of the individual? Where, spiritually speaking, is the nearest subway?

I also considered the possibility that she was part of a conceptual art piece, maybe an "interpreter" hired by the artist Tino Sehgal. Sehgal did a piece recently at the Guggenheim called *This Progress* in which interpreters—one of them was my friend's teen son—asked museum visitors questions like "What is progress?" and followed them up the museum's spiral ramp until another interpreter took over. Maybe Sehgal's new work was being secretly unfurled over campuses of higher learning. Maybe, in fact, this woman was not an interpreter herself but part of the conceptual art advance team. Maybe I was being interviewed for an interpreter position.

Now a job was on the line. I love to get jobs. Getting jobs is like winning domestic arguments on a grand scale, and then getting paid for it.

So. Did I imagine God as a woman? I didn't. When urged to envision God, or the aura God exudes, I understood that aura as male, maybe because the only people who use the word "God" in a question such as the one I was asked by the Japanese woman tend to be Christian. But I didn't want to give the Japanese woman this hackneyed answer. I would never be hired.

Instead I said, "I'm not sure."

"According to Scripture," the Japanese woman said, "God is referred to as both Our Father and Our Mother."

"Oh," I said. Now I was wondering: maybe she was a feminist activist?

The Japanese woman could see I was confused. I was clearly a novice. I was not the erudite liberal arts student/ professor she'd hoped to encounter.

She regarded me with sympathy.

"Do you *believe* in God?" she asked.

I heard this question as "Do you even know who God *is*?"

I was in too deep. I didn't have answers to her questions. I had too much e-mail to answer to answer her questions. I was no interpreter. I already had a job.

"I'm sorry," I said. "I don't think I'm going to be able to answer your questions today."

JUNE 18

Today I biked to a vintage store. I bought

· a deco rhinestone lipstick case, mirror broken, "as is" price of five dollars
· a red tin of cookie and sandwich cutters for twelve dollars
· a painted French serving tray for too much money (or maybe not; the owner of the store

made me feel better about the price by saying of
the tray, "it's probably much older than I think")

I also bought a garnet and rhinestone necklace. It's cos-
tume, from the '40s, not valuable, and it matches nothing I
own, but what swayed me was the weight of it. I brought it
home. I preferred looking at it to wearing it. I kept it spread
over the top of my dresser as interior decoration. Then I
considered giving it to my mother for her birthday. She was
about to turn seventy. My husband and I were throwing
her a fancy dinner, and turning our house into a three-
star restaurant run by children. But was this enough? I
worried that I needed to give her an object to commemo-
rate her birthday. A dinner party was too ephemeral a gift.
She wouldn't catch accidental sight of it and remember . . .
Me? That she'd turned seventy? Neither of these are
things she's likely to forget.

Still, the tradition with landmark birthdays is to give a
gift that presumes the receiver needs reminding that they
remain beloved and alive. I thought I'd give my mother this
necklace. But while I never wore it, I found, for whatever
reason, that I didn't want to give it away. I told myself, *You
didn't buy it* for *her, and it's not a true present if you didn't
buy it with the person in mind.* This gift was technically a
regift, from me to myself, and from myself to my mother.

I concluded: I definitely should not give her the necklace. And yet I still couldn't firmly commit. I changed my
mind daily. I thought, *She's turning seventy—does she really
want an old necklace? Wouldn't she prefer something more
fun and modern? If I give her this necklace, won't I offend
her by implying that she's no longer young enough to wear
fun and modern jewelry?* I thought, *I'm a vintage-wearing
person, but she is not a vintage-wearing person. Maybe the*

objects of dead people freak her out. I thought, *If I like it,
she probably* won't *like it, because we don't have the exact
same taste in jewelry. I have given her jewelry in the past
that I've never seen her wear (and that I would wear), and
she's given me jewelry in the past that she would wear (but
that I never would). By this logic, I should not give her the
necklace. Except that I didn't ever wear the necklace. This
suggested that she would like it and thus I should give her
the necklace.*

I did not give her the necklace.

The night of her birthday dinner, I dressed up. Because
I was still uncertain about my decision to keep the necklace, I wore it. I thought to myself, *If she doesn't comment
on my necklace, it means she doesn't like it, and I made the
right choice.* But I often compliment people on items of
clothing they're wearing because those items look great on
them, not because I think they would look great on me. I
compliment a woman on her ring when I can sense that
she is proud of or excited to be wearing it. I want her to
know that her positive feelings about herself are effectively
communicated to me through the object transmitter she's
put on her body.

If my mother complimented me on my necklace, it
could mean that she herself desired to wear it, or it could
mean that she appreciated how *I* wore it. If she said nothing, of course, this would mean unequivocally—she did
not like it, not on me, not on her.

We met for cocktails on the front porch as the child
staff readied our table. My mother said, almost immediately, "What a pretty necklace!" I tried to divine how she
meant this comment. It was pretty on me? It might have
been pretty on her? I demurred. "It's just some cheap thing
I found at a vintage store." It was cheap. But I was trying

to make it sound less desirable to her, and also to reassure myself—I hadn't been cheap when I'd failed to give it to her.

Today I realized it was July 19. This hasn't been the case in pretty much forever. For years I've gone days without knowing the date. I exist in relation to dates I've missed. Suddenly I am forty. Suddenly I was forty a long time ago.

The same is true with minutes. The first occasion I had to notice minutes was when I worked briefly as a hostess in a restaurant. The owner was Lebanese; he spoke French and rode a motorcycle and told me that my outfits weren't sexy enough for me to capably say, "Your table is ready." I hated working there for many reasons, but mostly I hated my time responsibilities—I could never lose myself in the work; I could never look at my watch and be amazed that three hours had passed. Quickly passing time stressed me out, because if time passed too quickly then people wouldn't have time to order dessert and time to pay their checks, and *come time* there would be no tables for the 8:45 reservations. I obsessively monitored the clock leading up to each seating—7:25, 7:26, 7:27, 7:29, 7:30. I never didn't know what time it was, not for one single minute did I not know. This made the shift crawl by. One night lasted a week. I quit after two days. A few years later I heard that the owner was killed on his motorcycle.

Once, however, I remember knowing what time it was for every minute, and yet this made time feel uncatchable, like a fistful of twenties the wind blew out of my hand.

(This happened to me once. My first three years in New York, I lived on an avenue lined with factories and through which the wind tunneled at high speeds. This was also the only time in my life I had fistfuls of twenties because I worked, after quitting my hostess job, as a waitress paid with tips.) I'd met up with a friend in L.A. She lives in London, and at that point we'd e-mailed each other many times a day for a year, but we'd only seen each other twice, for about three days each. Nonetheless, we'd fallen into an intense friendship. We were so intense in L.A. that people mistook us for lovers. We drove to the desert for the weekend, and stayed at a very small spa hotel where all the rooms faced inward toward a thermal pool, and the high desert wind, though hot, blew through our rooms and made air-conditioning seem silly, or at least unhealthy, so we left all of the windows open. The wind was so strong it blew the water glasses off the table. It blew open our books and sped-read the pages. A marine from the local base, on leave with his wife, stayed in the room opposite ours. He liked me because I am blond and marine-friendly. He did not take to my friend, who is darkly elfin, androgynous, and wicked. We decided to mess with him. I had a very good time flashing my wedding ring and talking about my husband while rubbing my friend's shoulders suggestively. Soon he started avoiding me. When I got into the thermal pool, he got out of it. The wind continued to blow. It blew through the days. It blew through the nights. Suddenly it was time to drive my friend back to the airport, and put her on a plane, and then probably I would not see her again for six months or even a year. On the way to the airport, she pushed to stop at a museum to see Christian Marclay's *The Clock*. *The Clock*—some call it an art installation—is also a twenty-four-hour-long movie that's a fully functional (and visual) timepiece. Every minute of a twenty-four-hour day is accounted for by a preexisting film clip, in which a clock or a watch appears (often during a dramatic moment, or what feels like a dramatic moment, in whatever film is being sampled—there is something breathless-making about time), showing the appropriate minute (1:22, then 1:23, then 1:25, and so on).

I drove speedily—we didn't have much time to see *The Clock,* and the more quickly I drove, the more time we'd have at the museum, but also the more quickly, it seemed, I'd be dropping my friend on the LAX curb. We arrived at the museum, parked, ran inside, discovered a terribly long ticket line, somehow located another not-so-terribly-long line, found a spot on a couch in the dark screening room, and watched. We'd decided beforehand that we had to leave at 3:45 for her to catch her flight. We passed our dwindling time together watching a visual representation of our dwindling time together. It confused my desire mechanism, and maybe rightly, because my desire mechanism was pretty confused. The movie made me so excited to see how the next minute (3:29, 3:30, 3:31) would be portrayed (what film clip would it be? Would I recognize it?), but I didn't want the time to pass because then we'd have to leave, and then I'd have to say good-bye, and then I wouldn't see my friend again for what felt like an eternity if measured by the time standards we encountered on that couch. Time crawled. Time flew. We broke our vow and stayed until 3:58.

JUNE 26

Today I ordered ten toy stethoscopes from a party supply company. I did this over the phone. Toy stethoscopes did not seem to be the sort of items that, if you ordered them online, would come. I often order things online that fail to come. I ordered a birth tub once. It disappeared in Tennessee. I tracked it like an air traffic controller does a plane that vanishes over the Bermuda Triangle, a series of regular blips that suddenly, like a heartbeat, stop. This was a very large item, not the sort of thing one could easily lose. Nor, though expensive, did it seem to be massively desired yet under-available. There is not a black market infrastructure built around birth tubs. Yet no one could account for the birth tub's whereabouts. My birth tub had dematerialized in transit.

This happens to me quite a lot, as I've said. Sometimes I'll place an order online and make my husband click the CONFIRM PURCHASE button, because he is confident and believes in ways that I don't, whereas the online commerce universe can sense my faithlessness. When I order things online, I am expressing my desire for an item I have never touched or experienced as a 3-D object, and to trust in the process requires the suspension of something I cannot fully suspend, even though I understand perfectly how online commerce works. As the object travels from the warehouse to me, it gains matter. Presumably it gains matter. But because I am faithless, my objects do not.

So I wanted to talk to an actual person about the stethoscopes. Conversations with strangers are so touching and intimate these days. Maybe it's simply that any conversation with a stranger, since such conversations are more and more rare, represents something you almost didn't do. *I almost didn't call you about toy stethoscopes.* Every item I've ever bought online represents a conversation with a stranger I didn't have. It's only when the system fails that you talk to people. Or exchange heated e-mails. I once bought some boots online that didn't fit, and I tried to return them, but I no longer had the original box. Because I no longer had the original box, I could not return the boots. I engaged in a lengthy e-mail discussion about this box. The box was worthless—it cost maybe two dollars at most—while the boots cost five hundred dollars. I had never before spent close to this amount of money on any article of clothing; this made me panic, and then become deranged. I wrote the online seller many deranged e-mails. Why should the boots become worthless because of a two-dollar box?

Once I failed to receive a pair of chairs from an eBay seller. She'd disappeared, and with my money. I left her phone messages. I e-mailed her. Finally, weeks later, she called me. We spoke at length about her life. She had a chronic female pain condition that flared at times, incapacitating her. Nothing eased the hell, not even morphine. I asked how this affliction had befallen her. She'd ridden horses as a child, she offered. Maybe that was the cause.

At the time of our conversation, I had just finished a book about a woman with an incurable headache. As I read this book, which chronicled the woman's endless cure quest, I became less interested in her pain than in my changing response to it. I began to think, as many of her doctors had begun to think, that maybe she was crazy or depressed. As her suffering intensified, and with it her desperation to treat it, I found myself increasingly doubting that she had a headache at all.

The eBay seller and I talked about how difficult it was to solicit people's sympathies over the long term. I admitted that I'm one of those people who harden in the face of other people's incurable pain. I start to blame them for failing to get better. Not to defend myself, I told the eBay seller, but I probably needed for my own sake to believe that I might be to blame for any of my future sicknesses; if I ever became sick, I could find comfort knowing that I was the crux of the problem and thus also the cure. I could just stop being who I was and get better.

We had a really candid conversation, the eBay seller and I, thoughtful and honest. When I arrived at her house to pick up the chairs, however, I found that she'd left them out on her lawn for me. When I knocked on her door to say hello, she did not answer.

Afterward, I told all of my friends about the eBay seller with the female pain problem. This story was good for a chuckle, and mostly at my own expense—no one was so incapable of the simplest online transactions as I was. Always my transactions failed, or became hilariously complicated. Even though none of my friends knew the eBay seller, I'd always felt guilty that I'd used her misfortune to make people laugh at me. Eleven years later, I contracted a strange pain down there, and I've never ridden horses. For three weeks I thought I had an untreatable, incurable condition. I thought I'd brought it on myself. I deserved it for making hay of the eBay seller's misery. It turned out I only had a tight muscle. I was quickly cured.

But because I did not have the proper faith to order these toy stethoscopes online, I called the company. The man with whom I spoke was very nice; he reassured me I'd receive the stethoscopes by the following Monday, in time for the Fourth of July parade. Then he said how odd it was that I, too, was ordering toy stethoscopes; his company hardly ever sold toy stethoscopes, yet in the past month there'd been a run on toy stethoscopes. We tried to figure out why. Many people were planning universal health care floats for their Fourth parades: this was our best guess. We didn't really have any other ideas. But I thought about the sudden popularity of toy stethoscopes for most of the day. There existed a reason for their popularity even if I didn't know it. Everything can be traced to its point of origin, and possibly to its point of disappearance. We know where things came from and where they are, even if those things have dematerialized in transit. I have become a location buff, possibly because I have a really good sense of direction. My interests and desires can be mapped, or mapped back. In parks, when people veer from the established paths and cut new ones through the grass, these are called "desire lines." Many people have the same desire when it comes to walking, which implies that we all want to get to the same place, and more quickly. Recently I desired to surround myself with the color cerulean. Six months later so did everyone else. Why did I crave cerulean just before everyone else craved cerulean? I try to crave colors and paths that other people do not crave. Right now, because I recently saw a '60s French movie in which the lead actress is wearing a union suit, I am craving a union suit. I am certain that come next winter, everyone will be wearing union suits. Will I get credit for wanting them first? Why do I need credit for my desire? It's ridiculous. But I do.

Today I took my kids to the cemetery to talk to E. B. White. E. B. White is buried next to his wife, Katharine Angell White, and their son, Joel White. I urge my children to tell E. B. what a great writer he is, because writers can never get enough reassurance about the importance of their work (even among dead writers this is true). Also E. B. White was a man of great humility; it is a privilege to live, for part of the year, a quarter of a mile from his grave, and to contribute to his eternal renown by remembering certain lines he wrote, for example these:

> *A person who writes of this and that stands in the same relation to his world as a drama critic to the theater. He is full of free tickets and implied obligations. He can't watch the show just for the fun of it. And watching the show just for the fun of it, once that privilege is forfeited, begins to seem like the greatest privilege there is.*

This afternoon, however, we were here to deliver a different message. Tonight there would be a reading in E. B. White's honor. This reading was meant to raise scholarship money for a local school—a private school—even though White, when he moved to Maine from Manhattan, sent his child to the local public school. I wanted to alert him, not to this irony, but simply to the fact that people would be reading from his work, and in not just one place, but in two. The Odd Fellows Hall was also hosting an E. B. White night. He was being remembered all over the place.

After I told him this, however, I felt horrible. Katharine, his wife, who is buried two feet from her husband, was a writer, too. She met E. B. when she was an editor, but she wrote a *New Yorker* column about seed catalogues and published a great gardening book. I hastened to compliment her as well. I told Katharine that she was also a great writer. But I'd already screwed up. My gaff was extra unforgivable because I am also married to a writer, and I am highly sensitive to the insensitivity of people who treat my husband as a writer in my presence while failing to treat me as one, even if they do consider him to be the better/more valuable/deserving of eternal renown. I never do this to other writer couples, no matter if I think one is superior to the other. If I ask one writer about her work, I ask the other writer about his work. When writer couples ask about or refer constantly to my husband's work and never inquire after mine, I begin to view their behavior as malevolent. One couple does this nearly every time we see them. Afterward, my husband tries to make me feel better by saying, "They probably think you're so confident and secure that you don't need their approval," and "Their behavior has no basis in reality." I argue that their assumptions about my confidence are eroding my confidence; that their reality is my reality when we're with them.

To be fair to this couple, this nerve is easy to strike with me. I am competitive with my husband, healthily so. He makes me push my brain to always be better. I perform the same function for him. But he is much less threatened by social inequalities than I am. He's not threatened by them at all. I do not often give him much of a chance, granted. When people start talking about my work in front of him, I quickly steer the conversation in another direction. It makes me uncomfortable to be complimented, but especially in front of him. I think, *I don't want him to feel bad,* even though there's been not a single indication that he's ever felt bad when people talk about my work in our presence, and not his. Only I feel this way.

My career competitiveness extends to my male friends. Once I overheard one of my best writer friends (a male) talking to another of our best writer friends (also male). The first friend observed to the second friend about a third writer (male), *He's not a threat.* Theirs was just harmless boy banter; my friends are too old to play organized sports, so their competitive energy must be rechanneled onto the athletic field of short-story writing. But it got me thinking. Did they talk to each other about me that way? Later I asked the first friend, *Am I a threat?* I asked it in jest but I was not kidding. I wanted to know, even though the question was, in some ways, moot. Obviously I love and admire my friend; obviously I am not out to threaten him or his career. But what I was asking without asking was this: *Do you feel endangered by the possibility that I might be as good as, or even someday more successful than, you?* And though I pushed him to answer the question using the same language he'd used with our other friend, my friend would only say, "Of course I admire your work. Of course I think you're great," but he couldn't say, *"You're a threat,"* I guess, because, on a fundamental level that has both something and nothing to do with writing, I am not one. Has any female writer ever been considered a threat by a male one? Aside from possibly Susan Sontag (surely someone had the good sense to feel threatened by her), I couldn't think of a single instance. We circled around and around the topic of threats, both of us feeling uneasy. Finally we agreed to stop talking about it.

Today I brought some objects to the Museum of Modern Art. Among them

> my great-grandfather's meat grinder
> the *l'amour fou* tap handle
> a ring
> the necklace I failed to give to my mother
> an air meter
> a doll-sized Webster's dictionary

This was not a hostile takeover on my part; I'd been invited to do something, to read or perform or something, in the museum. I put my objects in the gallery where an exhibit called *Inventing Abstraction* was being shown; to get to this gallery, you must walk through a doorway over which appears the Kandinsky quote "We must now, then, renounce the object." The first time I visited the show, I misread the quote as, "We must *not,* then, renounce the object." I thought this was so balanced and open-minded of Kandinsky; even while penning a perception-altering manifesto, he was committed to seeing all sides and including everyone, even those idiot still-lifers clinging to their skulls and their rotting fruit. *It's okay, you people who love your objects—you're included in our revolution, too.*

Later I realized what Kandinsky had actually written. And I felt insecure. And then hostile. My mistake reminded me that I am not by nature a manifesto writer, in that I do not want to hurt people's feelings or make anyone feel left out. I once wrote a manifesto, in which I tried so hard to be unbiased and fair. I suspect now that if I'd been rabidly biased and wickedly unfair, I'd have been better heard.

So maybe there was a tiny bit of hostility and insecurity involved because I'd been retroactively disinvited to the secession that happened, granted, decades before I was born. I am an object person. I cling to things. As a child I clung. Not for status reasons. Plain anchor reasons. Those objects that provided me with stability were rewarded with my protection. My bedroom lamp, for example. It broke. Possibly it was fixable, who knows; my parents were not handy. They fully knew what they were never doing. A broken lamp would stay broken. Better to remove the failed object from the premises. We removed lots of failed objects. A large porch, for example. Easier to tear off a giant, wraparound porch that was as sizeable as a cruise ship deck than to fix it. (To be fair—*fair*—there was no money. Removal was the only option.)

But when my lamp broke, and when I knew it would be thrown away, I put it in my bed. I slept with the lamp until I was promised: the lamp would not be thrown out. Lamps are shaped like people; they have heads. The sight must have been Duchampian (or Dalí-ian)—a wife lying in bed next to her husband who has been turned into a lamp! And the wife back into a girl!

My mother agreed not to throw away the broken lamp. As mentioned, I've won nearly all the domestic battles in my life. Perhaps this was the first.

So Kandinsky. MoMA. I decided to bring my objects to the abstraction show, fuck Kandinsky. Times had changed. Sure, in Kandinsky's day, the ability to speak via telegraph and then telephone, the ability to dematerialize yourself or to move your body (by trains) at higher speeds to distant places, this was an exciting life enhancement. The quickness with which words and people traversed time and space helped spread abstraction as an idea. (Next to the exhibit entrance was a huge diagram—it resembled the route maps that airlines print in the back of their in-flight magazines—consisting of points and lines, showing who had spread the idea on which continent and to whom.) Swifter connection represented possibility and promoted thought contagion. It still represents possibility and promotes thought contagion, but things have become endangered. Literally, *things*. Extinctions loom everywhere. "Evacuation of the object world" is how the curator of the MoMA show described what the abstractionists were up to. Once this felt exciting and liberating. To be free of all that weight and volume, and from the hell of what a friend of mine calls "object management." But now the whole world is being evacuated of things. Who needs abstraction now? Each day brings another tsunami wipe, or it can, on certain days, feel that way. Recently I picked up a book of matches and thought, *Soon we'll be saying, "Remember when we used matches?"*

Before bringing my objects to MoMA, I took them to a psychic because I wanted her to tell me about their histories. There's a practice called psychometry that purports to read the energy film left by former owners on the objects they once possessed or simply touched. I brought my objects to a woman named Durga. We sat across from each other at a fluorescent-lit table as though she were about to do my nails. She was blunt and no-nonsense; when I gave her an object to read and she wasn't receiving, she'd say, "I'm not getting anything," or, more crankily, "What do you want me to tell you about this?"

We also talked about synchronicities and how, the day

before I contacted her, a friend had given her my novel. That a psychic should be reading my novel was not so strange for me (my novel was about psychics); flipped, however, the scenario did seem synchronistic. Imagine you are a psychic and suddenly the author of the book you've just received calls you out of the blue.

"Even for me," Durga said, "this is an unusual degree of synchronicity."

By the time I met her she'd read part of my book. She had some factual bones to pick. For example, she told me that the psychic ability to see numbers was very rare (one of my characters psychically receives a serial number). "Numbers have very low numinosity," she said, which sounded so oxymoronic. (I later looked up "numinosity": it means "of or relating to a numen." I looked up "numen": it means "the spirit or divine power presiding over a thing or place.") "Only one psychic could see numbers," she said. She'd forgotten this famous psychic's name.

Two weeks later she wrote me an e-mail:

> Dear Heidi,
> The man whose name slipped my mind on
> Monday, the famous psychic who could see
> numbers inside an envelope, Ingo Swann passed
> away yesterday. Sorry to be the bearer of bad
> tidings. I always wanted to meet him, we had many
> friends in common, but never did.
> Best, Durga

Because this e-mail arrived from a psychic, I thought it might contain a hidden message. What was Durga really saying? What synchronicities were encoded here? Ingo Swann died on 1/31/13, and the number 13 (as well as any numeric variations including 1s and 3s) is a meaningful one to me, and has been since the late '80s, before Taylor Swift's mother probably even began menstruating. The book party at which, arguably, my career as a paid writer began happened at a club called "13." But probably the only secret message the e-mail contained was this: people can seem to be meaningfully near you, you can seem fated to meet them, but the connection, even today, maybe even more so today, because we assume the likelihood of connection, can fail to be made. Durga was connecting me to her failed connection. As is frequently my response when a person reaches out to me, and this reaching out deeply touches me, and even honors me, I do not reciprocate. I never responded to Durga. Whatever connection she sought, I did not allow it.

SEPTEMBER 9

Today I tried again to read *Pages from the Goncourt Journals.* I am reading a lot of journals and diaries right now—by Kafka, Woolf, a white Russian named Maria "Missie" Vassiltchikov, the Goncourts. The Goncourts were two brothers who aspired to be famous writers but instead only hung out with famous writers—Flaubert, Balzac, Proust, those guys. Not a shabby life, bouncing around the Paris literary scene of the nineteenth century, but a disappointing one for them. They wanted more, or rather different, fame. They wanted more timeless literary cred for their novels. Unfortunately nobody talks about their novels (not so much then, is my understanding, and definitely not now), but I have been told by many people how wonderful their journals are; how the true Goncourt genius lay, tragically, not in the many mediocre fictions they spun and co-spun, but in the reportorial acuity displayed in the journals, their bitchiness and their gossipiness.

For a long time, I did not want to read the Goncourt journals for fear that I would suffer the same fate as these pitied, embittered brothers. Their failure is a contagion to which I feel a greater susceptibility. I have been told, for example, that I "should receive a MacArthur for my e-mails." This was meant as a compliment, but I heard it as an insult. By reading the Goncourts' book, I risked suffering the same fate they did. After I am dead, my books of collected e-mails would be passed around and enjoyed at the expense of my other work, and every time anyone complimented my amazing books of e-mails, my accidental oeuvre, while overtly not complimenting my novels, they would do so with an implicit sigh—*poor thing.*

The other insecurity is reader-related. Everyone loves the Goncourt journals, they just love them! I, however, don't love the Goncourt journals. My failure of affection has nothing to do with the period nature of their language and observations—Sei Shōnogan, the famous Japanese courtesan and author of *The Pillow Book of Sei Shōnogan,* is older than the Goncourts by a few thousand years, and I totally relate to everything she writes. I just don't understand what's so great about the Goncourts, even though I've tried to read them repeatedly, and I've traveled with them to other states and other countries, because I don't want to miss my chance. Suddenly, here, in the Balkans for a literary festival, because of the perfect collision of barometric pressure, and air/water density, the smell of *this* burning trash, I will understand their greatness!

Today, however, I decided my failure has nothing to do with air pressure. I will never understand. But I wanted a good reason to abandon these Goncourts for good. I found one on page 18, which proves how little traction I ever got in their book. Which proves I did not give the Goncourts a fair shake before I concluded, definitively, that it was okay for me to give up on them. On page 18 the Goncourts write,

> Woman is an evil, stupid animal. She is incapable of dreaming, thinking, or loving. They can't create any poetry or things of that nature except what they are educated to create. The female mind is inherently inferior to the masculine mind. Women are also overly self assured, which allows them to be extremely witty with nothing but a little vivacity and a touch of spontaneity. Man on the other hand is endowed with the modesty and timidity which woman lacks. Women are unbearable if they try to act educated and on the same intellectual level as men.

To object to this kind of antique woman-hating, on principle, would make me too humorless to be endured. Who cares if the Goncourts hated women; so did everyone back then. So probably does everyone now; I suspect the Goncourtian attitude toward women, give or take many conscious degrees of vitriol, to be shared by a few of my friends' husbands, all of whom I'm fond of, in my way. I enjoy a misogynist so long as they have a wicked sense of humor and know, on some level, that they're pigs. This is why I enjoy Philip Roth but not Saul Bellow or James Salter. I recall a time in my midtwenties dating career when a suitor, typically around the third date, would give me a James Salter book. Salter articulated these suitors' internal lives (or their fantasy of their internal lives) without their needing to. Inside, they saw themselves as earnestly arty fighter pilots with souls too deep for any girl to plumb. Salter was their intimacy shortcut. They could hand me a Salter book—supposedly a "gift"—and say without saying, *This is me. I might someday say stuff like "Women fall in love when they get to know you. Men are just the opposite. When they finally know you they're ready to leave."* I appreciated the overture; it prompted me to be expedient in breaking off with these men. Salter helped me see so clearly the unendurable life these men and I would have together, not ever laughing about totally unfunny things.

NOVEMBER 3

Today I gossiped with a new friend about the illness of a woman we scarcely know. She and I are both living in a German villa along with a lot of academic policy experts and, in my case, my family. (We are here because my husband received a fellowship from the academy that occupies this villa; the academy awards people, for the length of a semester, money, housing, and food.) The sick woman— she is German—disappeared from the villa a few days after we arrived. This was over two months ago. No one knows what is wrong with her. We've asked around. Not even her close friends have a clue. Her story, we assumed, given the secrecy surrounding it, must be incredibly worth knowing. (My friend could offer this single detail about the sick woman: "Her husband was killed a few years ago in Antarctica.")

My friend, who is Italian, wondered if the refusal to discuss or acknowledge sickness was a specifically German trait. She herself had recently fallen ill; she said she couldn't *stop* talking about her illness. She couldn't stop calling people and telling them how sick she was, and how scared. She narrated in detail her sickness to everyone who would listen. Now she is better, sort of. She'd lost her innocence. Health, she now understood, is the pause between afflictions.

I'd recently lost my innocence as well. I was an illness iconoclast until I wasn't. At the age of forty-four, after decades of health so entrenched it was mistaken for chronic, I, like her, became sick.

The word "sick," however, doesn't accurately describe what befell me. I had pain. I had pain all the time. I was informed by doctors that I would have all-the-time pain for the rest of my life. They used the phrase "pain baseline." I'd played basketball and tennis in high school. I felt as though I was being initiated into a strange endurance sport, one without a clock or any means to keep score and end the match.

I did not deal with this news well. I asked my husband if he would mind if I killed myself. I tried to sell him on the benefits of my suicide; this stricken, whining person, who wants her around? I described to him the far greater damage I'd inflict on our children by living. By *insisting* on living, rather than taking an elegant bow (the elegant particulars had yet to be worked out). To *insist on living,* I lobbied, was sheer selfishness.

I did not want to be selfish.

Eventually I stopped thinking about suicide. Instead I became regularly beset by deep topics like time. I said to my husband, "Perhaps I am meant to be one of the great convalescents." By which I meant writers who popularized the lap blanket or wrote in bed, and whose literary greatness was proportionate to their physical misery.

So I filled my time with thoughts about my possible future greatness, and about time. Time, since my getting sick, had assumed a new shape. It was no longer linear; it did not cut through my day like a road. I did not see time ahead of me. I experienced time on top of me. I experienced time underneath me. Time became a hollow, vertical enclosure. I moved up and down inside this enclosure; occasionally I would remain stationary, or stable, at a fixed altitude that might be called "the present."

But because of the pain, I was vulnerable to sudden and extreme altitude shifts. As I dropped or ascended through the enclosure—my tube—I registered the change in air pressure physically. My stomach lifted to my throat. I often experienced my life in fast-forward, as though hurtling toward my death. Not that I cared about dying. What I could not bear to witness was the previews of other deaths that would, if I chose to stick around, precede mine. The eventual death, for example, of the affection my young son feels for me. Suddenly he wasn't next to me spinning tops. Suddenly he was grown. I did not experience the incremental shifting of his fondness toward me as he became four, and then five, and then twelve, and then thirty-six; I experienced it in a fraction of a second. I experienced it like a stabbing. This little boy whom I was, in the present, gamely entertaining with toys. He was already gone.

The same with my daughter, and my husband, and my parents, and my career, and the tree outside my window.

Everything around me sped up and vanished and then, when my altitude stabilized, reappeared, but something had changed. Everyone and everything existed as a future ghost to me. This sounds unpleasant. It was. However, I was so acutely *alive* during those four weeks. The pain of my aliveness was occasionally unbearable. I'm not referring to physical pain, though I experienced that too. I'm referring to emotional pain. To the emotional intensity that the passing of time should incessantly inspire; to the sickening countdown that every person should be registering every moment of her so-called aliveness, but is she? Until I got sick, I wasn't. How had I been so immune?

And then—I got better. I'd been misdiagnosed. With distressing quickness, time resumed as a road along which I traveled unthinkingly; when I had a spare reflective moment, and I rarely did, I'd turn my head to the side to admire the blur.

I am no longer immune, however, to the occasional plummet in time altitude. A plummet happened the other night. I found myself lying in bed and thinking about Mexican wineglasses, the green kind with the air bubbles. They are the size of goblets. I'd put a lot of identity stock, at one time in my life, in Mexican wineglasses. I'd bought some in my twenties, and they represented a pinnacle achievement in self-realization. Thinking of these wineglasses reminded me of a trip I'd taken through Mexico with a boyfriend when we were both in our twenties; we'd driven a two-piston rental through mountain ruts. We slept in fields. We emerged in a town with white walls and cafés, and were there also Mexican wineglasses? Did I buy mine there? I don't think so. I only remember a photo I took in that town of a white adobe wall and, rising above it, a crucifix atop a church dome. I was not religious, yet the photograph was so religious that I felt I shouldn't or couldn't be as fond of it as I was. But now, lying in bed and thinking about wineglasses, I found myself thinking of this photo, and the girl who took it, and that town—I'll never know its name—and I felt the kind of longing for that girl/town/ photo I feel for my children at night when they are asleep.

OCTOBER 26

Today I read a book written by a man I used to know. When I'd known him I was a certain kind of woman, or girl, that I'm not very proud of having been. I was a woman who used men. I used them quite knowingly. I didn't ever try to fool myself that I wasn't using them. Nor did I feel bad about my behavior. I felt that it was my due, though I don't know why I felt I was due anything. Men had done nothing to make me feel owed. Men had mostly been nice to me.

When I met this man, I had just moved to New York. I was temporarily crashing with an old friend who lived in a narrow three-story house located in the middle of a block in Little Italy. To get to this house we had to walk through an apartment building, out the other side, and into the court-yard where the slender house seemed to break through the cobbles like a tree. My friend and I shared a bed, and the bed was white, and a white sheer curtain billowed weakly over us at night, because there was a heat wave, and the house had no air-conditioning, and the windows, despite the staler air in the courtyard, were always open. Mean-while, on the lower levels of the house, people drank red wine and did coke until morning. I just wanted to sleep.

I'd moved to New York to become serious. Soon my friend and I would find a very serious artists' loft together. (We would have to interview with the loft's banker landlords to prove that we seriously were, or seriously wanted to be, artists. We would have to sublet the extra bedroom to an actor from a teen movie with a serious cult following, and who desired instead to be a serious concert pianist.)

I was not planning on having a New York boyfriend because I'd left a serious boyfriend in San Francisco. We were in love and intended to spend the summer together. But this meant I would have to survive in New York for the bulk of the year alone. I did not function well alone. I had not been alone since I started dating in third grade. I could count my alone days on two hands. I always had friends; I was never *alone*. But whenever I didn't have a boyfriend around I panicked. My future unspooled blurrily and I was felled by psychological vertigo, it was like standing on the sill of my loft windows overlooking the Holland Tunnel and the Hudson and the old printing press in the building opposite mine that respected no work hours—it was just on and on and on and on.

The man who wrote the book I read today had the misfortune of becoming the designated New York person who made me less fearful and lonely that year. I was never unaware that he wanted to be my boyfriend, and I was never dissuading him of his desire. I needed that level of devotion from him; a mere friend would not do. I gave him the hope that if he waited for the countrywide distance to dull my affection for my real boyfriend, he was next in line. He'd get the rest of my heart and all of my body.

He would get neither. He was one of those men I wanted to want to fuck. He was never a temptation even though we found ourselves in erotically and romantically charged situations where the minor sticking point of "attraction" should have been immaterial. Once when he was house-sitting for a friend with a penthouse apartment overlooking Central Park, we decided to drag a mattress onto the roof and sleep outside. Nineteen years later, I recall that night as one of the most magical nights I've spent in the city. And yet there was no sex. I experienced no desire. It was just me and a boy on a mattress in the air, the noise and the heat of the city billowing beneath us, keeping us afloat, and what a waste it was.

Also he was fun and funny and he had excellent friends. Oh, the poor men who have excellent friends. This man was friends with writers who were older, and already ruined by booze, with sloppily intricate bohemian approaches to love and to work. Once they had a Super Bowl party, not an ironic one. (These were sporty-spirited bohemians.) At halftime we went to the park and played touch football. We divvied into teams. My team captain had boyish hair and a boyish way of rousing us to achieve the highest possible level of sportsmanship, despite the fact that we would certainly be crushed. I recall thinking what a great dad he'd be someday—a fun and self-deceivingly optimistic dad, not one of those grumpy dads, the ones for which everything appears as an impossibility. Even a sandwich is impossible.

Eventually, when my California boyfriend and I split up, I started dating this future great dad. I did not date the man who thought he was next in line to date me. I did him the even greater disservice of dating a man he'd introduced me to, because he'd so thoughtfully included me in his life when I didn't have much of my own. All of it was shitty, so very shitty. And yet I did not feel shitty. Neither did any of my friends feel shitty when they used men like I did, and worse. One of my friends who got a lease in an uninhabitable factory tempted a man with great plumbing and electrical skills to fall in love with her. She kept him hooked on hope until he'd renovated her space, then stopped returning his calls. If I judged her, perhaps it was because I was trying to make myself feel less guilty for not feeling guilty when I'd behaved similarly. I'd never gone that far, I told myself. I'd never used a man to do something I might have paid another to do. I could not pay a man to be my friend and to introduce me to fun people. I could not pay a man to make me feel less alone. That was different, wasn't that different?

JULY 31

Today my friend told me about her gay male therapist crush. The crush seems mutual and for obvious reasons safe for all involved. Their relationship sounded so enviable. Recently, after a ten-year hiatus, I'd decided to go to therapy again. I made this decision abruptly, at two p.m. on a Thursday. I left the library. I went home and checked my insurance's website. I found an eligible provider within walking distance. I called her. She answered. She said, "Can you be here in an hour?"

The therapist, I'd discover, was a 1950s-era bohemian now in her seventies. She lived in a massive rent-controlled apartment on Riverside Drive that smelled of mothballs. She wore plaid shirts and jeans; she had wispy honey-colored hair that she seemed not to have brushed for decades, and that she'd twisted into a tiny knot atop her head. She had a crisp Katharine Hepburn properness to her speech.

She was also possibly senile. She seemed always to have left something she needed in another room. In the middle of our first session, her doorbell rang. It was a girl in her late teens. I heard the therapist whispering with her in the foyer. When the therapist returned, she told me that she'd forgotten she'd scheduled an appointment with the girl during my time slot. "But that was *weeks* ago," she said, as if it were the girl's fault for booking so early. She told me that the girl had abandoned college after less than one semester; that she was confused by life. The therapist did nothing to hide her disdain for this girl's problems. She seemed to be suggesting that we were working on much more vital and complicated problems. *Adult* problems.

I quickly understood that I would never tell this therapist much of anything that mattered to me. I'd talk, but I would not seek her counsel or advice. Our hour crept by. The hour felt like three hours. I had to tell her about my "family of origin," and she drew facile connections between my behavior and my relationship to my parents. At the end of each of our four sessions—I saw her only four times— she would pronounce that I needed medication, and that talk therapy was pointless for people like me, at least until I was on drugs.

I also sensed she didn't like me. Or maybe it wasn't that she didn't like me—she felt overwhelmed by me. In truth I was pretty unstrung. Normally it takes me months to reveal any emotion to a therapist, if I ever do; I once had a therapist who accused me of treating our sessions like a cocktail party encounter. This was not an inaccurate description of how I viewed our meetings. I adored this therapist. I joked that I paid her by the hour to be my pal. I wanted to be the patient she most looked forward to seeing; I strove always to be entertaining and never to be a drag. I took tissues from the box next to her couch only when I had a cold.

Meanwhile, I showed up to my second appointment with this new therapist in hysterics. I'd been buying a coffee at the Cuban place around the corner from her apartment when I'd received some bad news that shouldn't have come as a surprise, but it did. I left the Cuban place without my coffee. I tried not to cry until I made it to her apartment. Then I lost it. I said crazy, nonsensical, not-entirely-true shit. I spun for her the most negative and hopeless account of my life and its prospects. I voiced interconnected paranoias. Once I started I couldn't stop. I gave myself permission to be the darkest, most repellant version of myself. It was liberating not to care, for maybe the only time in my life, what another person thought of me.

The two appointments that followed were awkward. I was embarrassed by my breakdown. To compensate I was chatty and witty and entertaining. I told stories about my most outrageous family members; I told *stories*. Not lies, exactly. But I emphasized the interesting and salacious parts. She asked me at one point, "Do you love your mother-in-law?"

The fifth time I went to her apartment, she didn't answer her door. I'd arrived that day with an ulterior motive. I'd brought a single shoe that I wanted to photograph on her couch. A German artist I admire often violates other people's houses with her personal belongings. She put her nightgown in a friend's closet and her diary under another friend's pillow. Her art is a form of burglary where she adds things instead of subtracting them. I planned to do this when my therapist left me alone in her living room to retrieve something she'd forgotten in her kitchen.

When she failed to answer the door, I wondered: did she somehow guess what I'd planned to do on her couch? Then, more logically, I figured, given her track record, had she forgotten our appointment? I rang again. Nothing. I went home. I thought she'd realize her mistake and call me to apologize and reschedule. She didn't. I started to worry that maybe she'd died. I Googled her name + "dead"; I found nothing. Maybe, I thought, she's just expecting me to show up next week, at which point she'll explain what happened. The day of my appointment I couldn't decide whether or not to go. I could have called her, but I didn't want to risk talking to her. (She was the only therapist on the planet who answered her phone.) I didn't go. Certainly, I thought, she'd call me now. After our first session I'd signed a contract committing me to pay in full if I ever missed an appointment without twenty-four-hours' cancellation notice.

The therapist did not call me. She never contacted me again.

Nor did I ever contact her. I was happy to have been freed from this unsatisfactory arrangement without needing to do or say anything (therapist breakups are such a meta-trial). I've often wondered what happened to her. What if she didn't have a stroke? What if she wasn't sick or hospitalized, and thus unable to make phone calls? What if she just genuinely disliked me? I had been to other therapists, most of whom I'd gotten along with well enough. But our relationships were predicated on my "putting my best face forward." When I was sad, I'd make jokes about my sadness. I'd been so totally hilarious when I'd talked to my pal therapist about my then-upcoming divorce. With this

new therapist I'd let my ugliest self show. Either she'd had
a stroke, or she'd died, or she'd simply decided: I cannot
help that woman. I cannot bear to be around that woman.

Today I visited a summer camp attended by a lot of
wealthy New York City kids. I had not been around so many
eleven-year-old girls since I was eleven. The campers were
composed, and stylish, and, sure, in the Maine woods,
where one of the main activities was "llama care," their pre-
ternatural confidence and sense of entitlement struck me
as pointless survival skills, but most of their lives weren't
happening in the Maine woods. I found myself harshly
judging these children. They would get everything they
wanted in life (real life), and would it even prove a chal-
lenge? Probably not as challenging as keeping the llamas'
fur from snarling. Probably not as challenging as sleeping in an incredibly spacious teepee. Achieving happiness,
well, that was another matter, but isn't it for everyone? In
this elusive quest, the wealthy are not especially burdened,
though perhaps they feel the failure more acutely. It is
maybe harder not to get something if you've mostly always
gotten everything.

Certain recent encounters with very rich friends (people who were rich from birth) have confirmed: we are, on a
basic psychological level, different people, and these differences can rankle me morally. My moral rankle, however, is
complicated. It's disingenuous. It's a form of self-loathing.
Because for many years, I wished more than anything that
I had been born rich. My family was middle-class and rich

by the standards of many, including my friends. (I attended a public school near the projects; my best friend lived in a near-derelict apartment building that, in keeping with the occasionally benevolent ironies of Maine real estate, had a beautiful view of the harbor.) But I knew my family could be much, much richer. As an eight-year-old my fantasy was concrete, modest, and thus not beyond the realm of possibility, except that it completely was. I wanted to live in an old mansion in Greenwich, Connecticut. Very specifically Greenwich, a place I'd never been. I chose Greenwich because each Sunday I read the *New York Times Magazine*'s real estate section. I cut out pictures of mansions for sale in Greenwich and tacked them to my bulletin board. I knew, even as a kid, that a belief in one's ceaseless entitlement could not be acquired later in life. Even if I managed to become rich, I would always be faking entitlement.

Whatever. I was happy to fake it.

Since my parents did not share my wealth fantasy, I eventually discovered boys to be the quicker route. In high school I dated a boy with money, or what counted as money in my town. He wore torn sweaters and drove an Audi and was adept at stealing radar detectors from the country club parking lot, a talent I understood as his form of artistic expression because he was rich. He didn't *need* to steal anything. (I was not wrong about his creative gifts; he would grow up to become a successful defrauder of insurance companies.)

After high school I fell in love with a rich boy from Virginia. (I didn't fall in love with him because he was rich; he remains, other than my husband, the love of my life.) Through him I lived the rich life I'd dreamed my entire childhood of living, sort of. Richmond was no Greenwich. His family owned (I can still remember) two

Audis, a Porsche, a Saab, and a BMW. They had a beach house, a hunting property, and a ski condo. That I loved him so much, and that his family was so warm and inclusive, meant that I fell into his world like a thirsty girl into a well. Every once in a while I'd poke my head out and wonder, *What am I doing here?* I couldn't have a conversation with his female friends without faking an identity of assumed ease and privilege (and ease with privilege). These girls flew to London for the weekend to shop for debutante dresses. Their debutante parties were decorated by set designers from *Cats*. (They had debutante parties!) All of his friends went to Ivy League schools, even the self-admittedly dumb friends. Where I came from, being admitted to such schools was like winning the escape lottery, and many smart people I knew didn't win, and ended up at the paper mill or a local community college. Every once in a while I'd call home exhausted and upset—upset by the amount of energy it took to fit in, upset that I cared to expend that energy in the first place. I think my parents were relieved by my periodic cracks. I imagine they otherwise thought they'd lost me to another planet, one to which theirs offered very infrequent shuttle runs.

Still, I loved this boyfriend; I was convinced I would marry him. This belief resolved certain anxieties and illogicalities (despite my desire to be rich, I wanted to be a novelist). Of the many pressures I felt as I one-eye squinted toward adulthood, the pressure to support myself, or the question of how I would do so over the long term (and in the manner to which I was newly accustomed) was not one of them. It's not as though I lost my drive. I made good grades because I always did. I overachieved because I always did. I got grants and pursued non-remunerative careers because that's what interested me. But to know in the back of my mind that I would always have a very nice place to live, and money to eat in very nice restaurants and to buy very nice clothes and to go on very nice vacations, well, this was extraordinarily calming to me.

At a certain point, however, wealth—not money but *lots of money*—started to represent, ironically, the inverse of possibility. It seemed oppressive; it changed people's circuitry. One summer, my boyfriend and I accompanied his family on a trip to Spain. We ate every meal with his family. His parents and I talked more than was advantageous, if we wanted to remain fond of one another, about important matters. His father was conservative; he was also extremely perceptive, altruistic, and intelligent, which these days does not go without saying. He'd grown up with nothing; he was a self-made man. Still, it was wearing and occasionally enraging to tussle with him on political and social topics while I was staying in the villa he'd paid for, and eating the many fancy meals he paid for. I felt guilty that I experienced anything other than gratitude toward him.

Two years later, my relationship with my boyfriend began to falter. I'd like to claim that this faltering had nothing to do with the fact that, once I hit my early twenties, I no longer fantasized about being rich. (I fantasized, at most, about being able to pay my bills. This seemed ambition enough where money was concerned.) Soon I would be dating a broke PhD student with a disregard for money so entrenched that he would spend a semester living rent-free in a tent pitched on the concrete floor of a friend's garage. I learned to be a different person through him, and maybe I accomplished this on my own, but it doesn't, even at a remove of a few decades, feel that way. I needed guidance. I was still at that point where a boyfriend was an opportunity to try out different identities, not just an opportunity to have sex and be loved. As my male friend in graduate school once said, "Men want a relationship, but women expect a *world*." I don't think, in other words, that my expectations were atypical, or that I was atypically using men as a means to better, or simply alter, because my goals had changed, my circumstances. According to this friend, I was behaving like every other woman he knew. I've never considered whether or not I provided the men I dated a new identity to try out. What would it have been? I was blonde and clever and fun, but I can't imagine that I changed a man's world as they often changed, or promised to change, mine.

MAY 2

Today I went looking for Sanchez again. Again I could not find him. Sanchez is a legend in this town, at least among decorators and used furniture salesmen. Sanchez is a reupholsterer and an impossible man to locate. I'm looking for him because I have a couch that needs reupholstering, and reupholstering, I'm starting to suspect, is a dying art, like blacksmithing or coopering. Sanchez might be dead himself. His cell numbers, the four I've got, are all disconnected.

I could just buy a new couch, but then again I can't. This couch has history. It is an heirloom of sorts, proof of the people my husband and I once were. Once we were people who cared about, granted, possibly the wrong things. We cared about couches. We wanted to stake our claim as interesting individuals by owning a highly unique couch. Then we became enlightened, or resigned. The couch's purpose shifted. It became defiled. Now it is used as a napkin by our children. For the past nine years, this piece of furniture has wiped mouths and hands and absorbed milk, all kinds of milk. This possibly makes the couch sound more disgusting than it really is, though in truth it is pretty disgusting. This possibly makes us sound like parents without boundaries, because who lets their children drink milk on a blue velvet couch which, when stained with milk, to be perfectly candid, looks as though people, and the assumption would be "we," have had lots of sex on it? And now we expect our guests to sit on this couch, atop these stains, while eating olives and cheese?

I know people often fail to find disgusting or shameful the revealing grime and sloth of their own lives. My friend with the apartment covered, quite impressively evenly, with a layer of dog fur, makes no excuses for her dog or for herself. My friend with the kitchen that stinks of compost from a filthy plastic bucket kept next to the stack of clean dishes. My friend with the long black hair (not her hair— whose hair is it?) cemented by dried toothpaste globs to the bathroom sink. These people are not apologetic. I am apologetic. They are not trying to cover up anything, as I am trying, quite literally, to cover up the daily evidence of our poor judgment, our pure exhaustion. That's what this couch is. A sign of exhaustion. I would rather not be needed for two consecutive minutes than have a beautiful couch. I would rather search for coats I don't need on eBay while milk is spilled than have a beautiful couch. I let the couch go because I felt confident that people like Sanchez existed in the world. Once I recovered my energy and my standards, I could enlist a Sanchez to reinstate my former self. No slip is permanent, right? But I can't even leave him a message asking for his help. I can't even hope that he'll return my call.

Today my friend is arriving from London to help me pack. I am in Italy, I have been in Italy for a month, working at an art colony, and together she and I are going to a different part of Italy (also to work). I am often anxious about traveling alone, so she has been requested to keep me company and prevent me, in theory, from being anxious. What I forget is that she often makes me anxious when I am with her. She has a hunger for adventure so extreme that my usual hunger for adventure becomes, due to reactionary prudence, squelched. If she suggests we do something, then I know it is my job to wonder, *Why is this probably a very bad idea?*

The last trip my friend and I took together was to see and experience a building. I'd heard about this building for years; I'd even written a novel that took place in this building (that I'd never, save in my imagination, visited). While living in Germany—i.e., nearby, relatively—I decided it was time to finally see it. My friend agreed to accompany me.

This building, in order to be seen and experienced, however, required great effort. My friend and I had to fly to Zurich. We had to rent a car and drive, in winter, on terrible Swiss mountain roads. Our arrival was adventure enough for me. I was happy to stay inside for the rest of our trip. We were there to see and experience a building; let's stay inside the building! (The building is a spa, but "spa" does not accurately describe the building. It is more accurately described as an art installation filled with water.) But my friend had other ideas. She wanted to explore the area. She'd found a place where we could ride a sled for six miles down an alp. She'd found a beautiful reservoir she wanted to visit. She wanted to leave the building we'd traveled all this way to see and experience, even though, she agreed with me, we'd never been inside a building like this in our lives. A building built for people. Why are most buildings *not* built for people? We asked ourselves this question over and over as a means of restating our astonishment. Most buildings are machines. They perform services. They provide heat and dryness and other basic functions that help with survival. This building provided so much more than survival. This building was like a bed or a sweater or an orchestra. This building took into account what your body wanted to do, feel, see, hear. After not too much time in this building we felt as though we'd taken hallucinogenic drugs. We simply could not believe how much this building intuited and addressed (and maybe, too, inflamed) every desire we possessed. It became overwhelming. We needed a break from the building. We needed a break from being so deeply understood.

Given that the six-mile sled run was closed (I tried not to seem excited by this news) we decided to drive to the reservoir. We asked a local man for directions. He warned that the roads, due to snow, were impassable. My friend pushed. Really? Were they really impassable? The man agreed to call the resident expert on road conditions. He would tell the expert the make of our car, and she, based on whatever fate algorithm she ran, would calculate our survival chances.

The woman said: with our car, we might be fine.

This did not sound like encouragement to me. To

my friend, it sounded like encouragement. Because I am scared of appearing scared, I agreed with her interpretation. I would drive us to the reservoir.

No one should listen to experts. The road was ice-shellacked, the road was steep, the road was barely the width of our car; to the right of the road loomed a cliff so steep we could see only air. As often happens in situations when reality becomes terrifyingly stark, I avoid panic by allowing metaphor to take over. It's not *I am headed up a steep and slippery mountain road and I cannot turn around* but *My life is a novel written by an author who might want me to entertainingly die.* My friend and I were no longer people in a car; we were characters in a plot. As characters in a plot, there was no escaping the fact that our story would have an ending. An *outcome.* Arguably, each day, at its conclusion, produces an outcome (arguably so does each minute, each second, each microsecond). But even when you're just a person (not a character, or a person who feels like a character) your day will end, and using the most basic (i.e., starkest) accounting model, one of two outcomes will befall you—you will be alive or you will be dead. Some days the luxury of other outcomes can obsess you—*Will he respond to my e-mail? Will I get enough sleep so that I can teach tomorrow?* Other days refuse to permit distractions from the most fundamental outcome options: alive or dead. On these starker days, you can begin to worry as characters in a book should worry. Your outcome, however it gets decided, might not be designed with your best interests in mind.

Then we encountered the tunnel.

It was not clear, at first, that the tunnel was a tunnel. The road simply disappeared into the side of a mountain. Preventing us from pursuing the road was a metal door.

The road here also widened. At this single point in our journey, it was possible to turn around.

"I guess we have to turn around," I said.

My friend thought otherwise. She'd read about this tunnel online. If we drove right up to it, she said, the door would open.

This seemed impossible. It was not. The door creaked and groaned as it rolled open, slat by slat.

We drove through. In the rearview mirror, I watched the door lower with the stuttering movements of a mechanism about to fail. The door resembled a jaw closing, and the tunnel, aptly, a digestive track. The stone undulated overhead, muscular and involuntary. Our outcome was being processed.

We drove a few kilometers. If we'd lowered the car windows, we could have touched the walls as we threaded the space between them. Finally we reached the exit, sealed shut by a second door. We approached at idling speed, hoping to God the thing would open. It did. We'd driven more deeply into the Alps but also more deeply into winter. The snow was abundant, the icicles thick and browned with age. We'd traveled through more than just solid matter to reach this place.

Behind us, the door closed.

We parked. We hiked, or tried to hike, but the roads were so slick we could only skid and fall. We eventually reached the reservoir. I tried to pretend I was enjoying myself. I wasn't. My friend teased me about being such a worrywart, and I finally stopped feigning otherwise and admitted—I wanted to go back. I did not find it fun to wait for our outcome to be decided. I wanted to *know* our outcome, even though the variables were tilting us toward the less desirable of the basic two. Slippery roads. Mechanical doors that might or might not open. This situation reminded me not only of being in a novel but of writing one. It is equally no fun to be the author of scenarios where only a number of small outcomes are plausible. I knew the horror from both sides. In part this is why I'd told myself I was no longer, or not for the time being, writing novels. When writing novels I cannot seem to escape the trap of a plot. I imagine a fictional scenario and so quickly the march of consequence takes over. Things happen and so then other things must happen. I spend so much time working in the guts of this machine I feel less like a writer and more like the engineer of a high-performance vehicle. I am stuck perfecting the mechanics of happenings and coincidence. This is how plots take shape and achieve viability, at least when I'm wearing the hard hat—coincidence, recursion. In my defense, I am simply being mimetic. My life seems marked by a high degree of coincidence and recursion and synchronicity (as Durga the psychic confirmed). I know no other means to achieve plausibility.

I would like to learn other means.

My friend teased me for being such a timid, neurotic freak. She did it good-humoredly. We got in the car. The tunnel doors opened. The roads remained roads and did not cede to air. Back in town, we made a sunny lunch of cheese and bread we'd stolen from the breakfast buffet, and drank vodka, and grew giddy. We'd survived! We ran through the town like lunatics. We'd survived! We hiked up a hillside and peed in a sheep barn. We ended up at a store that sold sweaters. We made the shopkeeper drink with us. We asked her lots of questions about herself. *Who was she, no really, who?* She was Danish, not Swiss. She ran a bed-and-breakfast with her (also Danish) husband. She said, after a time, "I like your scarf." I was wearing a striped knit scarf. I told her that I'd bought it a few weeks ago in Berlin. I told her that I'd Googled the designer afterward to see what else she made, and everything was ugly, and this made me wonder if maybe I shouldn't love my scarf as much as I did.

The woman asked to see the tag. "Ah," she said. "I know that woman. She used to sleep with my husband when we lived in Copenhagen. It's true, her stuff is shit."

We wanted to ask—when did the designer sleep with her husband? While he was her husband? Before he was her husband? We left the shop in a whirl of questions. The day was not yet over—our outcomes, in theory, had yet to be decided. There could be an avalanche! My friend could get another stupid idea! But I suspected we were safe. We'd already had our unlikely coincidence, our moment of synchronicity or recursion. The machine had run its course. Our deaths would not be the likely outcome today.

JULY 14

Today I met for coffee a friend who, a few years ago, told me the most perplexing lie. She told me she was having an affair with a married man at work. (This part was true.) The only other details I gleaned from her confession— offhandedly mentioned—were these: The man lived in Connecticut. He had three children. She told me enough about him, in other words, that I could sleuthily Google her small company and discover his identity if I wanted to. Was I supposed to do this? I wasn't sure. To be safe, I didn't. I would respect, as she apparently wanted me to respect (since she hadn't outright told me his name), both his and her privacy.

A week or so later, however, I decided oppositely. She'd felt bound by discretion but, at the same time, badly wanted me to know. Maybe she'd made a promise to the man, who was married and obviously trying to keep things under wraps, not to tell anyone, not a soul. She'd given me the search terms so that she could tell me without telling me. Obviously she *expected* me to Google her love affair. I did. The only man at her company who lived in Connecticut with three children was named Ryan. Ryan, I now knew without her needing to break her vow of secrecy, was the man in her office with whom she was sleeping.

A few months later, I was shopping with this same friend. (Obviously we are not such close friends that we see each other frequently.) I asked her how "things" were going. She said she was in love but miserable, and that the situation had become really complicated with Nick's wife.

"Nick," I said. "Who's Nick?"

She seemed surprised that I shouldn't know who Nick was.

"Nick's the guy," she said, leaving the rest unspoken. Nick's the married guy I'm having the affair with.

We kept shopping but I was quietly confused. I'd Googled all of the men in her workplace. I knew enough about Nick, in other words, to have confidently excluded him as a suspect. Nick lived in Brooklyn and had two kids. And yet she'd told me that the man with whom she was sleeping lived in Connecticut with three kids. Ryan was her only coworker who lived in Connecticut with three kids. So she'd known that if I Googled her affair using the data points she'd provided, that I'd be steered toward the wrong man. Had she done this on purpose? Was this a test? If so, had I passed or had I failed? Years later, I still don't know.

OCTOBER 30

Today we are assessing the damage from the hurricane. We have brown water flowing from our faucets but we do have water. We have lights and heat and Internet. We no longer have half of what was once a whole tree outside our windows. To bemoan the partial loss of a tree when others have lost whole homes is ridiculous, but I am bemoaning its loss (I've told myself) as an object lesson to my children, who cannot understand loss on a grand scale and so must learn to comprehend it in smaller increments. They must learn about loss through a tree.

The tree is the reason we moved into this apartment; I have said many times, "Without this tree I do not want to live here." I have spent nights worrying that something will happen to the tree; it will grow sick and die, a taxi will lose control and mortally wound it. The latter worry is not far-fetched. Our windows overlook a cursed T intersection. A girl was killed by a falling chunk of cornice at this intersection. A man in a helmet catapulted from his motorcycle and landed facedown in the intersection, many yards from the point of impact, and appeared to have dropped from the sky. A taxi lost control and rear-ended a FedEx truck and took out a pedestrian waiting to cross the intersection. The intersection is the site of many car accidents. While cleaning the kitchen or making the beds, I have often heard the sound of brakes and crunching metal. The tree protected our home from the chaos. It filled our windows with white, or green, or red, or a hatching of bare sticks like the fingers you put over your eyes during the scary parts of horror movies. We had to crane our necks to see the bodies.

But now half of the tree is gone. During the storm, a large part of it lay in the street like the man hurled from his motorcycle. I didn't even realize it was *our tree*—I thought it was a weaker sapling, hauled wholesale from the roots. When I ascertained that it was ours, I wanted to go outside and investigate even though the hurricane was still raging. My husband observed, "If you die out there, your death will be so stupid." I waited until the wind subsided a little. I ran out to see what remained of our tree. Not a lot.

This morning I prepared my daughter and son for the possible death of the tree. I tried to make them understand how long the tree had been there, and how old they would be before, if in fact we lost it, another tree could grow to be as large. How to make people who don't understand time feel a loss that is best measured in time? It proved tricky. The only way to demonstrate the loss was to dramatize it. When the tree crew arrived to remove the half-tree from the street, I stood on the windowsill in my pajamas and watched. I acted sad because I *was* sad. Our tree would never be the same. It might even die. The damage wasn't insignificant. I wanted to be the conduit of sadness—and of passing time and mortality—by interpreting the significance of the potential loss of the tree for my kids. I could tell this wasn't happening. I could tell they were more interested in my reaction to the tree. I thought ahead to a point in time when this behavior might become symbolic of who I was or, depending on my life status, am. I do not think it unwise to view all children as future tattletales.

Such a perspective forces you to better (and with greater care) *behave,* lest your conduct be chronicled later, and prove revealing in ways you did not intend. If and when my daughter told her own children about her memories of the big hurricane, maybe the only takeaway she'd recall would involve me. I was the object lesson. *My mother was undone by the possible death of a tree.*

JUNE 27

Today I talked with a woman about ghosts. We were sitting in the shadow of a large building that is reputedly full of them. We wondered if people mistook for ghost sightings what was, in fact, a primal fear response to poorly arranged rooms. The appearance of a ghost was really just the cave brain responding with a potent visual alarm. The cave brain whipped up a ghost when a room lacked escape options, or when it featured too many unprotected entrances through which a saber-toothed tiger or a rapist might prowl in the dark.

I told this woman about a room in which I repeatedly, or so I believed, saw a ghost. The room's bed, I conceded, was in the dumbest place. The door was to the right of my head; when I was lying in the bed, the door was actually, by a few inches, *behind* me. I'd awaken every night in a state of panic and look to the door, where I saw a figure briefly coalesce from the darkness, then vanish. But I understand now (or think I understand) that I saw no ghost in that room; my brain was just keeping me alert to bad possibilities, tigers or rapists or whatever.

Then I told this woman my theory about rooms, and

why some rooms immediately feel like home while others, no matter how long you live in them, never do. Maybe ghosts are to blame, or a lack of egresses, but possibly, too, there was, I had recently decided, the issue of light. Growing up, I slept in a room that faced west. From the age of four to the age of eighteen, I opened my eyes to the same message: something better was happening elsewhere. I had to seek out the sun (presuming there was one); otherwise I had to wait for it to come to me. All sorts of bogus long-term psychological effects could be generated from such regular conditioning. To awake to the west has, maybe, imprinted me with certain personality traits. I am always thinking: where I am is not as good as where I could be. I must, from the moment I open my eyes, be on the move.

This sounds like an optimistic mind-set. It's not. It's neurotic. It's crazy-making. Especially since I don't particularly like the morning sun I feel so compelled to seek. Regardless, I only feel at home in places that face west. I currently live in an apartment that faces east. Despite my best attempts to comfortably inhabit this apartment, I have failed. I've faulted the gray paint I chose ("November Rain," clearly formulated for seasonal depression junkies or, more damningly, per a decorating blog, "for the sage green set"), the window treatments (there are none), the fact that our books are kept in the guest room and so sometimes it looks like nobody interesting lives in our home. There's sun upon waking, yes, but it feels like a reward I do not deserve and don't want.

Probably it's due to some combination of light and egresses and ghosts, but for sure I experience a panicked flight reaction when I enter certain interior spaces. I told the woman about a room to which I recalled suffering an immediate allergic reaction. I had just married my first husband. We'd blown all of our money on the wedding and had just a few hundred dollars left, and so we decided to spend it at an old inn in Camden, Maine, with cheap off-season rates. My first husband called these three days our "mini-moon." The moment I entered our mini-moon room, however, I needed to leave it. For no apparent reason I felt on the verge of hysterics. Or maybe there was a reason. The room had been renovated so that, while legitimately Victorian, it now vibed faux-Victorian. I worried that this room would reify what I already felt—I did not belong in this marriage. I was faux to my core. If we stayed in this room, I thought, my first husband and I would be divorced by sundown. I made up a story about how I needed a bathtub and not a shower with massaging jets. The porter showed us a second room, one that still had its old clawfoot tub, and one that didn't make me think, *We are doomed*. This room faced west.

Still, the west-facing room could not protect me from all bad omens, and Camden, in late October, plagued by rain, was full of them. My first husband and I read books each afternoon by the fire in the inn's library, and drank tea. I was reading a biography of Edith Wharton. Wharton, I learned, married a man she did not love because she felt societal pressure to do so. (I didn't feel societal pressure to marry my first husband, but I did feel pressure, most of it self-inflicted.) She had a fulfilling life despite her bad marriage, and, besides, she wrote many novels, which is what I hoped to do. Maybe, I reasoned with myself, I hadn't made a terrible mistake. Maybe a bad marriage would prove good for my career, too.

Aside from wedding decompression, my one goal in Camden—a town with many used bookshops—was to locate an out-of-print memoir. Published in the 1940s by a woman who never wrote another book, this memoir detailed the story of a wife (the author) and her husband, who fled Manhattan to homestead in Maine. The husband came from a wealthy banker family; he had artist ambitions, as this variety of black sheep usually does. Their remote, falling-down house—on a point of land accessible only by boat—became, after the adrenaline high of their escape subsided, the site of their marriage's unraveling. Only the seeds of the unraveling are present in the memoir. On the last page, they are still happily married. In the hermetic world of the book, their love persists. In reality, they grew miserable. I know because Maine is a tiny state and the couple's decline into unhappiness remained gossip nearly sixty years later. The friend who'd told me about the book had met the husband, by then in his eighties and a widower, at a dinner party. She found him scary, she said, broody and embittered. So great was the couple's marital misery in the remote house, in fact, it was rumored the husband had murdered the wife (she died under mysterious circumstances).

On the third rainy day of our mini-moon, I decided to search for this book in the local used bookstores. The first bookstore didn't have a copy of the book on the shelves, but I figured I'd ask the salesperson if she knew of a copy lingering in one of the many unpacked boxes. When I told her the book's title, her eyes—they were white-blue, the irises seemed to spiral toward the vanishing point of her pupils—got really wide. She didn't have a copy, she said. But she knew the book very well and had read it many times herself, because the woman who'd written it was her aunt.

I couldn't believe it. The woman, also stunned, nonetheless seemed so excited to talk to me about the book. Yet she didn't say a word. She just stared at me expectantly, as though I were the person who might enlighten her about her own relative, and her eyes spiraled more quickly, and the whole situation grew surreal and uncomfortable, and without learning anything more about her aunt, I left.

We did eventually, due to our own growing misery, get divorced, my first husband and I. The end of our marriage came as no surprise to either of us, though he and I maintained different perspectives on the cause of death. He blames this and that marital moment of callous disrespect or unintended harm as the cause. I take the more deterministic view. Our divorce seemed at the time, and still seems to me, to have been fated from the outset, though I know this fate is unrelated to Edith Wharton, or to randomly meeting the niece of a woman who might have been murdered by her husband, or to the fact that we were supposed to spend our mini-moon in that first, terrible room.

SEPTEMBER 5

Today we had dinner at the German villa in which we are living until December. (Technically, my family and I are not living in the villa; we are living in a small cottage by the gate. We do, however, eat meals at the villa.) This villa was built in the late 1800s and has a WWII-related story I've been told secondhand; roughly it involves the Jewish family who once owned the place and the gratitude they felt toward the avenging Americans, who, after the war, used it as a rec house for military personnel and filled it with Ping-Pong tables. When the Americans left, the family, in order to ensure a future of continued German

American ideas exchange, donated the villa to an American ambassador who turned it into an academy (minus, sadly, the Ping-Pong tables). This story, or some slightly more accurate version, is how the villa came into my country's possession; this is how I am being served a fancy dinner in it.

Most everyone living at this villa is an expert on foreign policy, on American and European intellectual history, on international economic issues, and on other topics I know nothing about. For months, my husband and I have worried that we'll have nothing to say to the experts at the many meals we're meant to share with them. Here is a good example of why we are worried. Last night my husband and I, in bed, Googled *WW1 why did it happen*.

At breakfast the other day, I chitchatted with an expert who was trying so hard to relate to me on my turf, such as he understood it; he said how much he appreciated having writers around because they added levity to the usually grave proceedings. But he also had such respect for writers! He brought up the fact that UNESCO had recently awarded *Das Kapital* a distinction, or maybe it was a prize. I asked if UNESCO only named nonfiction books as winners of this distinction or prize, and he replied, "Oh no, they've also named . . ." and he cited a very long title in German. I admitted that I had never heard of this book. He repeated the title. I said, "I'm sorry, I don't know it." And then he said, "It's the incredibly famous Middle High German epic on which Wagner based *The Ring* series." I said, "Oh, right, *right*!" The expert seemed a little crestfallen. He could forgive me for failing to be an expert in his area of expertise; he seemed slightly less willing to forgive me for failing to be an expert in my own.

(I have just looked up the UNESCO distinction/prize

the expert mentioned. It's an international program called the "Memory of the World," the stated goal of which is as follows: "to safeguard the documentary heritage of humanity against collective amnesia, neglect, the ravages of time and climactic conditions, and willful and deliberate destruction." What the Memory of the World program does not safeguard against is the failure of seemingly very educated and memory-loss-aware people to have read or even heard of these works to begin with. It does not safeguard the documentary heritage of humanity against people like me.)

By the night of the first dinner—today's dinner—my anxiety about socializing with these experts was chart-breaking. I figured the best I could do was make jokes and then more jokes. Or I would—since I'd recently started taking longish swims in the Atlantic Ocean—talk about sharks. I would cite shark attack statistics for the lake we could see through the dining room windows (*since before the beginning of time, no shark attacks on humans have been reported in this lake*). Fortunately, I was seated near an architect (I could talk buildings) and the fourteen-year-old son of a Chinese foreign policy expert (I could talk *Hunger Games*). I was also seated near a man in a banker's suit who was probably younger than me but who felt, categorically speaking, like a no-fun uncle. He introduced himself as the villa's CFO; we talked grounds, we talked improvements and expensive plumbing disasters. I decided to introduce the topic of the automatic mowers. The villa's property has a pair of automatic mowers—each is a three-wheeled robot the size and shape of a small ottoman. They are otherworldly to some—my son calls them "the zombie mowers"—and too human to others—my daughter and I have given them names and noted their different personalities. The mower who works the grass patch on the upper grounds we've named Schultz; Schultz is lazy and spends a great deal more time in his recharging hut than does the mower we named Greta, who tirelessly works a hilly, and much vaster, grass patch on the lower grounds. She is always mowing, even on weekends. She is dogged and uncomplaining, but my daughter and I have sensed her world-weariness. Greta long ago accepted her lot in life. Schultz, meanwhile, does the absolute minimum to get by.

I brought this up to the CFO; I thought he might want to know, from an insider's perspective, how certain of his employees were performing.

He said, "Well that's very interesting," and proceeded to tell me that in fact *Schultz* had been performing much better than Greta. And not only that, but Greta and Schultz were in competition with each other; this was their trial period. When the period concluded, only one of them would get the job. (Not one of *them*. Technically, two mowing companies were in competition for the villa's mowing contract.) At the moment, it appeared that Schultz had it in the bag. As people say of slam-dunk job candidates, *It was his to lose.*

This upset me. I couldn't help but think: *How typical.* First, how typical that a man (Schultz) does no work at all and is considered the superior candidate, and the woman (Greta) works and works and works yet is still not "good enough" to get the position. Greta's dedicated hard work even seemed, to this CFO, a strike against her; what a shitty mower she must be if she can't accomplish the job in half the time, and spend the rest of her day in her recharging hut, sucking down electricity! (I am failing here to interrogate the fact that it was my daughter and I who assigned gendered names to these mowers. I honestly cannot remember if we did it before or after we got to know their different personalities.)

I said to the CFO, "I don't see how your data is remotely reliable." I pointed out that the two mowing jobs were hardly comparable; Schultz was responsible for a small, flat, cleanly geometric patch of lawn, while Greta's patch was three times the size, irregularly shaped, and half overtaken by a steep hill. "If you're going to compare them, you must switch their spaces. You must make Schultz mow the big and hilly lawn, and give Greta the flat, small one. It's otherwise not fair."

I almost said, "It's practically inhumane!" This villa takes its humanitarian concerns very seriously. Many of the experts invited here have dedicated their lives to improving conditions for humans. To let such a travesty occur just beneath the vast windows of the dining room in which many Nazis had once dined (also directly across the lake from the Wannsee Conference house, in which some famous Nazis met to discuss the "Final Solution") and where we were currently enjoying chanterelle consommé, well, I didn't have to rub his nose in the irony.

The CFO looked at me. He said, "You're right to point that out."

I felt proud of myself. I honestly thought he might offer to hire me (another job won), or tell me that my true talents were being wasted as a writer—I should be in human resources or business management. Now Greta would have her chance, and she would succeed, or she wouldn't, but regardless, I hadn't stood passively by while she was passed over. I had saved her from injustice! Then I realized I'd accomplished no such feat. *You're right to point that out.* The CFO's statement was without content; it held no promise or reassurance or compliment. In fact, it was a total brush-off; possibly even his sentence contained some hidden irritation. *What do you, a writer, know about groundskeeping budgets?* His statement was the discomforting equivalent of what certain people say after I give a reading at a library or a bookstore or wherever. They are politic. They are careful to deliver messages so hollow that they beg to be filled with unstated criticisms. These people do not say, *I love your work,* or *That was so great.* These people say, *How wonderful it was to hear you read.*

NOVEMBER 14

Today the weather in New York was drizzly and cold, and I was reminded of a semester I once spent in France. When I was nineteen I lived in a French town called Blois, and for four months the weather was rainy, gray, densely cold, the kind of cold that penetrates to the body's core and must be leached out by a hot bath. Fire won't do. Clothing is useless. Once your bones have been breached, hot water is the only cure.

While I'd been scheming for years to get to France, I'd had a miserable time that semester and the weather was only partially to blame. I'd left in America a boyfriend to whom I was more attached than I otherwise might have been because I'd gotten pregnant a few months earlier. When a nineteen-year-old good-college-attending girl gets pregnant, she tells herself she has no option but to undo her mistake. She is pro-choice (she's driven many hours to attend rallies), but she prefers, because it is easier on her conscience, to think of herself as choiceless. Her life trajectory, such as she understands it, decrees: abortion is the sole outcome of this scenario.

No girl I knew, in other words, had babies, but more

than a few had had abortions. I'd attended two abortions before my own. I'd been invited along to do the driving, and hold the hands, and sit afterward in the bars and fetch the drinks. The boyfriends, though informed of our activities, were never present. Abortions are women's work, I guess.

Regardless, in France I was more fragile than usual. I missed my boyfriend to the point of illness. I talked to him weekly on the phone in the cold French house I inhabited with a man named Girard and a woman named Marie. I lived in a basement room that was doubly cold and also damp. After I hung up with my boyfriend I'd descend to the basement and lie on my bed and feel the weight of the house pressing down. It would be months before I'd see him. I felt so homesick I might have been five years old. I'd halfheartedly tried to find a love substitute in France among the twelve students on my semester abroad program, I discreditably had. But the cutest guy was pretentious and insecure, and the second cutest guy was Austrian and impenetrable. Instead I developed a close relationship with our TA. Halfway through the semester, she let me wear her best sweater basically every day. We'd each been wearing the same small suitcase of clothes for weeks at this point; other people's clothing was, more than it usually is, a break from ourselves. Our identities had been winnowed to four shirts, two sweaters, a pair of jeans and a skirt and one pair of boots, all of which stunk of nightclub cigarette smoke. The TA's sweater was nicer (in our opinion) than any other sweater worn by a foreign exchange student in Blois—and maybe in all of France—that winter; we each coveted it. That she'd awarded it to me was the equivalent, if we were still at our American college, of an older boyfriend giving a girl his torn and stained canvas jacket to wear, the one everyone knew, by the unique pattern of destruction, was his. In my mother's generation, men gave women their school rings, or their varsity jackets, if they were athletes, in order to claim ownership, and women wore them, well, I don't know why. To prove they were desirable enough to be claimed? When I was in high school, I borrowed and wore my father's clothing more than I wore my mother's. At the time I saw my preference for my father's clothing over my mother's as a logical extension of a tomboy childhood. But maybe it wasn't just about that.

During our school holiday, my TA and I traveled together to the South of France and Spain and Mallorca. We were living off of our respective summer job earnings, and to make the earnings last we subsisted on chocolate bars and baguettes and shared a hotel bed. The TA had the same taste in architecture as I did. We chose shabbily romantic places, the evocative atmospheres of which made me miss my boyfriend so much that, when trying to fall asleep each night, I imagined his plane crashing when he eventually flew to France to meet me in May. I stayed awake until three a.m. worrying this hypothetical into existence. Every day I despaired at sundown. In a few hours, I had another appointment with scenes of his demise.

One night when the TA and I were in Nice I awoke to find her sobbing in our bed. She refused to tell me why. I started guessing. I thought maybe if I stumbled upon the trigger for her distress she'd be spared the burden of articulating it. We'd both been reading a Jean Rhys novel called *After Leaving Mr. Mackenzie,* about a depressed woman who stays home and drinks and grows yet more depressed. I was so emotionally destroyable at the time that I thought it wise to stop reading it. My TA had bravely finished the novel earlier that week; the dysphoric aftereffects were still lingering, perhaps? Also she had a sort-of boyfriend she'd left in the States. Possibly she missed him? Possibly he'd failed to write her or call her enough? I knew the damage that night could do to a boyfriend.

These were not the reasons. Finally she said into her pillow, angrily, "You look so much prettier in my sweater."

I didn't know how to respond because I knew, even then: She was lying. She was one of those women who did not compare herself to other women; she just confidently *was*. Also, we were not competitive over looks or over anything. We both knew: She was more beautiful than I was. She was also smarter, and funnier, and more mischievous and braver and way better at French. She was better at all languages, even nonexistent ones. We often killed time in train stations pretending to be people we weren't. I'd pretend that I was her mute sister, and that we were from Estonia or Finland or some country with a language no one in France was likely to speak. She'd engage in conversation French men at station cafés, and then "translate" for me what they were saying into "our" language, i.e., her very plausible-sounding gibberish. My passive role was not to laugh, a role that proved not so passive, a role that was arguably the harder of the two. We once tried our ploy with the roles reversed, with her as the mute, me as the chatty sister. But speaking fake languages is as hard as speaking real ones. It required grammatical and sonic improvisational skills I didn't possess, and this failure proved to us, yet again, that she was my superior. She was my TA in school and in life.

Which was why I knew she was lying. What did she care how I looked in her sweater? Regardless, I didn't press her. We fell asleep. We awoke to a mild awkwardness that dissipated by breakfast. We never spoke of the incident again. We don't speak anymore about anything. We had a falling-out ten years ago, when my first husband and I got divorced, and I didn't tell her before I left him that I was leaving, and I didn't tell her where I'd be disappearing to for a few months. She left messages that grew increasingly angry. I got angry at her anger. In retaliation, I didn't call her back. I knew I'd be seeing her at a wedding in a few months. We could resolve our differences wearing formal dresses in an atmosphere padded by mandatory joy. At the last minute, however, she canceled. Not even the bride knew why. Eight years later I ran into a mutual acquaintance on the sidewalk who gave me her e-mail address. I sent her an e-mail. She never wrote back.

Years after the night in Nice, my TA became a lesbian, which was no great surprise to anyone, or it wasn't a surprise to me.

The friends to whom I tell the Nice story, a story that now concludes with my TA's and my "break" and her eventual gayness, jump to the obvious interpretation. "She was clearly in love with you," they say, and I lead them to conclude this. I would never say it myself, but I like to hear it said. I would never say it because I don't believe it's true. When I remember what my TA said and the anger with which she said it—*You look so much prettier in my sweater*—she was angry that the sweater didn't turn her into the person she still, given her strict family and also, frankly, the times, hoped she'd be—straight like me. She had everything on me but this: I was a straight girl who'd had an abortion and missed her boyfriend. I was a straight girl looking pretty in her sweater.

August 3

Today I went to a neighboring town to see the gallery opening of the woman inundated by motherhood and to hear another woman read. This town is as close to fancy as Maine can muster. It is also very literary. The poet Robert Lowell used to live in this town, ergo his second wife, Elizabeth Hardwick, lived in this town, and so did Jean Stafford, his first. Jean Stafford wrote a short story published in 1978 called "An Influx of Poets," about the inundation of poet guests to her summerhouse, and the subsequent ruin of her marriage.

> Cora's marriage to the poet Theron Maybank
> dissolved after five years in an awful Maine
> summer, right after the war. Every poet in America,
> it seemed, came to visit. They sat around reading
> their own works aloud, not listening to each other.

I will never write a story called "An Influx of Fiction Writers," even though there are many fiction writers in my town. More come every year, but we don't sit around reading aloud our stories to each other. Mostly we talk about old barns and how to keep them from falling down. Maybe this is our coded way of discussing how to prevent, given our dangerous summer numbers, the future dissolution of our marriages.

This fancy town is also a famed warfare site, and not only of the domestic variety. I've been told the history of this town. A Revolutionary War–era something happened there. The battle of something. During the war, people floated their houses here on boats from (or maybe to) Quebec. Or from (or maybe to) Massachusetts. They were either too sentimental to leave their houses where they'd built them, or they were too cheap to build new ones. When I think of this town, the image that comes to mind is a harbor clogged by floating houses, and people in tri-corner hats yelling at each other, "Watch your front porch, asshole!"

Subsequently, or not, the town consists of mainly colonial-era houses, and all of these houses are white because of a town ordinance. There is no town ordinance, however, governing public drunkenness or bad art. Most galleries sell the art of the vacation spot. Postcard-equivalent landscape paintings. Sculptures so figurative they appear Duchampian. A "Tea Cup" or a tea cup?

The art was not bad at the gallery we visited. My friend's art is there, and she is a really good artist. She makes bleak and lonely paintings that I can't help but unimaginatively view as representations of her maternal experience.

The energy on Main Street was scatty. There had been "feeder races" that day. Sailors had been fed into a boat on the other side of the bay and ended up here. Not much feeding occurred on board, but lots of drinking had. Some of these sailors landed at the gallery where there was more wine, and also chalk for the children. The drunkest sailors drew on the sidewalk with the children's chalk.

But I was also in town for the fiction reading. The reading was held in the white Parish House on the town green. The writer was Jewish. Her stories were about Jews in New York. She said the word "Shabbat" a lot. Behind her podium hung a portrait of a man from the 1700s. The parson, maybe? He stared disapprovingly at the woman throughout her reading. Who on earth was this New York

Jew reading her fiction aloud in the parsonage? Wasn't there a town ordinance governing this?

Afterward, a handful of us went to dinner at a Victorian inn. We were greeted by a woman who resembled a governess. More portraits stared at us throughout dinner. I did not know most of the people at the table, and so I found myself explaining myself a lot. One woman asked me where I spent my summers. I told her the name of my town. "Ah," she said. "And is yours a *heritage family*?" I had no idea, I told her—I had never heard this term before—but I guessed not. If she'd known my last name she'd never have asked me. *Julavits* is not heritage for anything you'd want to boast a historical connection to in these WASPy parts. Though maybe she did know my last name, and this was her indirect way of asking: *Are you Jewish?* I was indirectly asked this question a lot as a kid. After the Christmas vacation, kids would ask me, "How was your *holiday*?" In middle school, a Jewish family moved into the house next door. They noticed our lack of a Christmas tree (we'd gone out of town to visit my grandparents who'd retired to Florida). We were understood to be Jewish by these neighbors, and my mother never had the heart to correct them, not even when they invited us to Jewish holiday dinners. There seemed no way to set them straight without lots of awkwardness or risking offense. (*You? I look nothing like you.*) At a certain point, it seems more polite to just become the person people assume you to be.

Today I went to a dinner party at Edith Wharton's house. I wish this were as it sounds—*Edith Wharton invited me for dinner!*—but it wasn't. Edith Wharton was dead this evening. She was seventy-five years dead. Instead I'd been invited by a Wharton scholar to celebrate the 150th anniversary of Wharton's birth. For sure I should have been up on my Whartonalia. I should have improved my knowledge of her life beyond "she had a crappy first marriage just like I did!" Fortunately, at dinner, I sat next to two kids, and instead of talking about Wharton we talked about our fears of bears and sharks. Because I am considering a long-distance ocean swim next summer, I was coming to know a lot about sharks. I knew, because an all-but-dissertation philosopher had told me, that since 1582 there have been only 133 reported human deaths caused by a shark. This did not make the kids, nor did it make me, less convinced that we'd be killed by one.

Then I chatted with the director of The Mount (this is the name of Wharton's house), and she had shark fatality–type numbers at her fingertips about Wharton, and she seemed mildly appalled I should know so little about the house to which I'd been invited, other than that Wharton had lived in it. Finally I escaped. I found a writer I've always thought to be very beautiful and affixed myself to her. This writer has a serene face, and no other writer I know is serene at all. Especially their faces are not serene. Because of her face, I remember very clearly the first time I saw this woman. This was, give or take, late 1997 or early 1998. I was waitressing at a restaurant owned by a former actress who required me to French-braid my hair. One night this writer came in for dinner. Everyone glowed in this restaurant—the lighting was incredibly flattering, and the customers always looked marriageable, which was probably why a good many of them came here to become engaged—but she glowed differently. Beatific, I suppose, is the word for her type of glow. Her glow was the glow of her spirit or her soul or something that went deeper than skin and diet and lighting.

At the time I hadn't published anything. I was too inhibited to introduce myself to people who I thought would have no interest in knowing me. I could give them a reason to talk to me by saying, *I am just such a huge fan of your work,* but that's brownnosing where I come from, even if you truly mean the compliment. For this reason I didn't introduce myself to Joan Didion, whom I'd waited on, and I didn't introduce myself to Bret Easton Ellis, whom I'd also waited on. I didn't say to Didion, "I can quote lines from your work." I didn't say to Ellis, "I snorted honorific lines off your book jacket." I said to Didion and to Ellis, "Would you like to see the dessert menu?"

I also didn't introduce myself to this beatific woman. I'd read her work in magazines. She counted as a star sighting for me. And she glowed, she was really so glowy. She was glow atop of glow. I remembered her so vividly I half doubted, now that I was seeing her again, that this encounter had happened at all. I have come to that point in my life where my memories have begun interbreeding. I'd seen her, somewhere, true, but maybe not at that restaurant, and the glowy nimbus surrounding her, maybe that was just more postproduction touch-up.

So I talked to this woman at Wharton's house. She told me about the smart life choices she'd made, which made

me realize that she wasn't inherently serene, she was purposefully and strategically so, meaning somehow serenity
wasn't an oxymoronic pursuit like it was with me, because
I just get so stressed out when I'm trying to fit yoga into
my day. We exchanged numbers so that we could go out
to dinner the following night with the other Wharton cel-
ebrants. We decided to drive to the restaurant together. I
picked her up. It felt like a first date. After dinner, after
we'd had some drinks, and as I was driving her back to her
hotel, we did the friend version of parking. We kept the car
running, and we sat in the dark and we talked. I confessed
to her that I remembered the first time I'd seen her, or I
thought I had. I didn't want this to sound creepy; I wanted
it to sound complimentary. *I remember the first time I ever
saw you! But maybe I don't remember seeing you—maybe
I just imagined it! Maybe I have a fantasy about the first
time I ever saw you!* I was growing creepier by the contin-
gency. But when I mentioned the name of the restaurant,
she stared at me differently. She said she remembered that
night, and she also remembered seeing me. We had seen
each other! Maybe she was having a false memory inspired
by my false memory, who knows.

She obviously worried that her remembering me also
sounded a little creepy—why would a semi-famous person
remember a waitress?—so she explained her memory by
saying, "You're just so distinctive looking." Which no one
has ever said to me before, certainly not all of those people
who claim that I look like their cousin.

Regardless, I started to think about women who look
at women and not because they want to sleep with them.
Some women some other women like to look at. My first
husband used to say, sort of jokingly, that women deem other
women beautiful only when those women aren't really. He

believed that women are sometimes so competitive that they can't admit that the beautiful women are beautiful; they can only call beautiful the not-really-beautiful ones. But I don't agree. The women I find beautiful are so beautiful that I never forget the first time I saw them. I wait for years to see them again.

AUGUST 17

Today I heard an ambulance siren. In New York, sirens are no cause for alarm, but in Maine they are cause. If you hear an ambulance siren, the odds are fairly high you'll know the person for whom the ambulance has been called. One morning a few summers ago, the town was crazy with sirens. Because we live close to the town center, we received texts from friends who live on the periphery. *What the hell is going on?* I drove to the post office to investigate. The postmistress told me that a kid had been hit by a car. "She's the daughter of a family that's visiting some summer people," she said.

I suspected from her description: the girl was my friend's niece. I drove to my friend's house. My friend and her children stood on the stoop watching the emergency workers pack up their stretchers and machines. The trauma was elsewhere now; here was just the trauma's queasy hangover. Everyone was too stunned to say much. The girl who'd been hit was unconscious. The man who'd hit her was very old, but the fault wasn't his; the girl had run across the street from behind a parked delivery van. The old man, in shock, had, on the spot, suffered a heart attack.

For two days the girl remained unconscious. Then she woke up and was fine. The old man who had the heart attack was also fine. As a result of this near tragedy, our town decided to hire a sheriff to lurk in the church parking lot and hand out speeding tickets (even though the old man, when he hit the girl, had been driving ten miles under the limit). One of the most vocal supporters of the sheriff got two speeding tickets in one day. My husband also got a speeding ticket. Now when the sheriff's in town, people text us to let us know he's been spotted, and to warn us not to speed. Sometimes when I'm driving toward the church, a local will flash his lights at me, alerting me that the sheriff's ahead. This incident has brought our town closer, but in a perverse way. We agreed to hire a good guy to keep our children safe from speeding cars. Now we've joined forces against the good guy to keep ourselves safe from speeding tickets.

Still, when I hear a siren, or when anyone in this town hears a siren, the kneejerk fear is, *Somebody's kid got hit.*

Today when I heard the siren, I'd just sent my kid and her friend on bikes to the store. They're seven and eight, but the road is busy, and the trucks drive recklessly. So I didn't think, *Somebody's kid got hit,* I thought, *Maybe my kid or her friend got hit.* I wondered if I should stop working and drive to the store to check on them. But I have so little time to work these days. A few hours at most. Chances are the siren was for somebody else. But what if it wasn't? What if, in order to guarantee fifteen more minutes of work time, I forfeited the chance to hold my daughter's head in my lap for the last three minutes of her life?

Instead of getting into the car to check on my daughter and her friend, I "checked" on them by devising a hypothetical scenario to test my preparedness for what might be awaiting me. If there were an accident, and if I were forced to choose one child to survive, would I pick my daughter or her friend?

I chalkboarded the problem thoroughly. This friend, a boy, is the only child of one of *my* friends; to take my friend's one child from her would mean she'd suffer far more than I would, in theory, since I have two children. I'd still be a mother; she'd be the widow equivalent of a mother. This is what the Israelis I know would recommend if consulted. If I used my theoretical lifeline to call an Israeli. You must sacrifice your child, they would say, because you have another one. The transplanted Israelis I know in New York are calmly practical when describing the reasons Israelis have so many kids. Chances are one or more of these kids will be killed while serving in the army, or by terrorist attack. Wise, thus, according to these Israelis, to have a lot of them.

I once ran the Israeli theory past a comedian I know who, when not being funny, can be usefully thoughtful. I was, at the time, interviewing everyone I knew about whether or not to try to have a second kid. The comedian sided with the Israelis. He claimed he had two children because, "if you lose one child, what remains is still a family."

But hadn't he seen *Ordinary People*? I countered. (Two brothers, one played by Timothy Hutton, are stranded on an overturned boat during a storm; the non–Timothy Hutton brother drowns.) The family would still be a family after one kid dies, true, but the remaining members would be fucked beyond any pretense of future normalcy. The parents would come to hate and blame each other like Donald Sutherland and Mary Tyler Moore came to hate and blame each other. The surviving sibling would try to

kill himself like Timothy Hutton did, or, best-case scenario, claw his way back to semi-functional lugubriousness
with the help of a therapist like Judd Hirsch.

Which was my long way of rationalizing: when weighing whether to sacrifice my daughter or her friend to this
probably nonexistent car accident, the fact of a sibling did
not, in my mind, disqualify my daughter from the survival
trials. In fact, the reason my friend's son was at our house
was because my friend was at the hospital for a prenatal
appointment. Assuming all went well, she'd be giving birth
to another kid in four months. Meaning, wouldn't it be
traumatic to fewer people if my daughter lived? Because if
my daughter died, her younger brother would end up like
the Timothy Hutton character, while my friend's unborn
baby wouldn't know what he or she was missing if his or
her brother died. He or she would be burdened by the
ghost of this dead brother, true, and that probably wouldn't
make for the lightest of childhoods, but the dead brother
would be romanticized as the best brother ever, and he
or she would mourn the brother's loss unconditionally,
whereas if the brother survived, he or she would probably
find regular reasons to hate him. Some siblings are thick
as thieves through adulthood, but how many really? The
percentage is low.

Now I was bored with this exercise. Now I was just
worried. Having wasted far more than fifteen minutes trying to make a decision that no one needed me to make, I
got in the car. I drove to town. A mile later I passed the
kids on their bikes, headed home. They stared at me dis-
believingly. My daughter looked flat-out pissed. The reason
I'd made them bike to town in the first place was because
I'd claimed to be too busy to give them a ride.

Today I received a text from a woman I have never
met. She is the ex-girlfriend of the current girlfriend of my
London friend, and this woman and I had both received
free tickets to see perform in Berlin the girlfriend of my
London friend's really close friend. We are thickly connected total strangers, in other words. We needed a vector
diagram like the one outside the MoMA abstraction show
to understand exactly how we did yet didn't know each
other.

We planned, via text, to meet before the performance
for a drink. I wrote, *i will text you outfit deets once i have
them—then you can find me*. This is how strangers find
strangers in my experience: I will be wearing a plaid coat, I
am short/tall/pixie-haired/will be carrying a red umbrella.
I am always curious to see how a person's self-description
is or is not helpfully accurate. It is the primary appeal of
meeting up with total strangers.

Two seconds later, I received a text. It said:

This is what I look like. . . .

Beneath the text was a photo of her face. I could see
her apartment's pink walls and black curtains. I saw the
corner of a pine bedframe. She wore a sweatshirt.

I was horrified. I actually recoiled. A line had been
crossed! Etiquette breached! You do not send a total
stranger a picture of your face!

Then, of course, it seemed so logical that she would
send me her picture, and so bizarrely coy and parlor game-
ish and prim of me to dangle the promise of a Haiku of my
future outfit.

Still. I was miffed all day. I was miffed at myself for being miffed. I was like an old person crabby at an ATM machine for knowing my name. My process had been queue-jumped. I prefer to meet the constructed person first. Her photo jarred me so deeply that, once I got to the concert venue—far into a neighborhood I'd never before visited, reachable by a train called "the Ring" that ran in a circle around the city in both directions, and the act, on the platform, of committing to one direction over the other had already been such a draining leap of faith—I realized I was never going to find this woman. I scrutinized her text photo again. This picture of her face, I realized, was completely unhelpful; it was useless, in fact. She had shortish dark hair, pale skin, and no makeup, but who knew what she now had on her face or on her head? Her lips could be metallic; she could be wearing a chef's toque. I stood on the sidewalk and stared at other people milling around the entrance. She could have been any number of them. I failed at finding her like I've failed so many multiple-choice tests. I failed with glee. A, B, C, D, I could argue with equal conviction for the rightness of each—and, because the form so irritates me, find myself feigning jubilant outrage at the limitless *possibilities for rightness*. She could be that woman or that woman; she could, at a squint, be that fucking *man*. I had to really stare at people and search in the dark for their faces. I felt like an identity pickpocket, rummaging through the nightclub's exterior shadows to pull from people what many, for whatever reason, kept hidden beneath hats and hoods. If I'd known she was wearing a raincoat, or that she was tall or short, or that she'd be carrying an I ♥ BERLIN tote, I could have narrowed her down; I could have, less molestingly, better sorted her from these other strangers. I tried for fifteen minutes. But I could not find her.

A face, I thought to myself with some satisfaction, is not the best way to identify a person.

I gave up. I texted her. *long + blonde + glasses + standing under a bright light.*

I could have said "green coat" or "black bag" or "only idiot wearing heels." To admit that I was long-haired and blond, I realized immediately after I sent the text, was to admit to being the last thing I usually want to be. I am not rebellious enough or daring enough to attempt prettiness in an unconventional way. But "long + blond + glasses + standing under a bright light" conveyed precisely how I felt on this particular sidewalk on this particular night. Glaring and out of place at a Berlin nightclub. Far from home, riding a train that travels in circles.

SEPTEMBER 7

Today I went to the doctor for a physical. I took tests to discover if I had diseases I am certain I do not have. Like AIDS. Even during the '80s, I never, save one time, worried that I'd contracted it, even though my friends had regular freak-outs and disappeared to the health services clinic to have their blood drawn after long nights of death-worry. In part I was not worried about becoming sick and dying because I never worried about becoming sick and dying. Hypochondria, until my recent health scare, was not a tempting velodrome for my neuroses.

But primarily I never worried about getting AIDS because I slept with extremely straight straight people. None of them used needles. None of them had been in moped accidents in Kenya, and so none of them had received sketchy blood transfusions in huts. I cavorted, or so I believed, with a low-risk crowd.

Thus, in my nearly thirty years of sexual activity, I've had only one long night of AIDS worry. This night was spent at LaGuardia Airport in New York. It was summer. I was trying to get back to New Hampshire, where I and fifteen other people slept on floor mattresses in a house hanging over a river. I'd been in Oregon visiting my boyfriend, who'd been living in South America for the year. He'd returned to see his family for a week, and we reconnected in his hometown like the devoted couple we were, though unbeknownst to him I'd been having sex with another guy. My boyfriend and I didn't have an open relationship, but I considered the vast distance (time zones and miles) between us as license to sleep with someone else temporarily, especially since I planned eventually to move to South America to join him. Especially since I planned eventually to marry him. I was totally committed to him while sleeping with another guy. This made sense to me then. It makes sense to me now.

Moreover I didn't love this other guy. He was more like a conquest. A class or maybe a social clique conquest. He was from Greenwich. His girlfriend prior to me—she'd grown up in Manhattan—had been dating "the Preppie Killer" Robert Chambers when he accidentally-or-not strangled Jennifer Levin in Central Park during a bout of rough sex. I continued to sleep with this guy I didn't love because he made me feel I was part of a world I desperately wished, at that time, to be part of. If it took sleeping with a man who slept with a woman who slept with a murderer, so be it. Now I was only three fucks away from Robert Chambers. Now I was practically at Dorrian's Red Hand, the Upper East Side bar that had served alcohol to underage prep schoolers the night Chambers and Levin hooked up. I had practically seen them leave the bar together. I had practically turned to my best friend, whose family owned a private plane and a captain's house on Nantucket, and said, *Something terrible is about to happen!* (Even when I fantasized about being on the scene that night at Dorrian's Red Hand, I was still little better than an outsider; i.e., if I managed to have any value at all in that world, it would have been as a spooky, future-predicting witch.)

So I was at LaGuardia. I had just left my boyfriend in Oregon and was returning to my not-boyfriend in New Hampshire. The heavens protested. They heaved a lot of lightning around. My flight was canceled. This tart would be spending the night in the airport, forced to confront her deceitful ways until dawn.

The best way to pass an overnight in an airport is with a junky book. I'd buy a mystery before the newsstand closed. That was my plan, but then I saw a copy of *Wasted: The Preppie Murder* by Linda Wolfe, the true crime account of Robert Chambers and Jennifer Levin. I'd heard about this book. I'd been dying to read this book. (Published in 1989, it has a goodreads ranking. One woman gave it three stars and wrote, "Very interesting true story but the ending is a letdown.")

I bought it. I started reading. I thought I knew everything about Robert Chambers, but it turned out I didn't. He'd been a drug addict and needle user. He'd been possibly bisexual in New York City in the '80s. Had I known these things I might have practiced safe sex for once in my life. My three-fucks-away-from-Robert-Chambers status initiated a long night of death worry. I could have AIDS! Heritage AIDS! I decided I couldn't stay in the airport, or I'd drive myself crazy, reading *Wasted: The Preppie Mur-*

der by the half-light of the closed concessions, anxiously obsessing about my death, and also the death of my boyfriend (whom I would have basically killed with my dishonesty), and how, if my boyfriend didn't break up with me for cheating on him and giving him AIDS, we'd have to forgo living in South America and instead spend our final days at an experimental treatment facility in Mexico, where we could still get married, and after our wedding, I would ideally die first, because I had, as a kid, read *Love Story* by Erich Segal upward of fifty-nine times, and I wanted my husband/boyfriend to be able to say at my funeral, "What can you say about a twenty-five-year-old girl who died?" and (even though I had given him AIDS), "Love means never having to say you're sorry."

I made calls from a payphone using a credit card I'd failed to make any payments on for months, but which, by some glitch, worked. It was a Saturday night, but I found some friends at home. I took a cab to their apartment. We went to an Irish bar and got drunk. I slept on their couch. By the next morning, I was cured of my worry. I continued to sleep with the three-fucks-away guy for the rest of the summer and fall. This didn't make sense to me then. It doesn't make sense to me now. Despite what I learned in the airport, I didn't get tested for AIDS for another three years. When I did, I was not positive.

NOVEMBER 16

Today I realized that I am not in a bad mood. I am something else. I am someone else. This happens to me as it happens to everyone. You are not you for months at a time. When you become you again, you can actually greet yourself. You can welcome yourself back.

In my mind my life was ending in small and big ways. I wasn't despondent over these endings; instead I was energized by them. Because of the joke I made about three-way sex in class yesterday, I was going to lose my job, and so I must start thinking of a new career. Because I am not myself, my husband would leave me in search of a woman who more closely resembled the one he married. Because my babysitter and I parted on strange terms, and because she still has the house keys, she was going to enter the apartment at night and kill our children as we slept, so I needed to protect them. When I told my husband why I was sleeping with our children and not with him, I expected him to understand my reasoning and appreciate my prudence. Because he is an incredible human, he did.

What is interesting about these alternate states of being, however, is that they never seem crazy once exited and viewed from a more sober location. Even when I return from wherever I've been, I understand why, when not myself, I do what I do and believe what I believe. I consider myself highly sane and competent for exhuming the possibility that my children might be killed from the lulling blandness of everyday life. I congratulate myself for my foresight. I think: *I want* that *person on my team.* She has all the angles covered. In her brain she runs a computer program to evade dooms no one has even considered. There's nothing she hasn't thought of, and thought of and thought of, poor woman.

Today I was seated at a dinner beside the sister-in-law of a friend. We talked about self-destructive New Age healers and whether or not old Hasidic men in Brooklyn speak to you only if they think you're a Polish prostitute, and she showed me pictures of her dog before she showed me pictures of her baby. Then we discussed the bath salts epidemic in Maine. My husband and I first learned about the bath salts epidemic through a local newspaper we'd purchased for the purpose of starting a fire in our wood-stove. My husband held up a front page with a photograph of a distraught woman and the headline, "Husband Hasn't Been the Same Since He Started Doing Them." "Guess what he's been doing?" my husband asked. I guessed cof-fee liqueur. I guessed Sudoku. "Bath salts," he said. Bath salts? We imagined a man lying in a tub filled with scented water, unable to get out. Within a week he'd have lost his job, and his wife would be despairing. She'd cry at the foot of the tub in which he floated, serenely pink, as the house was repossessed and the children taken by social services.

The article did nothing to correct this assumption of ours. (We eventually learned that bath salts are typically snorted, that the high is a cross between meth and acid, that they can inspire people to eat the faces off of other people.) For days we believed that poverty-stricken people in Maine would get into a warm bath one day and never get out. Did this seem so implausible? It didn't to me. Bath salts are a dangerous temptation in our household. My hus-band and I take turns before dinner disappearing into a salted bath. There is never a compelling reason to get out, not for the first forty-five minutes at least, until the water starts to cool and you're vaguely reminded that you like the life you've built with your spouse, at which point you consider the possibility that it *might* be worth leaving the tub in order to maintain it. But if your life sucks and you hate your spouse? Yes, I can see a bathtub being a perfect place never to leave.

So this woman and I talked about the local bath salts epidemic. I didn't know anyone who did them, but I'd once given a ride to a woman who'd been on them, I told her. She wanted to know the story of this woman. It was late at night, I said. My husband and I were returning from a dinner party and realized we were out of gas. We stopped at the automated pumps where there is always classic rock playing, where the lighting is always blue and bright, where it is always like an underage nightclub. On this night the pumps were playing Fleetwood Mac. I noticed another car parked just outside the illuminated area. One back door was open. The car appeared to have been abandoned, until, when I looked up again, I saw a lone woman zombie-shuffling toward the pump island.

"Help me," she said. She spoke from beyond the grave. *"Help me."*

I asked: How could we help her?

"Help me," she said.

My husband and I exchanged a confused look.

"Can we call anyone to help you?" he said.

This time she heard us. She freaked out. Her face spasmed.

"My dad will kill me if he finds out," she said. "He will fucking *kill me.*"

(I told the woman with whom I was having dinner: "Mind you, this woman was easily forty years old.")

We asked the woman where she lived, she answered vaguely, we calculated based on these vague descriptions that her house wasn't too far out of our way. We offered her a ride, even though my husband worried, given the woman's tenuous grip on her surroundings, that she'd never be able to locate her own driveway, and that we'd be carting her around all night.

I drove. My husband sat in the back because he hates making small talk with strangers on street drugs with whom he is, by the laws of vehicular proximity, obliged to chat. We also figured he could restrain her from behind if she went nuts. We'd already shared a knowing glance—*bath salts, clearly*. Given we had no experience with the bath salt high, we thought we should be prepared for anything.

Once we were driving, her brain notched into a manic groove. "You have no idea what happened to me tonight. You have no idea. You have no idea what happened to me tonight." This refrain persisted for seven miles. She'd grabbed my husband's hand over the back of her seat; she violently caressed it. "Shit Louie," she said. "That's what people say down south. Shit Louie. Shit Louie. Shit Louie. You have no idea what happened to me tonight."

At this point I wanted an idea. The reason I'd agreed to give this woman a ride was, yes, because she was in a bind, but the repayment for my generosity should be her story. What happened tonight? I half suspected there'd been a dead body in her car. She'd killed her boyfriend, maybe, for refusing to drive her home.

As we neared the town where she lived, her energy changed. She grew distracted. Her scatty brain got ideas it couldn't articulate. She held her purse in her lap; she slid one hand inside of it. I sensed an impulsive act brewing. For the first time, I got scared. She was going to pull a gun—the gun with which she'd killed her boyfriend—and now she was going to kill me, or my husband, or herself. No target would prove compelling until, in a random millisecond, it became unbearably compelling. She started repeating, menacingly, "I owe you big-time. I owe you big-time. Shit Louie, I am going to give you *the best present ever.*"

The ride ended uneventfully. She located her driveway. She lived in a trailer, a nice one. She hopped out of the car and suddenly seemed as harmless as a drunk teenager relieved to be home. "I am going to give you the best present tomorrow!" she said again, forgetting she had no idea who we were or where we lived.

I concluded by saying to my dinner partner, "And for sure the woman was on bath salts!" I felt a little bit guilty having wasted so much time telling her this story. It starts promisingly, but the end tells nothing. "Very interesting true story but the ending is a letdown." I hadn't turned the deflation of events into a moment of unexpected revelation. I could see the woman trying to apply the right kind of curiosity, because I hadn't properly directed it. Her curiosity passed over the bath salts woman and landed on me.

"I can't believe you gave her a ride," she said. "That says a lot about you as a person." I thought she was going to compliment me on my selflessness, and I would then counter with the usual demurrals. *She was so desperate! Anyone would have done what I did!*

"Either you're stupid," she said, "or you're just really nosy."

Today my friends and I swam the entire length of the harbor, and out into the Reach, and around the point, and to the beach where my friends are staying. As we swam past the docks, we chatted with the people on them. "George," we said, as we neared the first dock. "When's your daughter arriving?" George replied, "Late tomorrow night. Would you like to take a rest here? Can I get you a drink?" We demurred. We had places to be! People to visit! As we stroked past I thought I saw George growing older and older. His grandchildren beside him grew older, too, taking his place before being replaced themselves by *their* children. It was like a trick of stop-time photography, everyone shading into everyone else. (It helped that I didn't have my glasses on, and that the members of George's family are tall and thin and slightly stooped, even the young. At a squint, they blend.) Near the yacht club dock we exchanged pleasantries with the commodore. "Where are you going?" he asked. "Out into the Reach!" we said. We swam and we swam. We waved to people on boats and deflected, with good cheer, their slightly concerned disbelief regarding our swimming project. Eventually, we reached our destination, and all of us were blue, and all of us concurred, "That might have been a little shorter, that swim." We lay on the hot rocks. We each drank a beer. Time passed. Time passed. I started to doze. The cold water had slowed our pulses but everything else spun at great speed. I worried I would awake to find myself an old woman, my husband dead, my daughter grown and turned into me. But life, when I woke up, was as I'd left it.

JUNE 28

Today I had a dinner party. I did not tell the people I'd invited who else was coming. I didn't want anyone to pre-Google anyone. I don't know why I wanted to control what my friends did or did not know before they arrived to my house. I do know that I treat the Internet as an oracle that one consults, like Laius, father of Oedipus, at his peril. Must I know my son will grow up to kill me? Or that my Amazon star ranking is on the wane? For this reason I limit my visits. I don't ask questions I feel I cannot handle the answers to.

I feel others should exercise similar caution.

A few years ago, when my son was in day care, I met the father of one of his playmates. I did not know at the time, but I would soon learn via parental gossip, that the man's wife had died when his daughter was two months old. "Gossip" is maybe the wrong word to describe how I came to know his history. No malice was intended. The chatter was in the service of protection. It prevented the unwitting from asking the father, "Do you and your wife live around here?" or asking the little girl, "Is your mother picking you up today?"

The gossip gave rise to further curiosity and specu-lation on my part, especially since I'd become somewhat acquainted with the man. I so badly wanted to know how his wife had died. Had she committed suicide? Had she been killed in a car accident? The man is an actor and his wife was a director of documentary films; they were, in other words, slightly more Googleable than other peo-ple. But Googling him seemed invasive; also, to learn the details about his wife would put me in the position, when he eventually told me these details, of pretending I didn't already know them. Unlike him, I am no actor.

I did not Google him. After a few more weeks of walking together and spending time in playgrounds, during which time he still hadn't told me about his wife, I considered that he possibly *hoped* I'd look him up online (as my friend having the affair with her married coworker had possibly hoped I'd look up her lover's identity online), as this would remove the burden of his having to tell me. He'd let the Internet do the disclosing for him.

I still did not Google him. My loyalty paid off. Finally, six months into knowing him, he told me what had happened to his wife. We were at a party. The ambient noise was such, however, that I couldn't hear him. What he was telling me was no doubt extremely heartrending, and so it seemed rude to say, repeatedly, "Sorry, *what*?" I pretended, for politeness' sake, to understand. I expressed regret and sadness and said, repeatedly, "Wow," and, "Oh my God." Then I went home and Googled him.

The Googling that might occur before dinner parties, however, confuses me more than the Googling of dead wives, especially since I prefer to have dinner parties where nobody talks about their careers. Isn't that the mark of a failed dinner party? When the conversations resemble job interviews? Wouldn't it actually be preferable, thus, to request that everyone Google the other guests beforehand so our tedious biographies won't need teasing out in person?

At my dinner party, however, I quite purposefully prevented any pre-Googling. To this dinner I'd invited a couple I didn't know very well along with some close friends, one of whom is a well-known writer. I didn't tell the new couple that this writer would be at the dinner. I thought I was omitting this fact as a means of showing how unimpressed I was by literary celebrity. I'm so unimpressed that when the new couple arrived to the party, I didn't disclose his identity, not even when I introduced him. (I said, "This is my neighbor.") To state his name, or so my thinking went, might be seen as name-dropping; there is little else in the world that I hate more. I went so far out of my way not to name-drop that I accomplished something even more pretentious. I also told myself that I was doing the new couple a favor. Fame basically prohibits casual conversation. What's your opening gambit with George Clooney? It's all so fucking awkward.

I also viewed my act of nondisclosure as an experiment. I wanted to see how many minutes or hours would pass before the new couple figured out who this writer was. What if they never did? What a great party that would be if we all just made jokes and shared no personal information, not even our names.

Predictably, there was much awkwardness. A lot of confused small talk eventually led to the writer's occupation and then his identity being revealed. By the end of the night, it was still unclear whether I'd done the couple a favor or a disservice. It was unclear whether they left that evening thinking that I was merely an eccentric hostess or a deeply messed-up person.

JULY 27

Today my husband and I watched the finale of *The Bachelorette*, Season Eight. The bachelorette, Emily, is a bright yellow blonde with fake boobs and a polite, little-girl demeanor. She has a daughter by her former fiancé, a racecar driver who died in a plane crash. (Her story, and maybe it checks out, and maybe it doesn't, and I don't care either way, is that she discovered she was pregnant a week after her fiancé was killed.)

We've known Emily, my husband and I, for two full seasons. We first met her on *The Bachelor*, Season Fifteen; she competed with seventeen other girls for the heart of Brad, such as it was. Even though she was chilly, and unforthcoming, and appeared to be one of those pretty women who'd never once had to make an effort in bed, and thus hadn't, she won Brad's heart. She took it home, she found it small and defective. Wisely, Emily ditched it.

Though she frequently demurred that the constant tabloid attention wasn't for her, she returned to TV a year later as the star of her own show.

Initially, we were disappointed in The Franchise's choice. Emily was pretty and likable, but she wasn't smart enough to be interesting or dim enough to be an accidental genius. We feared that she would sit around in a sparkly dress and let men fawn over her, even the asshole-ish and the ill-intentioned. This would be the dramatic highlight, we figured, her failing to understand that some men, just because they liked her, aren't good people.

But Emily surprised us. She proved to be a much tarter apple. She had wit and sharp retorts, she gave men shit as a way of flirting with them (and some men were so thick they neither understood that she was giving them shit nor that she was flirting with them), and she totally knew who the scumbags were.

Tonight, on the final episode of her season, Emily had to choose between Jef, a boyish entrepreneur whose family owned a gazillion-acre ranch in Utah, and Arie, a handsome racecar driver. The obvious choice was Arie because Emily wanted to fuck Arie, and historically the bachelors and the bachelorettes choose to marry the people they most wanted to fuck, even if that person is despicable.

Emily, meanwhile, had zero chemistry with Jef—they bird-pecked when they kissed; they had nothing to say to each other—but she *wanted* to want Jef. Her desire marked her either as a climber and a gold digger, or as an ambitious woman who privileges over sex and love not money per se (though Jef was certainly rich, and also a Mormon whose mysterious socioeconomic situation—the big house, the many children and women—*The Bachelorette* found it wise to represent in general yet in its specifics ignore), but exposure to new experiences. Arie's career as a racecar driver meant he'd be traveling much of the time; in effect, she'd still be a single mother. Also, as noted, her dead fiancé, the father of her daughter, was a racecar driver. While dating him, she'd hosted her own cable show about car racing. I imagined her thinking about Arie and the future he offered her: *done that.* She wanted to try something new. Emily is a beautiful enough and smart enough woman who can have any man she chooses, and also, via these men, any life she chooses. She chose a life over a man. She chose Jef. (Cue my grad school friend, *women expect a world.*) Wasn't this so ambitious of her? Wasn't this savvy and self-knowing?

Recently I went hiking with a woman whose daughter is friends with my daughter. This woman is beautiful but haplessly so. She cannot dress herself; she has no clue about hair. She told me about an old woman, a famous heiress, that she'd worked for when she was in her twenties. The old heiress advised her to use her looks to get ahead while she still had them. She told her there was no shame in doing this, and that she, the heiress, was bored by women who thought they should handicap their best assets on the principle that doing so would be unfair, or that the spoils they achieved would be less valuable.

My friend said, "I had no idea how to do what she was talking about. I had no idea how to use my looks to get anywhere." This might sound insincere; it isn't. She really doesn't know how. Funnily, her daughter, who is eight, already knows how to use her looks as the heiress recommended her mother do. The mother could take lessons from her eight-year-old daughter. So who can say where this knowledge comes from?

I have the knowledge, but to what degree I put this knowledge to use is debatable (i.e., I have a debate about it with myself). My parents like to tell of the time I came home from high school and announced that I wanted to dye my blonde hair black so that people would take my mind, my brilliant teenaged mind, more seriously. My desire was hollow. Or rather my desire was other than it seemed. I *desired* to be a teenaged girl who could destroy her most compelling teen asset. But I was never her.

JULY 22

Today I wrote a long e-mail to my London friend. Sometimes I spend more time writing e-mails to this friend than I do writing what I'm supposed to be writing. I justify this time expense by viewing these e-mails as a substitute for my otherwise nonexistent epistolary record. Regularly I'll put my friend's name into the search bar and read what I wrote to her a year ago. I'll be reminded of a good meal I'd forgotten about, or that last August I was kind of blue. My friend from London is an excellent e-mailer—she's inquisitive and hilarious; she uses ALL CAPS when she's trying to make a POINT. She comes from an Australian family of rain people. She forwards me her mother's vacation-planning e-mails as proof of her bloodline's savantism. Her mother, prior to a family vacation, will research a rental property and draft for her sons and daughters an account of the house and its recreations worthy of a presidential advance team. For example:

> PRAWNING
> *Best done in a boat. However can wade out from*
> *northwest side of bridge. Must have a good light*
> *and it must be on a moon free night. There are 2*
> *prawn nets in shed. The prawns swim out on the*
> *outgoing tide—i.e., I think best just after the tide*
> *turns—check this at Tackle World.*

We share evidence. We exchange phone photos of our outfits. She sent me pictures of her wedding dress, which she'd borrowed from the '80s singer Sade. We explained ourselves to each other. Our histories. When did we lose our virginity, and to whom? Why did my first husband and I divorce? What happened to the guy she married in the Sade dress, through whom she got her UK passport?

Our e-mails have proven to be an important archival exercise because I'm starting to forget important life events. The reason I'm forgetting is because it's been a while since I've articulated my life history to anyone. The depth and range of the intel I was meant to provide to my London friend—this I hadn't done since I'd met my second husband. It was fun to do it again but it was also hard. Especially over e-mail, or especially in writing, and especially when you are a writer. It was hard to tell the truth, is what I'm saying. I tried to tell it, but I was aware of how each sentence had a million conditional offshoots. Like if you were to diagram a sentence for meaning, rather than grammar, that's what each sentence might have resembled. I was trying to be charismatic, and in doing so I probably didn't tell the truthiest truths. I never made stuff up. But I did strive to be entertaining. Such embellishments do not constitute lies. They constitute your personality. But your personality can seem like a store front for lie vending if what you've said threatens to find a wider audience.

I once arranged to meet a friend at a bar. He was supposed to interview me for a magazine—we were meant to have a "conversation" between writers—but our endeavor was doomed from the start. The bar I chose turned out to be much louder and scarier than I'd recalled. It opened at eight a.m. By four-thirty p.m. the clientele were drawing shivs over the jukebox queue. We ordered drinks and tried to make the best of it, but his tape recorder wouldn't turn on. Instead we used my phone to record our conversation. We talked about books and writing for about five minutes before sliding into the sloppy, erratic rhythm of our surroundings. We talked about the things you talk about when you're drinking bad vodka. We remarked, with some amazement, that neither of us found any of our young students attractive, and never had. Weren't professors supposed to want to sleep with their students? What was wrong with us? We discussed one disastrous man's disastrous love life. We discussed alcoholics we knew. When we were leaving, I realized I'd forgotten to shut off my phone after the brief books discussion concluded, and that our entire conversation had been recorded. Meanwhile, the file was due to one of the magazine's interns the next day for transcription. I panicked. Probably this intern wouldn't do anything with the file, but who knew? He or she could forward it to someone, and soon we'd be reading on the Internet damning shit about people attributed to us. Nothing I said on that recording differed from what I believed; I stood by all of it. But the way I'd articulated certain truths—there was falseness involved. There was a *persona* involved, one that I used with this friend, and that I used with other friends, too, but I did not use it with everyone. My friend and I considered pretending that the recording had failed, that there was no interview, sorry. Then, at home, I figured out how to split the file. It necessitated erasing the parts I supposedly no longer wanted. Suddenly, however, I was loath to lose them. It reminded me of the newspaper sections I never care to read until I am kneeling by the woodstove, balling them up to start a fire.

JULY 23

Today I am not going to a yard sale. I have not been to a yard sale all summer, even though I am fanatical about yard sales. I am also very gifted when it comes to yard sales. I can case the tables of junk and instantly locate the four items that don't immediately appear interesting—a pitcher, a raincoat, a jigger—but are. Seconds are all I require. It's like what happens when I go to an art colony and I sweep the dining hall and identify the attraction threats. My body responds to people and objects erotically, and within a micro-span of time. When my friend, who suffered from strange food allergies, visited a holistic healer, she was asked to bring samples of the food she normally ate. The healer would pick up her jar of peanut butter, or her bag of jasmine rice, and hold it against my friend's body, and pronounce, "The body likes this," or "The body doesn't like this."

My body works this way.

But this summer I have sworn off yard sales. I see the handwritten placards—9AM—NO EARLY BIRDS—nailed to the electrical poles. I feel the rise in my pulse like a libido spike, and I say to myself: *No.* I am going to have a healing summer, one absent unnecessary stresses. Yard sales are stressful. I feel like the character with the superpowers who, after she uses these powers to stop a villain, collapses in a heap.

Also, yard sales are sites of potential confrontation. One year there was a yard sale at a house that was always perfectly painted and the lawn perfectly mown, but no one ever lived there, not even during the hottest weeks of August. Then a sign announced there would be a yard sale at this house and I knew: it would be a good one.

I was right. It was one of the best yard sales I've ever been to; the competition, as it can be in Maine, was intense. I had to double my usual speed of identification, because stuff was disappearing fast. I found an iron bed within two minutes of arriving. It could have come from an infirmary, or a Victorian orphanage. It was narrow and long, custom-sized for a serpent. The odd proportions and level of disrepair (not terrible) announced to me: this is the item you must stand next to, and thereby risk losing all other good items.

I stood next to the bed and tried to flag the person with the sales tickets. Meanwhile, a woman I know approached me. "Are you getting that bed?" she asked. "Yes," I said. "Oh," she said. "My husband was supposed to get here early to buy it." She explained that there had been a preview of the sale, and that they'd gone, and they'd agreed to buy the bed for their small son.

I am usually the first person to cede to another—the more advantageous place in the checkout line, the last scone—I do this because I enjoy making other people happy. I enjoy the friendly exchanges that result from this kind of giving. But sometimes I give away things I want for myself. I do this because I hate social awkwardness and then afterward I hate myself for being such a coward.

This time, however, and maybe it was because we were at a yard sale, and because the rules of yard sales are understood and respected by everyone in Maine—*I got here first, piss off*—I did not budge. I said, "I'm sorry." I wasn't sorry that I wasn't giving her the bed. I was sorry that she wasn't married to a man who better understood the rules.

The story of this bed has become legion among our friends. Or rather, my "cutthroat" behavior has become legion. I put "cutthroat" in quotes because my friends are not criticizing me. They enjoy teasing me about my refusal to give away the bed. It was so out of character, my failure to cede the bed to a couple who would use it year-round rather than just during the summer, a couple who probably makes a fraction of the money my husband and I make. All these factors rendered the story even more delicious for my friends to tell and retell.

But my failure to give, in this instance, wasn't a failure of generosity. It wasn't a "cutthroat" desire to beat someone, or a crazy quasi-erotic need for an object. The truth was that I wouldn't respect myself if I gave the woman this bed. I wouldn't respect myself for being incapable of saying, "I really want this bed, I won it fair and square, and I am not going to give it to you out of guilt." (I basically said this by saying, "I'm sorry.") If I'd given the bed to the woman, I'd have done so passive-aggressively. I'd have done so to make her feel bad for making me do something I didn't want to do, and that, by the laws of Maine yard sales, I didn't need to do. But if I'd given her the bed, she wouldn't have felt bad, not for a moment. And I would have felt like an idiot for giving up a bed to make a point that nobody got, not even me.

SEPTEMBER 12

Today my husband and I went on a date to the Wannsee Conference house. The Conference house is on the opposite side of the German lake from where we're living, and is a villa much like ours, save for the fact that in its dining room on January 20, 1942, Eichmann, Heydrich, Müller, and other notable Nazis gathered to draw up their official Jewish extermination plan, euphemistically referred to in the conference minutes as the "Final Solution." (I have since learned a bit more about the history of *our* villa. During the war, following its seizure from a prominent Jewish banking family, our villa became the home of Hitler's "economic guru," a man named Walther Funk, whose work for the Third Reich earned him the name "the Banker of Gold Teeth," a moniker referring to the practice of extracting gold teeth from concentration camp inmates so that they could be sent to the Deutsche Reichsbank—of which he was president—and melted into bullion. So the similarities between our villa and the villa across the lake, one can assume, extend beyond architecture and water-front proximity. Though I have no doubt that the topic of extermination was, on numerous occasions, also discussed in the dining room of our villa, these remarks were unofficial enough that no museum is warranted to memorialize them.)

To get to the Conference house my husband and I biked past rowing clubs and yacht clubs and mini-schlosses, and along the way my mood started to tighten. I could not entirely blame Hitler. This just happens on some days, even when mass murder tourism isn't on the date docket. We rounded the corner onto the street where the S-Bahn is located, and the mean beer-and-wurst seller I've made it my goal this fall to befriend, and it was as if I'd pedaled into an unpleasant new weather system. I saw my husband biking ahead of me and decided, because I had no better explanation, that he was somehow to blame for the alienation I'd been vaguely sensing all day and that had finally coalesced into the more solid (and paranoid) beginnings of a depression. By plain virtue of the fact that he existed and he loved me, he was at fault. I thought of the recent invitation he'd received to go to Paris, and of the many readings he's giving in Germany and elsewhere in the upcoming weeks. Here, in this country, at this villa, I am a spouse; literally, this is how I am referred to on the villa itineraries he has received, i.e., "dinner for fellows and spouses." My spousehood even required documentation. We had to produce a marriage certificate in order to secure my official welcome. (Apparently many people try to pose as the spouses of fellows; the fakes must be ferreted out.)

None of this, until today, had bothered me.

We arrived at the Wannsee Conference house; we parked our bikes. Standing in the beautiful gardens, reading the history of the villa on a placard, I was struck—as most people who visit the villa, at least according to the placard, are struck—by the uncomfortable collision of "idyll and violence." This made me think of my husband's and my favorite movie, an Austrian film in which a lakeside summerhouse is invaded by murderers who first toy with the family before killing them one by one, including the child. Years ago, when we were first dating, we rented this movie—from a Maine video store stocked with old blockbusters and about six foreign films—knowing none of the plot in advance. The title was in German, the blurbs and the descriptions were in German. We met this movie cold.

In the gardens, I made mention to my husband that possibly the director of this movie we'd seen so many years ago had been thinking of the uncomfortable collision of idyll and violence prompted by the likes of the Wannsee house. If I'd been a critic in Austria or Germany writing about this movie when it first came out (in 1997), I'm sure I would have thought about idylls and violence, and how, not so long ago, many people were hanging out in lake houses or regular old houses while elsewhere people were definitely not doing that.

What I was not saying but trying to say: *We are on a sort-of date at the Wannsee Conference house, but I am struggling not to feel really alone here, and also not to be angry at you for absolutely no reason.* This movie is important to my husband and to me. It signals that we had a history of liking things together, and of seeing the world similarly. I needed reminding of that.

But I also wanted confirmation that my inexplicable, unjustifiable resentment of him was explicable and justified. I was fairly committed to this mood I was in; I less wanted to overcome it than I wished to stumble upon an excuse to more fully realize it. So I lay in wait. There was no escaping me. My husband said of my observation about idylls and violence, "That's not what that movie was about." Then he told me what the movie was about. This, at least, is how I chose to interpret his response.

I grew indignant. As if I needed anyone to tell me what that movie was about! I recalled another movie we'd watched together in our early days, in which a New Age character says to his non–New Age dinner guest, "That's funny, you're telling *me* about chakras."

This was my inner chorus as we walked through the Wannsee Conference house and took pictures of anti-Semitic children's books. *That's funny you're telling* me *about chakras. That's funny you're telling* me *about chakras.* I also sensed—or wished to sense, in the interests of fully realizing my bad mood—an increasing emotional divide between us. My husband stopped talking to me; he wandered off on his own. This sounds ridiculous, and is ridiculous, but I decided that my husband believed he had a deeper connection to the material and the exhibit because he is half-Jewish and I am (possibly) not Jewish at all.

In my head, I started a fight with my husband. I argued in favor of my possible Jewishness, and thus my right to walk around the museum as his equal. The spelling of my last name was created on Ellis Island, and only the direct descendants of my great-grandfather have the exact arrangement of letters; phonetically, however, there exist many potential "relatives" in the States, and every one of these potential relatives is Jewish. I am occasionally contacted by members of these phonetically identical families whose names are spelled "Shulawitz" or "Jewelowicz;" they say, "I heard you mentioned on the radio.

I thought perhaps we might be related." Recently I was asked to be on a panel; when I declined, the organizer said, "Could you possibly recommend another female Jewish novelist?"

(Also—this is unrelated yet somehow not—Hitler and I share a birthday. This has always made me suspect that people subsconsciously believe I am somehow complicit in the killing of Jews. It has also made me vigilant with myself. According to the laws of horoscopes, I might be an enthusiastic organizer possessed of incredibly bad ideas. Every instance of group inspiration requires a gut check. *What are the possibly really negative long-term ideological ramifications of this Fourth of July parade float?* If I were Jewish, I would be relieved of a great deal of probably pointless self-doubt.)

I trailed my husband. I continued our heated dispute to which only I was party. In my head I said to him: Does having two one-quarter Jewish children give me rights to a Jewish connection? Did the failure in the 1970s of Portland, Maine's WASPiest law firm to hire my father, maybe because he was presumed to be Jewish ("How was your *holiday?*") give me rights to that connection? What about the fact that my best friend in graduate school so believed I was Jewish that she mocked me for being a Jewish denier, and would pick up from my desk the old daguerreotypes of my just-off-the-boat-in-nineteen-oh-whatever relatives on my mother's side, the schnozzy Dabelsteins, and point at them and say, grinningly, and with fake credulity, *Not Jewish!*, and then point to photos of my dark-haired father and dark-haired brother and exclaim with the same expression and intonation, *Not Jewish!* The name "Julavits," as she likes to point out, is doubly Jewish. My name, she says, is basically *Jewjew.*

I followed my husband into the dining room. Aptly, the question of defining Jewishness was a primary preoccupation of the Wannsee Conference. The conference minutes are basically dedicated to solving the problem of who counts as Jewish, who only partially counts as Jewish, and who does not count as Jewish at all. Proposals for determining the sub-, and sub-sub-, and sub-sub-sub-"degrees" stretched, under glass, on side-by-side typed sheets of paper, the circumference of the large room. For example:

(2) TREATMENT OF PERSONS OF MIXED BLOOD
OF THE SECOND DEGREE
Persons of mixed blood of the second degree will
be treated fundamentally as persons of German
blood, with the exception of the following cases,
in which the persons of mixed blood of the
second degree will be considered as Jews:
(a) The person of mixed blood of the second
degree was born of a marriage in which both
parents are persons of mixed blood.
(b) The person of mixed blood of the second
degree has a racially especially undesirable
appearance that marks him outwardly as a Jew.
(c) The person of mixed blood of the second
degree has a particularly bad police and political
record that shows that he feels and behaves like
a Jew.

In my head I argued my case to my husband: all of my fully Jewish friends think I'm Jewish! (2c, "behaves like a Jew"). Some of my nearest relatives appear to be Jewish! (2b, "racially especially undesirable appearance that marks him outwardly as a Jew"). The first guy who ever went down on me was Jewish! (Certainly this "deportation"-worthy transgression was covered somewhere in the minutes.)

Afterward, my husband and I biked to the grocery store. I was feeling excluded, still, and wanted to address that feeling of exclusion by highlighting how totally not Jewish I supposedly was (wasn't?), and how far apart from one another my husband and I were on this date. I tested; I poked. I remarked on the malevolent stylishness of Hitler, and that I understood how people were (to tragic ends) seduced by his aesthetic bombast and precision. My husband said that Hitler's aesthetic didn't appeal to him at all. By this he was saying (I thought) that he was better than those people who found it seductive. That he was better than *me,* because I claimed to understand how a person, back in the day, might, at their peril, be seduced.

I cited the many scholarly books written on Nazi style by people who were smart and knowledgeable; on the basically irrefutable intellectual proof that the Nazis were aesthetically intoxicating, to which he said, quite innocently and also correctly, "I just don't think that anyone would join the Nazis because of the way the party looked." At which point (we were now in the berry aisle at Kaiser's, our local supermarket chain) I blew. I said, *Of course* I wasn't saying that people joined the party just because they liked the uniforms and the fucking interior decor. I accused him of reducing everything I said to the claims of a simpleton; that he refused to have a conversation with me, or a discussion with me, that he was only interested in staking out his belief territory, and in so doing relegating me to a belief territory that was boneheaded and morally weak (I might have been seduced!). I was trying to *talk* to him and to emotionally engage with him (by attacking him, but whatever); he, meanwhile, just wanted to tell me who he was, or who he'd have been, in the face of Hitler. He was defining himself apart from everyone, but especially apart from me.

My husband was totally surprised, as he often is when I explode like this. I tend to give no hint of disturbance until I am massively and performatively disturbed. He was also mortified that this fight should be happening in Kaiser's, and within earshot of many English-speaking Germans. He said in a low voice, "Please, let's not fight about Hitler." (The other day he said to me, "Please, let's not fight about military time.")

I countered that this "fight" had nothing to do with Hitler; that he'd started behaving like an intellectual separatist while we were talking about movies in the Conference house gardens. I told him I had been really insulted when he'd told me what the movie we'd watched many times together was "about."

"I know what that movie's fucking about," I said.

As he must do in these situations—What else is there to do save divorce me? I really did pick a fight with him the other day about military time—he approached me calmly. He tried to offer an honest, outsider perspective. He promised that he hadn't committed any of the crimes I'd pinned on him. He said, quite objectively, "I think you're just looking for reasons to be offended."

He really did not offer this observation accusatorially. He offered it kindly, as an explanatory diagnosis that might provide me some relief. It didn't give me relief, but it did give me pause. Was I looking to be offended? I knew I was in a terrible mood. A terrible yet officially documented *spousal* mood. At the admissions desk at the Wannsee Conference house, my husband whispered that he'd been invited to speak at the Wannsee Conference, and I'd missed the joke entirely. My response was: Really? He'd been invited to speak there, too? And I hadn't been? I wanted to say to him: I'm not looking to be offended. I'm really not looking. It's just that when I opened my eyes today, offense was all that I could see.

JANUARY 3

Today I tried out a new space in the library because my old space, the one with the catwalk, is going to be ruined. Not according to the loud librarians who, in an officious pack, roamed the room and pointed out its flaws. To them, this room will not be ruined; it will be improved. The librarians have tacked a sign to the bulletin board explaining their intentions. "The catalog has not been updated since 1985," says this sign, "and information in the catalog becomes increasingly inaccurate and obsolete every day." The card catalog is a threat to truth and relevance! It is a constantly intensifying, present-tense menace! It *becomes*. It does this *every day*.

Now I am in a different catwalk, one threatened only by obsolete books. I have read many of these books; I seem to have landed in the women's studies nook of the Dewey decimal system. HQ 1236.5–HQ 1665.15 are my coordinates. I was a women's studies minor in college. I can't recapture what made me want to study women, but I remember wanting to do so from my very first semester. I tried to convince a friend from my dorm to take a class with me. I was scared to do it alone. "Fuck no," she said. "I hear women touch each other in those classes." She was hyperbolic, this friend, tall and mouthy. She'd go on to play rugby, and do heroin, and marry a scruffy mountain genius, and raise chickens in the city.

I signed up anyway. On the first day of class, everyone already knew everyone. My solitude was conspicuous. Minutes after I sat down, the woman behind me began playing with my hair. She ran her fingers through it. She began to braid it.

After I recovered from my surprise (and the annoyance that I'd have to admit to my friend, *you were right*), I found her attention so relaxing. This woman was welcoming me in the way that women welcomed all newcomers into the women's studies cult. Braiding a newcomer's hair was a time-honored ritual, I'd probably soon learn, practiced by the Native Americans (for whom our college was founded, in part, to educate) to initiate strange women into their tribes.

I turned to thank her.

The woman blanched.

"Oh my God," the woman said, horrified. "I thought you were Daphne!"

Her embarrassment yielded to suspicion. What kind of person lets a total stranger braid her hair for five minutes *without saying anything*? I was so not a feminist! I'd let any old person touch my body! I would endure the invasion in silence! I would probably even enjoy it!

I don't think this woman and I ever spoke again during the two years we occupied the same small campus. There's no recovering from certain shames.

But this Daphne person I might have been. I didn't know Daphne at the time. I would soon find out how totally not-Daphne I was. Daphne was the Gwyneth Paltrow of our school. She was white-blond and grew up on Park Avenue and attended an expensive private girls academy and was a lesbian. Her lesbianism did not appear to be about desire or preference, but probably neither would her heterosexuality be, if she practiced it. She was beautiful without seeming to suffer the needs of a body. She was ascetically thin with an expressionless face that might seem sociopathic or enlightened, depending. She ran feminism on our campus like Tilda Swinton ran her Utopian island community in the film adaptation of *The Beach*. She was everything I wanted to be in 1986, so I was flattered to be mistaken for her. Now I'm embarrassed that Daphne was the person I most wanted to be mistaken for. Since 1986 my desires have been updated quite regularly—on a daily basis, even. Does this constant updating make me more or less accurate and obsolete? I am not sure.

NOVEMBER 4

Today I was making breakfast when a man floated past my window. I hadn't slept well. It was all I could do to feed the people in my home. My brother, who is staying with me because he has no electricity in his house and likely won't for many more days, said, "They're doing something to your tree."

This was very bad news. Since the hurricane took down half our tree last week, the half that remained possibly wasn't doing well. I'd convinced myself that its health, or people's perceptions of its health, said more about the perceiver than it did about the tree. The trunk had once forked into two segments pointing north and south. The northern segment was gone; the southern segment, lacking its counterweight, *might possibly* be listing at a more acute angle to the sidewalk. I'd stood beneath it daily and tried to ascertain whether this listing was real or imagined.

"I wouldn't stand under that tree," an old lady said to me one afternoon.

"Why not?" I said.

"It's going to fall over," she said. She was optimistically pessimistic, the way old people in New York can be.

"It just looks like it's falling over because half of it's gone," I said.

You also look like you're falling over, I wanted to say to her. *You're lucky people on the sidewalk aren't assessing your survival chances.*

"It's always been this way," I said.

"Really?" she said. "It always touched this building?"

"Yes," I said. "That's my building. Those are my windows. It's always touched my windows."

The woman shrugged. She wasn't going to quibble with the so-called expert. But she wasn't altering her opinion. This tree was coming down.

The airborne man started up his chain saw. I abandoned breakfast. I took the elevator downstairs to talk to the tree crew. The worker guarding the sidewalk confirmed: the old lady had been right.

I returned to the apartment. I didn't think twice about breaking down in front of my brother; he regularly, when we were kids, witnessed me losing my shit over a misplaced pencil or a lost shoe, objects that solicited my grief more intensely than did the death of our family pets. Still, he hasn't seen me cry like this in thirty-five or more years. I called my husband (he was in Maine). He professed shock over the tree's total removal. "That seems unnecessarily brutal," he said.

Outside the window, the dismemberment began. They

removed the limbs one at a time; they fed each limb into the chipper.

"Maybe we should all go to a park," my brother suggested. My brother is a formal fellow. He's not often outwardly emotional but he is always very empathic.

Of course we couldn't go to the park. We owed it to our tree to stay. I took photos of the view out our window that would never again be the view out our window. I documented the stages of disappearance. Its total goneness looming, I returned to the sidewalk to ask the crew if they would give us a round of the trunk. "So my children and I can count the rings," I said. "They're just so broken up over the loss of our tree." My children didn't give a shit about the tree and its rings. But I figured the crew would be more willing to override whatever rules the city had against handing out tree parts to civilians if they believed the solace and education of children were at stake.

I carried the trunk round upstairs. It was really heavy. My brother and I examined it. "How do you know which marking is a ring?" he said.

My idiot brother. I swore we'd counted tree rings as kids; we had a dead tree in our backyard that had always been dead, dead and even barkless, and yet we'd hung a swing from it and used it like a regular alive tree until it leaned dangerously and we had to cut it down. We'd counted the rings on the stump, or that's what I recalled.

He was right. The rings weren't clearly demarcated. So many activities that I remember being easy and self-evident when I was a kid turn out not to be. I tried to do tombstone rubbings recently. I tried to lift newspaper print with Silly Putty. I tried to make a Christmas ornament out of a burr and cotton balls and toothpicks. All attempts failed; each failure sent me running to the Internet for answers. How had we managed to do tombstone rubbings without a discussion forum determining what kind of paper works best, what kind of charcoal? How had we successfully made pathetic-looking Christmas sheep?

I refused to consult the Internet about tree rings. "When the wood dries," I said, "we'll be able to see the rings."

My brother shoved his laundry into bags. He shoved his kids into coats. He planned to return to his cold house to tough it out for a few more nights. He and I grew up in a cold house; we are used to sleeping in cold houses. Still, he seemed melancholy. He talked about wanting to throw a proper party for his son, whose birthday fell on the second day of the power outage, before they'd relocated to my apartment. Also they had just moved back east from California and didn't know many people in their new town yet. When his son woke up on his birthday, my brother said, he waited patiently for the festivities to start. There were none. They had no electricity. They had no friends. Finally his son asked, "Where are all the kids?"

My brother, half in his own coat, teared up. I don't know that I've seen him cry for thirty-five years. Perhaps it is due to the rawness of the times that we're made so sad by missed birthdays and dead trees. There's an election in a few days and everyone's on edge. Our city has escaped ruin, but for how much longer can we keep escaping? If another storm doesn't level it, then a terrorist attack will. The sudden impassibility of the same downtown neighborhood has coupled attacks by humans with weather, past and potential, in our minds. I think we are all thinking: our days here are numbered. The old ladies are walking

around making their optimistic pessimistic p
This city's coming down.

Today I trespassed at twilight. Twilight is the ideal
time for pretending you live somewhere you don't. The sky
guard is changing, security is relaxed, and everyone's just
had a cocktail. In the gloaming, there is slippage. In this
particular gloaming, I pretended to live in a Maine summer colony that's in my town. Maine has many summer
colonies, most of them built at the turn of the last century,
most of which resemble adult camps. Each house has a
decrepit porch with hard wooden chairs in which relax-
ation is meant to occur. The words that spring to mind
when I look at these cottages are "backgammon" and
"wife-swapping" and "gin." Families have been swapping
wives over backgammon and gin for generations. They are
heritage families, I suppose. I know some of these heritage
families. Heritage families tend to fray, and fight, and go
spectacularly broke. They fail to fix rotting sills or replace
window screens. This adds to the charming unattainability
of such properties. You cannot purchase a century of hostility and neglect; you cannot purchase houses in which
first editions of *1984* and old family letters are left unprotected, even when the houses are rented to strangers, as
many are, in order to fund the most urgent repairs and the
paying of taxes. To care so little for history raises the value
immeasurably.

My friends are renting one of these houses; ergo we'd

established a trespassing foothold. Just before the moon rose, we decided to walk to a nearby cottage we'd heard was for sale. My friends called it the Boston Marriage cottage because it was once owned by two women of independent means. We walked down the dirt lane carrying wineglasses so that we could *pass* as well as trespass. Open container strolls marked us as natives. We wondered about the origin of the term "Boston marriage." Even though we had iPhones in our pockets, we preferred to hazard guesses. It would not be passing of us to Google a term we'd presumably used so many times without knowing what it meant that we no longer harbored any curiosity about its origin.

The Boston Marriage cottage was located on Mandalay Lane. Mandalay! Colonialism was so predictable. *Manderley,* the name of the house in du Maurier's *Rebecca,* seemed the shrewder and more literary fit, with its haunting of the new generation by the old, also its themes of passing and identity concealment. We were all the second Mrs. de Winter that night.

There was no "For Sale" shingle in front of the Boston Marriage cottage, which made us wonder if it had been sold, or if it had never been for sale in the first place. My friend, who hails from a multigenerational family of landowners in a historic area outside of Philadelphia, assured us that a sign would be gauche, or an indication of financial vulnerability. Their neighbors in the colony would gossip condemningly. *Who would bother selling such a worthless thing?* Only the desperately desperate.

We walked around the Boston Marriage cottage and peered into the windows. We sat on its deck and enjoyed the view. We guessed at the problems given its age and location. A complicated septic situation. Rot, infestation,

unbearable neighbors. These seemed minor ᴄ
given the price, which we'd heard was reasonaʟ.
guessed at the future problems that might mar this ᴄ.
tage were my friends to buy it. Men who never wanted
to come and weren't handy. Close-quartered children who
quarreled when the fog parked in the harbor for days. My
friends—both are women, best friends since girlhood—
began scheming to buy this cottage together. They both
had husbands. But they had yet to replace one another.
Who ever replaces their friends with a lover? These two
women took nearly all of their vacations together. Their
individual families coexisted as a larger, extended family,
headed by two matriarchs. We finished our drinks on the
porch. My two friends reasoned that they were the cottage's heirs apparent. "We basically have a Boston Marriage," they said.

JANUARY 5

Today I tried again to read the Goncourts. I know
I said I'd definitively given up on them, but this is the
beauty or the lameness of me—there's no shortage of second chances. Every petty, embittered person should want
to date me. Every petty, embittered person should write a
book I hate because I'll keep trying to read it.

It has been a few months since I gave up on the Goncourts; today I thought about them, *Maybe they'd changed.*
Or maybe I'd changed. I reread books to measure my
degree of difference from myself. During my twenties and
thirties the book I reread most often was a biography by
Jean Stein, edited with George Plimpton, called *Edie: An*

American Biography. Edie Sedgwick, often described as "one of Warhol's factory girls" (this is my description—a shocking number of people do not know who Edie Sedgwick is), lived a fast, sad life, dead at twenty-eight of a drug overdose. Despite my PhD-level familiarity with all extant images of Edie Sedgwick, the images that appear in my head when I think of her are two: (1) with a peroxided pixie cut, doing a ballet move atop a coffee table in black tights; (2) head cocked like a cute dog, hair long and brown, looking up at the camera, wearing a flowered, normal dress. Between those two images exists the identity spectrum she traveled during her life, though this does not take into account certain images further out on the spectrum, for example, stills of her topless and drugged out at the bottom of an empty swimming pool (from the film *Ciao! Manhattan*), or shots of her immediately following the Chelsea Hotel fire, her burned hands wrapped in dirty gauze, looking like a boxer wearing too much eye makeup and also, though not by human forces beyond herself, defeated.

I first read *Edie* in college. My roommate found a copy in a dingy, low-rent part of Vermont, a part that hugs the railway lines and the river, a part where it is always, psychically speaking, mud season. Among the old towels and the kitchen tin she found this book. It was out of print. So far as we knew, there was only one remaining copy in the world. My roommates and I all read it. We all wanted to move to New York and be lauded and exploited by an artist and wear black tights and little else. Ambitious though we were, this one time we dreamed about becoming famous for having produced or accomplished nothing.

Also, Edie and I shared a birthday. This coincidence was the equivalent, in my mind, of a knighting; clearly, I was destined to be Edie's successor. This also meant Edie, like me, shared a birthday with Hitler. Somewhere within our essences, the ones determined by constellations, we might harbor a dormant evil. A mutation of circumstance could set it off. Could we safely endure for a lifetime without waking it?

Edie maybe didn't think so. I felt it was important to study her and to learn, perhaps, how to better cope with our cosmic birthday inheritance. But really what I studied was how I might fulfill a fantasy I never knew I had until I read *Edie*: I wanted people to want to photograph me because I represented energy. Cultural energy. I wanted to possess and transmit cultural energy that, ideally, wouldn't produce another national socialist movement. I guess, thinking more broadly, Edie didn't produce or accomplish much, but she did *exude*. Why get hung up on production and material accomplishment? Let's look at what Hitler produced and accomplished, and let's wish he had slightly less of a production and accomplishment fetish. Who cares about a bunch of books. Edie left spooky and beautiful images of herself. That is more than I've managed to do.

Later, when the Internet happened, I bought my own copy of *Edie*. It remained my practice to regularly read it because every time I did my reaction was different. I could use it as a barometer of who I no longer was. Early twenties: I want to be Edie. I want to be a drug addict. I want to end up at the bottom of a swimming pool with a male model cooking my dirty underpants in a cauldron. Mid-twenties: These earlier goals start to seem somewhat less like "goals." Late twenties: Edie and also Warhol are starting to bug me. I covet only Edie's body and her earrings. Thirty: I decide that all of Edie's problems are because she comes from old money, and I've been developing theories about money and how money, especially old money, can be bad for children, even though all I ever wanted as a child was to come from old money. Early thirties: I feel guilty for thinking so harshly of Edie. I see her as pitiable, a product of bad parenting, because a seriously crazy bunch of humans raised that girl. Her father was vain and also possibly/probably/definitely molested her. He was an obsessive tanner. His nickname was Duke. The children called him Fuzzy. One of her brothers killed himself; another died in a motorcycle accident.

Midthirties: I start to get interested less in Edie the life than I am in the structure of *Edie* the book—the many gossipy voices all talking about Edie (the book is an "oral history," i.e., a bunch of interviews edited into what appears to be a continuous conversation among many people). I think to myself, *Someday I am going to steal this structure.*

Around this time I loaned my copy to a good friend. I kept the dust jacket because I didn't want her to tear it. Ten years later, the dust jacket is all I possess. Acquaintances return books. Friends never do.

Fortunately, at a public reading I gave around the time I last saw my copy of *Edie,* I mentioned during the Q&A that the book I most treasured was *Edie.* A woman in the audience e-mailed me the next day. She was a novelist; she'd been asked to write the screenplay to an Edie Sedgwick biopic. She offered to hook me up with the director in case I might want to write the screenplay in her stead. I didn't want to write it, but I did want to meet the director. The director had known Edie in her worst days; he'd been criticized (by some) for taking advantage of her at her most pathetic and putting the sad spectacle on film. Also I was about to spend a month in L.A., where the director now lived. I contacted him. I told him I was very interested in his project. Hollywood, in my scant experience, is an industry consisting of projects—defined similarly to the way Mainers define projects. Passionate enthusiasm and commitment is expressed in the name of negligible material results. Twelve years after buying the lumber for his porch project, my neighbor still hasn't built his porch. After a while the lack of a porch is not a daily reminder of what should be but of what *might be*. It's a form of promise. What's to hope for once the porch is built?

We arranged to meet at the director's house to talk about the screenplay. He lived in the suburban-seeming flatlands of L.A., his house hard to discern behind the bamboo forest overtaking the property. The roots were slowly upending his foundation like a tooth under a tooth. The floors, because of this slow incursion from below, pitched up and down, and walking through the house I felt like someone trying to reach an airplane bathroom during a turbulent flight. The director was a fanatical collector not just of movie posters and movie memorabilia but also of American bulldogs. One very old, incontinent bulldog had been urinating throughout the house (and presumably other bulldogs before him), and the whole place, windows darkened by the thick stalks of the jumbo bamboo, stank historically. The house extended like a tunnel to an even more lightless inner chamber where his videotapes were kept.

The director was, I think it is fair to say, a man who had not received all that life had, at one time, promised him. I can't explain, even after knowing and meeting him, why. He was charming and generous and alarmingly smart. He possessed in his head an archive of American culture spanning decades. I suppose, yes, he was a little overwhelming when generously sharing his enthusiasms, and maybe, even in a process town, a bit too enamored of process. But he knew everyone who was anyone from the '60s, '70s, and '80s. He had *proof* of everyone.

What I mean by proof. Among his many interests were Kung Fu films. In the '80s he'd obtained the rights to a popular Chinese series and, with the help of a partner, reedited two episodes into a single film with an English-language sound track. This movie was very influential. Around the time when I met the director, he'd recently been contacted by a young and very famous *auteur* for permission to use a clip from his reedited Kung Fu movie. The director was thrilled. He'd wanted to meet the auteur for years. He told the auteur that he had footage of Uma Thurman's mother breast-feeding Uma Thurman's brother. His thinking: the auteur was obsessed with Uma Thurman. Imagine what an opportunity this presented! To see footage of the naked breasts that had nursed Uma Thurman! He told the auteur that he could see this footage if he came to his house. Then the director would sign the papers and give him the permission he wanted.

This is, I think, give or take, what eventually happened.

The director and I spent a lot of time together that month I lived in L.A., though we barely talked about the screenplay. Maybe he didn't want to make the movie any more than I wanted to write the script for it. One day we hung out with a deranged actress he thought might be good for the part of Edie; she wore a Mexican sundress and talked for uninterrupted hours about herself, though not one detail of her life do I retain. Often the director told me stories about the talented people and the untalented people. And about those who'd made it and those who hadn't. He was outraged on behalf of certain geniuses who had never gotten their due. He never once expressed bitterness on his own behalf, but I suspect the director believed, and I believed it too, that he'd been unfairly deprived of opportunity and greatness. Far stupider people had succeeded where he had not.

At this time, I had not yet read the Goncourts. Only today did I read the following page from their journals because I am giving these brothers, these viperous, sulky brothers, a second chance:

> *If I were really wealthy, I should have enjoyed making a collection of all the muck that celebrities with no talent have turned out. I should get the worst picture, the worst statue of this man and that, and pay their weight in gold. I should hand this collection over to the admiration of the middle classes, and after having enjoyed their stupid amazement at the tickets and the high prices of the objects, I should let myself go off into criticism composed of gall, science, and taste, until I foamed at the mouth.*

Were the director and I still in contact, I might send him this quote. We're not. Promise has a shelf life. Without ever stating as much, we both knew he was never making this movie about Edie. But he was not as close to her life as I would get. A few weeks after meeting the director, my friend's husband, also an Edie fanatic, suggested we drive a few hours north to Santa Barbara and visit the ranch where Edie grew up. We chose not to worry ourselves that the ranch had been donated, by the Duke Fuzzy Sedgwick estate, to the nearby university for agricultural experiments, and was surrounded by a fence. We parked on the roadside. We ignored the NO TRESPASSING signs. We pried ourselves through the gate. We hiked down to the house, we looked into all the windows, we saw the fireplace where the Sedgwick family photograph with Fuzzy reading a book to his many (not yet suicided or motorcycle-killed or overdosed) children, was taken. Then we got busted by the caretaker. He gave us hell. We apologized, and he offered to show us around. He didn't understand what we were there to see, however. We were not there to see how nonnative grasses behave when planted in Southern California. We were not there to see how formerly extinct varieties behave when reintroduced to their homeland. We were there to understand why the native promise of this one woman, it had long ago been proven, did not survive.

JULY 3

Today I went to a barbeque wearing a hospital bracelet. I'd gone to the ER a few days earlier to get antibiotics for a case of strep throat. Normally strep throat does not require a visit to the emergency room, but we are in Maine, and we don't live here full-time, and the doctors here aren't accepting new patients, and my doctor in New York refused to phone in antibiotics without examining me, and so I had to go to the ER.

I'd been to this ER eight years ago. All of my information dated back to that time—my old address, my old insurance, my old doctor in New York. My old doctor's name was on the bracelet they taped around my wrist; on my discharge papers, it was suggested that I follow up with my old doctor once I returned home. Unfortunately, my old doctor was dead. He was killed riding his bike in Manhat-

tan about six years ago. He was a beloved family physicia
of the sort that is not bred any longer, and thus his demise
was newsworthy, inspiring many articles in the papers. In
New York his tragedy had been well documented and long
ago accepted. Not so here.

The secretary requested I update my information
when I settled my bill. Because of my dead doctor, I nearly
didn't. In Maine, computers function as keepers of nostal-
gically outmoded ideas and things, kind of like historical
societies. But I needed to input my new insurance company information, so I updated everything, including the
name of my old doctor. Next time I visited the ER, there
would be no trace of him.

I kept the ER bracelet on my wrist. Partially I wore it to
make myself feel less terrible about erasing him. But I also
wore it because of my failure ever to properly thank him for
his doctoring while he was alive. He bent over backward to
help me, not that I needed his help very much, but when I
did, he gave it. I'd repeatedly said to my husband, "I need
to write him a note to tell him how wonderful he is." I
never wrote a note. After he was killed, my husband made
me feel better about the note I never wrote by saying, "I
bet he received so many notes like that." But what if other
people assumed as I did, that all of his patients sent him
notes, and thus they did not need to send him one? Maybe
he'd never received a single note from anyone.

So at the barbecue many people asked me about the
hospital bracelet, including a woman who, after I told her
the story of my dead doctor and my subsequent guilt and
how I couldn't, because it was the final connection I had
to this man, cut the bracelet off yet, she said, "Wow, that
was not what I was expecting to hear." She declared that,
due to this bracelet story, she would need to totally rethink

ht I was. I didn't ask how I'd formerly been
w I'd be re-categorized based on this
.

d a piece by Julian Barnes about the
an Freud. Barnes writes,

> *In one version of the philosophy of the self, we*
> *all operate at some point on a line between the*
> *twin poles of episodicism and narrativism. The*
> *distinction is existential not moral. Episodicists*
> *see and feel little connection between the different*
> *parts of their life, have a more fragmentary sense of*
> *life, and tend not to believe in the concept of free*
> *will. Narrativists feel and see constant connectivity,*
> *an enduring self, and acknowledge free will as*
> *the instrument which forges their self and their*
> *connectedness. Narrativists feel responsibility*
> *for their actions and guilt over their failures;*
> *episodicists think that one thing happens, and*
> *then another thing happens. . . . Narrativists tend*
> *to find episodicists selfish and irresponsible; while*
> *episodicists tend to find narrativists boring and*
> *bourgeois.*

These two approaches might typify our differences as
people, this woman and I. She's episodic, I'm narrative. I
see connections everywhere. She's a woman who has lived
many fantastic yet disparate and self-canceling lives. She's
a rebooter, a category shape-shifter. I entered a track in my
twenties and stayed on it and on it. She's my occasional
fantasy; I don't know if I'm hers. But I suspect this is why
our relationship is strained occasionally. We remind each
other of who we aren't. I am herself betrayed. She is myself

betrayed. I don't know for a fact, but I can bet she's told herself, or told her husband, that she's relieved she's not me. I have told my husband that I'm relieved I'm not her. I only sometimes mean it.

AUGUST 19

Today I met a reclusive writer/editor who lives in our town. I've been hoping to meet him for years. The closest I've come to meeting him is seeing his name written on the DRY CLEANING READY list they tape to the cash register of the general store when the shirts come in.

I finally met him not at the general store but at the boatyard. I was wearing a bathing suit and the writer/editor was fully clothed. It seemed inappropriate to be meeting this man in my bathing suit, primarily because this is not a dock where people are often seen wearing bathing suits, and secondarily because this man is ninety-seven years old. Plus my bathing suit is ridiculous on so many design levels; my left breast pops out when I shrug, or when I inhale, or when I put my hand on my hip. For swimming it is completely stupid, but it is a one-piece and thus more sensible than a bikini, and so it is the suit I wear when I swim to the Goodale buoy. Today this is what I intended.

I tried to cover myself with my arms as I shook this man's hand; I told him how excited I was to finally meet him. I asked how much time he spent in Maine (as opposed to New York, where he also lived); he said he'd been here most of the summer. He made reference to the fact that, after the recent passing of his wife, Maine seemed the pleasanter place to be.

Coincidentally, three children and I had visited his wife's grave earlier that day. We'd gone to the cemetery to bring flowers to a number of people: E. B. White and Katharine White; also the "youngest person in the cemetery" (given the youngest members tragically warranted little more than an INFANT tombstone, this superlative status proved impossible to determine); and the grave of the bootlegger whose name I stole to give to my daughter. I'd specifically shown the kids the writer/editor's wife's grave, because, since last summer, it was new. He had a matching grave beside hers. It was also new. I suggested his wife might qualify as the "youngest" in the cemetery (in that she was the newest member) and was probably deserving of flowers. She got some. Then the kids noticed that the writer/editor's grave did not have a death date on it yet. I explained that this was because he was still alive. I explained that people sometimes buy and erect their tombstones before they die. This confused them. The existence of a tombstone for a not-yet-dead person wasn't the source of their bewilderment. What bewildered them was the etiquette involved. They had put flowers on his wife's grave. Should they put flowers on his grave too, even though he was not yet in it?

A brief discussion ensued. "It's rude to put flowers on the grave of a person who's not dead," declared one kid authoritatively, putting the matter to rest.

I wanted to tell the writer/editor about our earlier visit to his wife's and his future grave, but I wasn't sure the story would come off as I wanted it to. Because I was wearing a bathing suit, I wasn't confident in my ability to walk the line between respectful and inappropriate. Would it make him happy to know that a few strange children had, just two hours earlier, put flowers on his wife's grave? Would he find it cheering or depressing to know that he had not met the requirements for flowers? I'd heard that he'd been bereft since his wife had died. That it was "a matter of time" before he joined her. I told him that we'd put flowers on his wife's grave, but didn't tell him that he had not yet qualified. Sometimes, I figured, people don't need reminding that they are still alive.

AUGUST 6

Today we tried to socioeconomically identify the people whose house my friend is renting for the week. My friend is an artist, England-born, contrarian. He paints representations of historically seismic thought shifts. His ability to contextualize data, and divine from it a visual map, is applied, in his off hours, to his immediate surroundings. He decided that the family from which he was renting his house was anti-intellectual, conservative, and Francophobic. The books in the house, he said, supported his theory, which he delivered as though it were the third law of thermodynamics (one of his favorite laws). I defended the family, knowing them not at all; bookshelves of summerhouses are filled with dishy nonsense, I said. They indicate how a person understands time that is meant to be wasted.

He fetched from the shelves a novel that appears in many houses around here because the novel is about this town, and the writer wrote about real people and changed their names, and so everyone bought the novel to see if and how they'd been portrayed. He read the first sentence aloud. "All places where the French settled early have corruption at their heart, a kind of soft, rotten glow, like the phosphorescence of decaying wood, that is oddly attractive."

This proved everything and nothing, and led to a conversation about *la tendresse,* which the artist refused to define, save to say, "If you don't know about *la tendresse,* you'll understand nothing about nineteenth-century French literature." Another friend explained *la tendresse* as the sexual education of French daughters by French mothers. Education of actual sexual techniques? we asked. Or just wiles? What class of French women inculcated their daughters via *la tendresse*? And what did this say about the man we knew who'd married and then divorced a millionaire and built a boat named *Tendress*?

This discussion, such as it was, dovetailed with a *tendresse*-related conversation I'd had two nights previous. In August, in Maine, it can sometimes seem that everyone everywhere is having the same conversation between the hours of five and eight p.m. The summer bleeds into an extended talking twilight. I was discussing with two women how best to raise a girl so that she won't become anorexic and won't approach sex guiltily, because many of us had mothers who came of age during an era when to have casual sex with a guy was thereby to inspire his disrespect, and to subsequently be seen as a woman of low morals, i.e., unmarriageable and worthy only of fucking. I admitted to telling my eight-year-old daughter, who has a great body but is no waif, that she shouldn't wish to be really skinny, because in my experience (I told her) once you start dating, you'll get a lot of action if you've got meat on your bones. I didn't say "if you look fuckable," but that's what I meant. I was insecure about my non-waify body when I was a teenager, but I had a boyfriend who guaranteed me that my body was "fuckable," and this seemed a decent runner-up distinction if I couldn't look like a model. I then emphasized to my daughter that her self-worth should have nothing to do with what other people thought (thereby contradicting myself); that she had to believe her body to be fuckable, i.e., if only she wanted to fuck it, that would be ideal, and that would make other people, girls or boys or whatever, want to fuck it more. Again I communicated all of this using none of these words. I admitted to my friends that maybe it was totally screwed up to mention this stuff to my daughter, and that I basically really didn't know how to talk about it at all. But now this conversation with my daughter could be viewed, more nobly, as my attempt at *la tendresse Américaine*. Set a good example. Want to fuck yourself so that others want to fuck you too.

APRIL 19

Today I wore a coat I haven't worn for years. My husband and I were headed downtown on the subway. I said to him, "I wonder what's in the pockets." I use my clothing as storage for important and unimportant paper scraps I might paste into a book if I were more organized. The contents of my pockets are like the diary I have, until recently, failed to keep. In pockets I have found movie stubs, plane tickets, to-do lists, e-mail addresses written on grocery receipts, business cards from people I have no memory of meeting, reminders that I used to have far more money in my savings account than I currently do, jotted-down directions (what was at 457 7th Avenue? Who was in Suite 23?). According to my pockets, I've been all over this city. I could mark these destinations on a map using pushpins, showing the shape of my travels over the past twenty years. These are my hunting grounds, though I have no memory, now, of what I was hunting.

Sometimes there is money.

So today I said to my husband, "I wonder what's in the pockets," thinking I would pull out the usual handful of oblique data points. Instead I found a folded piece of 8½ x 11 paper. I assumed it was the Robert Frost poem I'd read at our friend's daughter's bat mitzvah. (I encounter this poem every two years or so. I keep it in a spring coat; I never can remember which one.) I was surprised to unfold the paper and discover our wedding vows.

"It's our wedding vows," I said to my husband. We'd been married in our backyard in Maine, and, yes, I recalled, when it had grown colder that afternoon, I'd put on this coat. This was now ten years ago.

I tried to read the vows but found I couldn't. I felt embarrassed, maybe because we were on the subway and in close proximity to many strangers, but then again we'd gotten married in front of strangers, people we'd literally just met when we'd moved, a month earlier, to Maine. We invited the strangers to our wedding, but I did not—out of shame, because I'd been married before and not successfully—invite my own family. I was trying to make a very small deal of this wedding. I thought I was being so sensitive by failing to include them in this really (I told myself) quite insignificant event. It wasn't worth the plane fare, I reasoned, plus I figured they'd wish to be spared the shame of witnessing their daughter or sister promise to unfalteringly love yet another man. Then the morning of the ceremony I realized how much this wedding meant to me, and how much I needed my family there, and how insanely thoughtless and stupid it was to think I could get

married, especially to this man, without them. I wept o_
the phone to my mother while the wind blew and the sun
shone and the yard was readied for a ceremony that she
would, because I'd wished to spare all of our feelings, miss.

In the subway car I handed the vows to my husband.
He tried to read them. He also grew uncomfortable. Why
was this? We'd been married by an Internet-anointed, ex-
fighter-pilot-turned-mussel-farmer; it had been up to us to
provide the ceremony's entire script. So maybe we were
made uneasy by what we'd written because we are writers. What writer can look at something he or she wrote
ten years ago and not feel that back then he or she knew
basically nothing about language or life? Or maybe my
husband, like me, experienced a little bit of personal mor-
tification regarding "our affairs." Though we're both highly
capable and responsible people in other areas (job, family),
we're unable to file our taxes without an extension. We're
unable to keep track of our Social Security cards or birth
certificates or car registrations or any of the official documentation one is called upon, with erratic infrequency, to
produce. When we recently needed our marriage certificate to prove my spousehood to the Germans, we were so
uncertain of its location that we began to doubt we'd ever
owned a copy. Then my husband stumbled upon it in a
cabinet used to store lightbulbs and chafing dishes. He put
it in a more sensible place and immediately forgot where
that was.

Another possible explanation for our discomfort: my
husband and I, on this day, were going on our first date
together in months. We've rarely been in the same city for
the last year and a half. I recently met him on the street to
exchange the kids when I was returning from a trip and he
was leaving on one, and the time window was so narrow

rendezvous on a corner, and hug hello and
      took his suitcase and got in my cab, and
      e and wheeled it home with our children.

      because we were just getting to know
      again after a few trying years of what my hus-
band called "corporation co-management." It was a bit like
having amnesia and being introduced to a total stranger
and told, "You're in love with this person. You've been in
love with them your whole life!" It's not that we weren't in
love, but we'd grown shy around each other. I think we
were slightly embarrassed by the baldness of the love proc-
lamations we'd written in our vows.

Or maybe it wasn't the baldness of our love proclama-
tions so much as the inadequacy of them. These words
we'd written were sweet and hopeful and well intentioned,
but they didn't come close to capturing the actual future
we'd built in the subsequent years. (Also we'd watched too
many episodes of *The Bachelorette* together. I fear we've
been forever ruined for love language by that show.) The
vows made me think of our barn. Our barn is built on top
of a pile of rocks. Basically someone just threw some big
rocks on the ground a few hundred years ago and built a
barn on top of them. People walk into our barn and they
can't believe how quiet and vast it is; it's got a hand-hewn,
holy feeling that a friend once compared to an old Swedish
church. When you peer underneath the barn sills you can
see the light streaming through from the other side. The
whole thing appears to be levitating on these inadequate
supports that once functioned as vows for the future. (*Here
there will someday be a barn.*) The engineering is inexplicable; it's a beautiful mystery. Our barn no longer needs
those rocks, if it ever did.

Today I took a bus with some secular pilgrims to the top of a Tuscan hillside. We were here to see a famous, pilgrim-enticing fresco I'd never heard of called the *Madonna del Parto*. Our head pilgrim told us why we should seek to see this fresco. Because it is one of the very few images of a pregnant Mary. Because it was painted by a man named Piero della Francesca. Because Piero was big on math and so, behind his expressive faces there is not emotion but the math of an emotion. He discovered the perspectival equations for happiness and worry and fear.

Like all good modern-day pilgrims in Italy, we prefaced our visit to the Madonna by eating and drinking and seeing ourselves into a stupor. We'd already visited (before our lunch of three pastas) a church and two museums. Our head pilgrim talked about the art we saw. She performed a very graphic mime of a fresco painter slicing a yolk sac with a razor blade. I'd taken notes on the back of a museum ticket that, a day later, would prove inscrutable to me. (*wear a hood—against germs—also so that you cannot be seen and thanked.*)

The point is: I was not primed to feel anything much at the sight of the *Madonna* except exhaustion and a little guilt from having done too much with my face that day (eaten and drank and talked and seen with it), but nothing with my head. Technically today had been a workday. I was supposed to be working; I am in Italy at an art colony and away from my children to work. For the past six months I have been swamped by deadlines and by job stress. I have had such job stress that, even while home these past months, I spent so little time with my children that they started to call me "dad." If I am not working, and getting ahead of the work and the deadlines, and by implication freeing up some future time I might be able to spend with them, I feel that I do not deserve to be in Italy. Also, my children are on the verge of not needing me at all. They no longer need me to read to them. They don't beg as much for me to sleep with them. To leave them for a month is to force them over a threshold they might otherwise cross more gradually. They will realize while I am gone that I am not much missed. When I get home, I will only be their maid.

But when I stepped over the threshold of the building in which the *Madonna* was kept—"kept" really was the word; she was hung on a wall and sealed off from the air and the humidity by a layer of glass and then another layer of glass, resulting in a viewing experience described by our head pilgrim as "trying to see a jam jar inside an aquarium"—I felt *overcome*. (The poet Jorie Graham wrote of Piero's *Madonna,* "This is / what the living do: go in.") "It was believed," said the head pilgrim, "that contemplation of the *Madonna*'s face could change the outcome of your pregnancy. It could change the outcome of your life."

Fortunately, the *Madonna* was preserved like a nocturnal zoo creature in a dark room. I could, unseen, fight to control my own face equation while the head pilgrim talked about the *Madonna*'s ermine-lined tent, the open lacings on her maternity dress, the color-coded angels.

The head pilgrim said that you could gauge the length of time it took to paint the fresco by the *giornate*—the days of work. You counted the *giornate* by the round swipes of plaster Piero put on the wall each day before he started to paint. It took Piero seven days of work.

I listened and looked and tried to distract myself. I still could barely keep my shit together. Why was I so undone? I did not want to change the outcome of my life (if "outcome" is understood to mean "my life right now"—i.e., I am currently *in* my outcome). People had written prayers on paper scraps and left them under the Madonna; weekly, the church burned the scraps so the smoke could deliver their messages to God. Many of these people were praying for a child. I wanted to leave, not a prayer, but a note of gratitude. I have my children, but I didn't want to feel about the *Madonna* as I did about my doctor who died before I could thank him. It seemed not unwise to deliver to the *Madonna* a retroactive prayer containing the hope that she could someday give me what I now had.

In the gift shop, I bought a postcard of the *Madonna*'s face. I saw it as an insurance policy in case "outcome" refers not to the life I'm in but to the one I'm eventually due. Who knows, in that case, whether or not I might need to change it. More than usual, my future concerns me. Since arriving in Italy, I have been beset by anxiety about my children's welfare. I am certain something terrible is going to befall them while I'm gone. It does not help that my husband is driving them a long distance for an upcoming weekend, and that I am particularly afraid of car accidents. I've begged him not to travel with them, though everyone in the family likes to point out that I'm the hazardous driver, not him. If anyone will kill our children with a car, it will be me. But I see things he doesn't. He might unwittingly kill them by failing to see! One of Piero's other fresco subjects, Saint Julian, whom the head pilgrim had taken us to view before lunch, had been jinxed as a baby by pagan witches; the jinx ordained that he would grow up to kill his parents. When older, Saint Julian left home, presumably to avoid this fate. He became a famous hunter. If you are hoping to escape a murderer prophecy, I'm thinking you should probably not put yourself in regular contact with weapons. Whatever. He did. He much later mistook his parents—sleeping in his bed—for his wife and her lover. He killed them.

Saint Julian was not seeing the future properly. He was not thinking ahead like I do. Maybe, thinking ahead, I really should have left a prayer under the *Madonna*. Regardless, I have the *Madonna*'s postcard face. If needed, I can meditate upon it. Behind her face hides the mathematical equation for worry that, if I study it hard enough, perhaps I can solve for myself. How to leave my children behind without this constant anxiety that they will disappear in my absence? Because of course this worry is founded; I will not return in one month to find the same children I left. They are growing older by the hour, by the minute. The head pilgrim told us of a time when the *Madonna* was packed into a truck to be shipped to the Met in New York for an exhibit. The women of the town freaked out. Without the *Madonna*—even temporarily—the crops would fail, and the families would fail. It's the women who fret about luck and how to keep it safe. It's the women who worry, behind protective glass, about future outcomes, their worry protected from dampness or mathematical dismantling. It's the women who foresee doom and take extreme measures to battle its approach. To prevent the *Madonna* from leaving, the head pilgrim said, the women of the town lay down in the street.

JULY 28

Today I am reviewing *The Address Book* by the French artist Sophie Calle. Calle found an address book on the street in Paris. She contacted the people listed in this address book. She interviewed them about their friend, the book's owner. Some claimed to barely know the man.

I imagined someone contacting me about a person in whose address book I might appear. A person I might now barely know. I thought of an old boyfriend with whom I've had no contact since we broke up. I have heard nothing about or from him in over twenty years.

"Boyfriend," however, is not the right word for what he'd been. He was the not-boyfriend I slept with when my real boyfriend moved to South America. Come midnight I knew which bar to find him in, and we'd spend an hour or so ignoring each other. Mutual neglect constituted fore-play. We were strangers hooking up every time, and even then, ambivalently. At some point one of us would give a sign and we'd inconspicuously leave together. I don't think I ever spent the full night at his apartment, or he at mine. After we had sex, whoever didn't live where we were went home.

This arrangement might make sense—if not in a moral sense, then in an erotic sense—if the sex was great. It wasn't. It was the least great sex I'd ever had in my life. Twenty years later the distinction holds. Maybe that's why I pursued a sexual relationship with him—I wanted to understand why I wanted to pursue a sexual relationship with him. The motivation was as cleanly circular as that. Whatever the reason, since this had never happened to me before, this kind of fascinatingly terrible sex, I blamed him. He was a prude. He wasn't comfortable with his body. He was unimaginative and inhibited. I felt confident that the fault was entirely his, and thus never worried that he'd told his friends how bad the sex was. I figured he didn't know from bad. My bad was his good.

Eventually we stopped sleeping together. (I no longer lived where he lived.) A few months later I heard he was dating a girl I vaguely knew. She came from a family in which the sisters and cousins were beautiful and sought after but she was only pretty at a glance. I also heard that they'd had sex on a pool table. This wasn't a pool table in someone's home; this pool table was in a bar, or what passed as a bar. They'd had sex on a public pool table! I became insecure and paranoid. Clearly I'd been the one erotically inhibiting *him;* clearly he'd known the sex we'd had was bad, and he'd probably told people about it because its badness really was that remarkable. A few years later he married the pool-table girl. Last I heard, he was a banker in New York like his father. I heard that he really enjoyed being a banker. I heard that he'd said, "I'm really good at it." This was edifying news. He'd never liked or been good at anything when we were together. He was smart yet adrift. I was honestly happy to hear he'd found a passion.

Then, for over two decades, I lost all track of him.

Today, inspired by Calle, I decided to find him. Was he still happy? I wanted to know. I Googled him by his given name. I Googled him by his nickname. No hits. I added to the search term. I added the town where he grew up, the college he attended. I added "banker." This led me to his father. His seventy-year-old dad had his photo and bio on numerous financial sites, while his son appeared not even to have a Facebook account.

I added his wife's name to the search—she was also from a fancy family. I figured she and my ex-not-boyfriend hosted school fund-raisers or joined country clubs or sponsored auctions to benefit wildlife preserves.

Nothing.

Didn't he have a job? Didn't he have children who played Little League or soccer? Then I got nervous. Maybe he'd died years ago, before obituaries were posted online. His wife had remarried soon thereafter and had a new surname. Surely a total online absence suggests you are probably not alive.

But nor could I definitively conclude that he was dead. Maybe, I thought, I was looking for a *technically* dead person. This guy had not grown up to be the person I'd assumed he would be—the happy banker with the country club wife. That person was gone, but a new person had taken his place. How could I look for *that* person? I tried to imagine what he'd have become if not a banker. (His father had been priming him since he was in elementary school to be his clone. But he wasn't like his father, or this, at least, is what he'd repeatedly insisted to me. Much of the attraction I felt for him originated from this struggle. I was going to help him discover his true artist self. He'd chosen me to have bad sex with because, for once in my life, a man was coming to *me* to get a world.) Maybe he'd woken up one day and realized, *I hate banking, and I'm about to be thirty.* Maybe he told his wife that he was thinking of quitting his job and starting a nonprofit to help poor people in Africa gain access to better dental care. Maybe his wife thought he was joking, or simply freaking out about getting older, and maybe she didn't take his threats seriously until she realized he was serious. Maybe she warned her father-in-law: *he's making a move.*

Maybe, when approached by his son, the amply warned
father refused to give him his inheritance; also he refused
to invest any of his own money, thereby forcing his son to
stay the course. Maybe when the son complained about
his father to his wife, pointing out how his father always
opposed him, not because he was right but because, like
a gorilla in the wild, he couldn't pass up a single opportunity to assert his dominance, maybe the wife said, "Maybe
your father *is* right." And maybe my ex-not-boyfriend told
his appearances-and-money-grubbing wife to go fuck herself, and maybe he appealed to his mother, who'd always
believed her son had it in him to be someone other than
a lesser version of his father, and maybe the mother gave
him the money to start his nonprofit, and maybe he moved
to Africa, and maybe he started a nonprofit that obviously
hadn't done very well, given that I couldn't find any trace
of it, or him, but maybe he'd at least met a girl, and made a
satisfying life with her that wasn't newsworthy, but maybe
it was proof of their uniquely sturdy happiness that it could
not be dispersed and disseminated, not even by the Web.

> *writing h3 life for him*

After a half hour, I gave up. I stopped searching for
him. I could have sent an e-mail to a friend-of-a-friend-of-
a-friend; I could have made some phone calls. I did neither. I realized I'd be disappointed if I found him now.
This was such a nice life I'd imagined him living.

AUGUST 22

Today my husband and I cleaned out our storage space.
It is not news that we have mice. These mice have feasted
on expensive baby clothing that no baby has ever worn;

they have crapped on my first wedding album. These mice are opinionated in all the right ways—Why designer kimonos for an infant! Why the marriage to that unsuitable man!—and still we must kill them. First we must embargo their bedding supply. We swept and boxed and taped and stacked. These tasks always take longer than they should; while killing is the order of the day, it is impossible to fully extinguish one's curiosity about one's own shat-upon past.

Old pictures confirmed to me that I wore glasses that did not suit my former face. What I found most disconcerting about my old (i.e., younger) face, however, is that it suggests I might have become a different person from the one I am. That face wore a lot of vintage men's outdoor gear. In general I look like I live in a place where it is always cold and about to rain, a place where fashion is a prophylactic against the elements and one's body is never revealed until the moment of intercourse, if then. I should have been the wife of a dogsled musher (I was dating one at the time); I should have watched birds or studied lichen; my body and my face should have grown bigger and bigger, rather than shrinking, rather than appearing, as my body and face now appear, as though I'm a practicing self-cannibal. The point at which that person shifted trajectories to become this person was not photographed or documented in the evidence boxes. Where or how she happened could not be ascertained.

I also found a file folder of short stories I'd written in my twenties. I had the same reaction to these stories as I did to the photos of my old face. I didn't immediately recognize the stories as mine. I had no memory of ever writing them. I thought they were copies of stories written by friends that I'd, for whatever reason, kept. But each fictional scenario closely resembled a real-life scenario from my twenties. One story was about a woman going to Alaska over Thanksgiving with a boyfriend she didn't love named Tom (I'd been to Alaska over Thanksgiving with a boyfriend I didn't love named Jim). One was about a woman playing craps in Reno with her husband (I'd played craps in Reno with my boyfriend). Also, the file was labeled "Stories in Progress." All signs pointed to the fact that these stories were written by me. But I had no memory of writing them. "In Progress" would seem to imply "failed" if the in-progress-ness has extended, without progress, over a twenty-year period. The struggle to make a story that's inherently shitty into a story that's inherently not, well, often the only good story to come from such a struggle is the story of the struggle itself. Yet I didn't remember the struggles I'd had with the stories in this folder. I didn't remember trying to fix these shitty stories in the loft I rented with my beautiful friend nicknamed the "Queen of Soho" and the Hollywood actor who wished instead to be a concert pianist. I remembered the actor's noisy espresso making and piano playing, but I did not remember trying to fix these shitty stories. I remembered the Queen's heavy footfalls and her incessant fax receiving, but I did not recall them as distractions from trying to fix these shitty stories. I remember weighing my hunger against the shattered concentration that would come from taking the scary freight elevator downstairs, and walking alongside the Holland Tunnel traffic, and buying a bagel from the corner store run by curt men from Beirut, but I did not remember doing so in service of fixing these shitty stories. I don't have an exact equation by which to estimate the time it took for me to fail for the thickness of this file folder, but a decent guess would be years. Which means I did not remember *years* of failing to write a decent story, which is what I most wanted to do at the time. How could I possibly forget this?

NOVEMBER 16

Today we had a dinner party at our small German house. We live up by the gate in what was once the gardener's shed. The house is so snug that my work desk is in the kitchen which is also basically our bedroom. While people ate cheese and drank beer, they examined the books on my desk. "This is a beautiful edition," said one woman of a book. "You're reading this?" said a man (a German) of another. The book the German man picked up was Leni Riefenstahl's memoir (called *Leni Riefenstahl*). Many years after her death, Riefenstahl remains, to understate matters massively, a controversial character. She was a film director (most famously of the Nazi propaganda film *Triumph of the Will*) and a dancer, and a first-class mountaineer. She might have ranked as one of the twentieth century's most bad-ass humans except that she was, as bluntly articulated by one of the "Gypsy" extras Riefenstahl used in a film before sending her off to a concentration camp, "friends with Hitler" and (again, to massively understate matters), "not a good person." For sure Riefenstahl is a curious case study of what people disallow themselves from knowing when that knowledge is incriminatory or inconvenient. I told the German I'd stopped two-thirds of the way through Riefenstahl's memoir. Her narcissism began to grate, also the tragically comic omissions, the alternating tone of self-aggrandizement and self-pity. Theatrically flawed people are fascinating, but only to a point. For me that point was page 459.

The man told me that his company—he owns a film production company—was making a movie about Leni Riefenstahl. (His was not the first Riefenstahl biopic project, he said. A famous and reputedly "intellectual" actress had been involved in an earlier Riefenstahl project; she'd finally quit because of the script.)

"What was wrong with the script?" I asked.

What was wrong with her script, he said—and what was wrong with his script, and what made Riefenstahl a tricky character to portray—was the character's failure to change.

"She was the same her whole life," he said. "She was just the same person." She only ever cared about making films. She only ever cared about her career. She was always arrogant, narcissistic, unrepentant.

Certainly I understood how this could be boring; hadn't I stopped reading her memoirs for similar reasons? All the same, the criticism struck me as a failure of imagination. (To be fair to this man, it was less his personal failure than a failure of the audience's or the "market's" imagination, to which, as the owner of a production company, he is beholden.) I countered like the teacher I usually am when I'm not with my husband on his fellowship in Germany.

Wasn't Riefenstahl's failure to change, despite the fact that so much change was happening around her, of potentially great moral and dramatic interest? Could you argue that she might be the *more* fascinating and enigmatic character than the character who, predictably, changed? Thomas Mann, for example, changed. At the beginning, yes, Mann failed to behave in a terribly brave or upstan‹ing manner; he was timid in the face of the Nazi rise. Maintaining his career meant more than speaking out on behalf of his friends and colleagues—some of whom were deported—or even supporting his children, who were actively anti-Nazi, and from whose activism he initially distanced himself. But after Mann was forced to leave Germany he made twenty-five radio broadcasts for Germans on behalf of the Allied forces, all of which began, "German listeners!" and which were scathingly anti-Nazi.

Mann's an example of the morally understandable and also the morally reassuring character. From personal experience, I can attest that it's uncomfortable to confront dramatic situations in which the "protagonists" are not redeemed, in which they are so self-absorbed that nothing penetrates their shell of self-interest and self-promotion, not even mass murder. But why must that make for a bad script?

On the morning of 9/11, my husband and I were charged with caring for the girlfriend of my sort-of cousin. While the towers burned and the death count, at that point, was estimated at ten thousand, she arrived at our house with a meditation candle and dessert. She worried all day about her relationship with my cousin. Did he love her enough? She just wasn't sure if he did. She pestered us with questions about my cousin as we walked to a clinic, as we tried to give blood. What did we think? What did we know? Did we think their relationship could last? Did we think he *really* loved her? Her character was so inconceivable even though it was standing right in front of us. We finally left her in our apartment and went to someone else's apartment. We had to escape her because she was so disturbingly unchanged. How could that be? How could

ln't and still can't make sense of her. Our
rstand makes her a regular character in
ves, the ones we tell about the weirdness
together. We talk about the woman who,
city was burning around her, stopped to buy dessert. Probably her life would also make for a bad script. Yet
I don't think there's a story we've told more often to others
than hers.

OCTOBER 10

Today I got an e-mail that said, "Good luck, pursecake!" This was the nicest e-mail I'd received in months.
Who knew me as "pursecake," besides myself? And not
even really myself? I'd had to change my usernames
recently, because my old ones no longer worked. I chose
"pursecake" because it makes me think of my daughter, for
whom we once made a purse-shaped cake, sort of but not
entirely because she loves money.

But who was wishing me luck? And luck with what?
With my hearing test at the ear doctor's? With the swanky
party I was attending later that day, and where I hoped not
to make myself look a fool? With remembering to pay my
speeding ticket before my license was suspended?

I checked to see who had sent me this e-mail. eBay
had sent it. eBay was hoping that I'd win a vintage tuxedo
shirt I'd bid on. Good luck, pursecake!

I should have felt deflated or idiotic, but I didn't. It
didn't matter that the e-mail came from eBay, and that
eBay was not a person. People's sincerity is sometimes
not totally sincere. There are complications, modulations.

People who wish you luck in winning don't always totally want you to win. eBay wanted me to win. eBay also wanted other people to win. eBay wants everybody to win! When eBay really wants everybody to win, the real winner is eBay. The sentiment was sincere. eBay wanted me to win this shirt. I did.

NOVEMBER 7

Today instead of working I watched YouTube interviews. For no particular reason I watched all of the interviews I could find by a singer I like and know nothing about. Now I know quite a lot about him. Before he became a songwriter and singer he was a drunk and a drug addict. Now he responds to interviewer prompts such as, "It's interesting that, in this song, you don't judge the teacher who raped you and then later killed himself," with stock recovery responses. *I was angry at others as a way to express my anger at myself. Now I've accepted who I am and no longer need to blame other people for my shortcomings.*

Until this year, I was not the sort of person to find sentences like these profound.

My best friend from college recently started saying such sentences. After years of psychotherapy, she's switched gears, found a guru. This guru has, as gurus must, an origin tale, a story tracking her path to enlightenment. Roughly it goes like this. Before she became a guru, she valued what people tend to value—love, money, real estate. Her first marriage failed. Her second marriage failed. She became a shut-in, subsisting on ice cream and pain pills. One day she awoke on the floor of her bedroom and saw a mouse crawling across a foot. She was filled with joy. She saw it as her job to love everyone and everything unconditionally, but her conviction was still challenged by old anxieties that cropped up every once in a while. She created a series of questions to ask herself whenever she felt tempted by real estate, or jealous of other people's money, or self-pitying, or hopeless, or if she could not find beauty in even the most agreed-upon beautiful things, never mind a mouse.

These questions she asked herself are now an official product, a mental map you can buy or a head dance you can be taught. I am sounding dismissive here, but I really don't view this guru's work dismissively. She has measurably helped my friend. I was hoping she might help me. I did not feel entirely ready yet to be helped, but I did feel open to the possibility—maybe this guru could make my life better, too.

Recently I met this friend and another friend at a cabin on the coast. The cabin was runty and constructed of press board and plastic and propped up by rusted propane tanks. The view was astonishing. We are scarcely ever together nowadays, the three of us; we are far-flung in more ways than just geography. When we do meet, confession is our shortcut to intimacy. We bypass the years and our widening differences by confessing. We confess and confess and confess. We confess about our bad behavior toward husbands, children, other friends, ourselves. We are each other's priests.

On this night, I had my usual confessions to make; I waited for my turn. Though the confessions on offer (I thought) were good ones, my friend with the guru seemed distracted. When I finished, she wanted to know with whom I'd shared one particular confession. She wanted to

know if I'd shared it with another woman I see more frequently than I see her.

I had.

The next morning I woke up to ocean and a painful
amount of sun. My friend emerged from the small back
bedroom; she announced that she'd spent the past two
hours asking herself the questions she'd learned from the
guru. She'd gone to bed upset last night by what she saw as
my betrayal (she understandably felt betrayed that I would
share news with this other woman before I shared it with
her); now, however, she was perfectly fine.

We ate breakfast. My friend was calm but also unset-
tlingly distant. I wondered if she'd experienced a moment
of acceptance in that bedroom; what she'd accepted had
something to do with my inability to stop disappointing
her. She was finally resigned to this fact, and her resignation required she stop investing any hope in me whatsoever.

Formerly I'd loved her guru. Now I was not so in love
with her. I was emotionally quite dependent on the dys-
function my friend and I had co-developed over the past
twenty-five years. I depended on my friend to get mad at
me for doing mostly totally reasonable things that I then
got mad at *her* for being mad about. I started to worry: our
durable friend romance, the one that survived, and even
thrived upon, our regular breakups, was finished. Her guru
had killed it. Gurus, I'd always thought, were so airy and
ephemeral—they encouraged your thoughts to drift around
wearing the mind equivalent of an Indian gauze dress with
a tinkling bell hem—but my friend's guru, it seemed, was
the most practical of taskmasters. She dressed people's
minds in an off-the-rack skirt suit and sent them to an
office job where they laid people off.

I tried to remain circumspect in the face of my friend's

resignation; maybe it was for the best. How much longer could we act like schoolgirls with crushes on one another? We were forty-four years old.

After breakfast we all three sat on the rocks. We arranged ourselves at distances from one another so great that we nearly needed to shout to be heard above the gulls. We were literally speaking over a small crevasse. My two friends assumed one plane, like jurors; I faced them with my back to the sun. They began to worry aloud about me. Their worry amounted to a personality critique, but whatever. They cared enough to care. After my close run-in with total guru annihilation, I thankfully accepted their concern.

Whenever I am not with them, they said, I am Not Me; I become a person they are certain, because they know me so well, I am not.

There is a complicated truth to these claims. Historically, when I am in a shallow tizzy, or just really depressed, I do tend to pull away from these two friends. Historically, the explanation for my disappearance has been: they know me too well. When I'm not interested in (or capable of) being who, at my core, *I am*, I steer way clear of the two people who hold me to this unappealing standard.

However—and maybe it was because the guru had messed with things, and so now our narrative seemed open to restructuring—a part of me wanted to disagree with this long-running interpretation. A part of me wanted to point out that this Not Me facet they strongly disliked— this "other" buzzy and irreverent me—was, if we were to deal in pure percentages, the person I predominantly am. I liked people, lots and lots and lots of them. I wanted people around me much of the time, and I wanted for the

most part to never directly speak about ser'
a serious matter arose, I wanted to dispat/
ous manner (which manner, in my opiniо,
theless result in its very seriously being dealt wɪ
they were saying, in short, I wanted to point out to tɪ
was this: we are worried about you because we don't like
who you are.

I said nothing. I chose not to seize the restructuring opportunity offered by the guru. Instead I listened; I
nodded. The sun was hot on my back. I was struck by a
guru-worthy koan to describe my current situation: *To face
away from the sun is not to hide from it.* My friends and I
have our friendship origin tales, just like the guru has hers.
These are our paths to enlightenment, or maybe just our
paths to this cabin, to this beach, to this day, to our girl-
hoods, to which we are fast losing the connection. I believe
it is not wrong to protect these stories, even if such protection requires a little dishonesty in the form of silence. I
did worry, however, that the crevasse over which we faced
one another would eventually grow too wide. As yet, it had
not. I was thankful for this. It was nearing noon now. My
shoulders were starting to burn.

JULY 30

Today I read a book while holding a fountain pen. I
often have a pen in my hand when I read. I am trying
to fool myself into thinking I am writing when I'm not. I
read with a pen in my hand because it helps me think. If I
underline a sentence, I temporarily own it. It's mine. I have

bought real estate in this book, laid down stakes, moved in. This does not mean I remember where I live. I turn the page. I lose my place.

I used to be more of a habitual loser than I am now. In the past, I lost everything. Official, identity-reinforcing objects such as my wallet, these I lost regularly. Often my wallet was found before I knew it was lost. One night I received an e-mail from a woman who'd tracked me down online. She said, "I found your wallet on the street." I thought: what is she talking about? I have my wallet right here. But I didn't.

I have also lost my passport. Once when I was twenty-four, and in Morocco, and traveling with my boyfriend and a woman whose terrible Arabic she made up for with outraged panache (she would ask a carpet merchant, when he told her the price of a carpet she wanted, "Am I a donkey?" and he would immediately halve the price), I discovered my passport missing during a sandstorm. We were in a Berber town on the edge of the Sahara Desert. We ransacked our hotel room as the sand hit the windows and sounded, apocalyptically, like rain. My passport was gone. This meant we could not go into the Sahara, as planned, in an old Mercedes driven by an old man we'd hired for the excursion, even though it was August, and eight trillion degrees, and when we told people our plans, they laughed at us, not because we were funny, but because we were stupid and going to die. This was their opinion and they were probably correct. The old Mercedes, the old man, our mettle—something or someone would have failed.

But now we could not go into the Sahara because I had a flight home in five days that required a passport. I was starting a new job. It seemed a very bad idea to be a week or two late for my first day of work, so the missing passport

needed to be dealt with. Unfortunately, the nearest passport office was a thousand miles away. We repurposed our
driver. We told him we didn't want to go to the desert—we
wanted to head north through the Atlas Mountains to the
nearest airport in Casablanca, so that I could fly to Rabat,
so that I could get a passport, so that I could then take
another taxi across the country to a Spanish principality,
and get on a plane home that was so indirect I would have
to first switch airports in London and spend the night on
the terminal floor.

So the driver took us north. In the High Atlas, we
stopped to look at carpets, and we sat around drinking
mint tea, and the woman asked, "Am I a donkey?," and we
left with four carpets. We descended the mountains and
it got dark. We drove up another set of mountains and at
around two a.m. the driver begged to rest, so we pulled to
the side and spread out our new carpets and slept for an
hour. Dawn happened. We returned to the cab and drove
down the last mountain into Casablanca, and we boarded
a very large white 747 headed for Paris and then America
but stopping first in Rabat, and when we disembarked in
Rabat, a city which to my memory looked and smelled like
a wetly rotting dock pylon, we checked into a hotel room,
and as the woman was looking for a sweater, because for
the first time in weeks she was cold, she found my passport.

We were dumbfounded. Who had put my passport
in her suitcase? The taxi driver? The carpet merchant?
Sometimes when you're in a foreign country, it feels like
everyone is in on a joke against you. My boyfriend accused
the woman—they'd been fighting—of hiding it on purpose. But to what end? She appeared guilty, true, but only
because she *was* guilty, albeit innocently, of harboring my
passport. Who knew what had happened, but now we were

stuck in this damp city, and we tried to believe that fate had intervened to make us change our plans. We might have perished in that hot desert. The sandstorm was a sign.

Loss, what I am trying to say, so long as you're dealing with objects, can be spun as opportunity. Because I lost my passport we did not die in the Sahara. Because I lost a cashmere cardigan at a bus stop in Hyde Park, and decided that the University of Chicago student who probably found it would, instead of keeping it, decide to sell it on eBay to make some pocket money, I discovered eBay, and truly feel that eBay has measurably improved my mental quality of life more than doctors or drugs. Because I lost a necklace in a river I learned that the state of Vermont has a scuba diving club. All of this does and does not explain why my mother-in-law, at my marriage to her son, read "One Art" by Elizabeth Bishop, the opening lines of which are

> *The art of losing isn't hard to master;*
> *so many things seem filled with the intent*
> *to be lost that their loss is no disaster.*

Nor does it explain how I lost my way today. I started writing because I was holding a fountain pen in my hand and a drip of blue ink landed on my sweater. Without thinking I stuck the sweater in my mouth. I sucked the ink like it was blood.

DECEMBER 9

Today I am working in the library of the German villa. I have my favorite spot. Next to me are books about Germany with titles like *Deutschland, Wo Ist Du?* and *The German Question and Other German Questions*. Usually there is an actual German in this library. The German is an architect. The German architect and I bonded a few weeks ago over a building we both liked and which I'd found in the nearby woods while on a bike ride. He said about the building, in his very kind way, "I am so happy you discovered it," which I interpreted as, "What a remarkable person you are for having the same good taste as me. I am so pleased we found each other."

Soon afterward, the architect and I both began working in the library. All day long we spend together. His living space in the villa, I gather (from reports) is very nice and overlooks the lake. We'd commiserated over the fact that working alone, even in one's lakefront suite, is not as appealing as grinding it out in the presence of others. We both needed someone with whom to share a glance when a man spent hours tuning the piano just outside the library doors, and then complained to a passing American, "This building is full of plaster, and plaster is the enemy of sound." We both needed to be guilted into working longer hours, or maybe we saw it as a competition. Who would be the first to leave the library when the Berlin sun set at three-thirty p.m.? Who would be the first to crack a Berlin beer? Who would be the first to cave to the library's chilly temperatures and start writing in gloves and a coat?

Soon this competition we were or were not in became a crush. My husband jokingly accused me. I denied nothing. It was no big deal; it was just another of my workplace infatuations. Also this architect is the age of my dad.

In the midst of what I understood as our mutual infatuation, I flew to Zurich to meet my London friend and see and experience the building/spa in the Swiss Alps. The architect was thrilled to learn I was going to visit this building that he'd already visited numerous times and

about which he'd written many papers. ("I am so happy
you discovered it.")

While in Switzerland at the building, I sent the architect an e-mail—my first-ever e-mail to him—wondering
about our cold library (had it snowed inside?) and asking
about a nearby restaurant he'd mentioned liking.

When I returned to the villa, the architect sent me
PowerPoint presentations about the building/spa and its
architect (whom he considered "the world's greatest living
architect"). I sent him photos of a Swiss house built into
the side of a mountain that, from a distance, looks like the
site of a meteor crash. The next night—after firmly and
energetically bonding over the world's greatest living architect, thereby cementing our love via the creative genius of
a third party—I ignored him. I couldn't help myself. My
teen mating instinct kicked in. (*La tendresse Américaine* on
which I was raised deemed you must strongly discourage a
man after you strongly encourage him as a way to more yet
strongly encourage him.) We were at dinner with a group
of people. I did not meet his eye. I very visibly engaged
others in conversation. I took great pains to appear to be
having quite a bit more fun while not talking to him than I
ever did while talking to him.

Our romance, such as it never existed, started to wane.
Either he realized that he really liked me and could not
bear to be ignored but also could not, in good conscience,
follow through on his desires (we were both married), and
so needed to "break off" this relationship we did not have.
Or he realized I was a ridiculous person who likes to play
games—card games, silly games of the heart, harmless, all
of them, but therein lay the problem: I was a frivolous person who just happened to share his taste in buildings. Or
maybe our infatuation was entirely one-sided. Even more

ridiculously, perhaps I've fabricated this entire situation, and he's simply confused but more likely uninterested by my middle-school bizarreness. Recently the architect sent an e-mail to a much older woman on whom I am certain he does not have a crush. He'd written to her about a Bauhaus building. She forwarded his note to me (she knows I am also a Bauhaus fan). I saw he'd written to her, of this building, "I am so happy you discovered it."

I am the only one working in the cold library today.

SEPTEMBER 6

Today I turned the wrong knob on my stove when I tried to boil water. The burner knobs on my two stoves are reversed. To fire up the front burner in New York, I turn the left knob. To fire up the front burner in Maine, I turn the right one. When I move from the apartment to the house (or the house to the apartment), I spend many days unthinkingly turning the wrong knob and igniting the wrong burner. Like a magician off her game, I throw fire where I didn't mean to throw it. I have to remind myself: You are not where you just were. Things are different here. I get mad at myself because I hate to waste time, even if it's only one one-hundredth of a second. I watched the Olympics this summer. One one-hundredth of a second is no joke. One one-hundredth of a second is the difference between gold and last place. I also hate to think about actions that shouldn't require thinking. I need the mechanics of my life to be effortless. When appliances don't work, I cannot be my best person. I actually become a bad person. I am not a patient mother when the machines, in addition to the people, require attention. I become like the real estate woman in Maine who showed me the Odd Fellows Hall the other day. The woman, nearing eighty, emerged from her car wielding a butter knife. (The hall has no keys.) She used the knife to jimmy the lock, but the lock wouldn't spring, and she grew frustrated, and I saw in her what I see in myself when plain things that should work do not—that I have the capacity to turn, with the quickness of a lightning strike, unkind.

But I am also reassured by my failure to turn the correct stove knob in New York. This meant that, though back, I was not yet *fully* back. Even though I'd already forgotten the calm of the past three months, my muscle memories had yet to be overridden. I am still in that place where real estate agents unlock empty houses with butter knives. My Maine neighbor, an occasional electrician, warned me when he changed our bathroom light from a pull chain to a light switch: "You'll be reaching for that chain for weeks." He was right. I was incapable of remembering the chain was no longer there. A year later, I still grope in the dark at the dark.

OCTOBER 15

Today I fought with my husband. He is on a diet, not for vanity's sake but because of a recent encounter with a scary illness. A person might think—given my own recent encounter with a scary illness—that I would unreservedly support his wellness pursuit. I do not. Until today I have *acted* supportive, but beneath my support a dark undertow lurked. I'd kept this undertow a secret from him. Instead

I confessed my baffling hostility toward his diet to my female friends. All of them, I was surprised to learn, are or were once involved with men who'd experimented with diets for reasons of health. I discovered that the male diet is a potent relationship disharmonizer. "Threatened" is the word that arose most frequently when I spoke to women about their male dieting partners, as in "I am/was threatened by his diet." The obvious interpretation of our reaction was this: we feared that our husbands desired to look slimmer and healthier because they'd met another woman and planned, once their transformation was complete, to leave us.

But we weren't scared of being left. Maybe we should have been, but we weren't. We were resentful. The dieting man does not eat the same food as the rest of his family— the diets we were speaking about were not "eat more healthy foods" diets. These diets required extreme abstinence and often had a cultish whiff to them. The adherents of these diets made YouTube videos that were both compelling and disturbing. People lost so much weight that their skulls shrank.

We tried to parse our feelings of endangerment. Was gender primarily to blame? By being on a diet, our husbands were (albeit for very different reasons) behaving like so many of our female friends, some of whom developed eating disorders and became incredibly boring. I was one of those women for a year. Luckily I was able to escape what is often, tragically, inescapable. When I emerged from my brief anorexia incarceration I thought: *Well that was a very huge waste of my time*. The monomaniacal dedication of brain activity required to maintain an eating disorder was an inexcusable squandering of one of my best brain years. Plus the obsession was inherently perverse.

Even though I was fixated upon nothing but my body, my brain was somehow totally disengaged, save intellectually, from its singular concern. My body, despite the molecular-level attention paid to it, belonged to a faraway creature, a numb, gray sylph.

Also I did not tell my friends, but to myself I admitted: I was jealous. I was jealous of Dr. Fuhrman, the man who masterminded the diet my husband is following. My husband seems to believe most everything Fuhrman says, and this affronts me because my husband doesn't believe most everything I say. My husband approaches my claims with a loving but skeptical eye. He doesn't *not* question what I say, but occasionally he believes certain ridiculous statements I make because I have probably exhausted him into a place of acceptance. Fuhrman's claims do not exhaust my husband, even though Fuhrman advocates something called "the Nutritarian Food Pyramid," which sounds to me acceptable only under circumstances of extreme exhaustion. Also my husband is not as sensitive as I am; he does not understand the title of Fuhrman's book—*Eat to Live*—as just so bitchy and rebuking.

"Because I'm eating to die," I said to my husband.

My husband is an alarmingly smart man; he's a unique thinker to his bones. He is, as a friend once said, a monk or a holy person who might better live in a tower or the desert. He thrives on discipline and solitude. Despite the fact that he has a family and a job and a wife who is always planning parties that he must cook for and attend, he manages to maintain his iconoclastic integrity. Most remarkably he can, without compromising this integrity, happily follow the occasional diet mastermind like Dr. Fuhrman. He has followed a few masterminds since we got married (these are not whimsical switches; he keeps up on the research and responds in kind). While I take pleasure (when I'm trying to reason him out of his health pursuits) in pointing out how, for example, he is able to endorse the belief "fruit is bad, never eat fruit," and then, after a mastermind shift, "fruit is great, eat as much fruit as you want," what I'm really expressing is insecurity. He can weather a belief reversal—one based on science, granted—without doubting the soundness of his faith or his mind.

I, however, am often insecure about what I believe. So, most of the time, is my husband. "Insecure" is maybe not the right word to describe us. We are avid second-guessers because, though we are both professors and thus must act as authorities in certain situations, we find certainty a turn-off. We love to take a conviction we might, for a moment, entertain, and then turn it on its head and make a joke about it. This joking is our form of the Socratic method. Our jokes are interrogations that help us to figure out what we care about, and where our faith, at the moment, lies.

His unfailing certainty about his diet, thus, made me feel isolated. I was making jokes no one got but me. I was making jokes that weren't, technically, jokes. They were criticisms driven by the fear that he was abandoning me to interrogate our future uncertainties alone.

Still, I tried to act supportive. Today I failed. I failed to act my best or at all. As my husband prepared his healthy dinner, and I prepared my moderately healthy one, I had what is best described as a tantrum.

Afterward I lay on the couch. My husband sat in a distant chair. I tried to explain why, when he was on a diet to manage his pain and secure his longevity—why, when he was trying his best not to more rapidly and miserably die—I was being so totally mean. I talked about how, *as a woman,* I'd spent literally decades around other women

luded) who cared too much about food. Who
er what they ate, and adhered to bib-lettuce-
only diets, and who became, over time,
unhappy and sexless and dull. After watching for decades
what I ate, I finally didn't give a shit. I'd been freed from
the female curse of perpetual self-dissatisfaction and pleasure denial. His caring about what he ate posed a threat to
my enlightened, non-caring state.

I then confessed that I was jealous of Dr. Fuhrman.
I further confessed that really I did not give a shit about
Dr. Fuhrman; my issues were related to my feeling excluded
and subsequently rejected by my husband. He'd found a
passion I could not share. He believed and I didn't. Once
we spent an entire summer making and eating elaborate
banana splits. Now we prepared side-by-side meals. We
parallel cooked and I couldn't help but extrapolate that
soon we would parallel *live,* and that our vectors would
someday permanently cease to cross. It turned out that
(contrary to what I'd said to my friends) I *was* scared of his
leaving me, but I worried he would do so by never breaking
up with me and never moving out.

My husband listened. He confessed that he'd been
unceasingly aware of my ambient enmity (my secret had
not been such a secret, it seems). He understood, now that
I'd explained myself, why. I think we are both worried
about the perils of parallel living because we share so many
parallels. We are so alike that we pursue the same passion
and work at the same university and raise the same children and have the same sense of humor. At the dinner parties I force us to throw more often than is probably healthy
for either of us, we are often the only two people laughing.
No one makes me laugh more than he does. But we both
worry, I think, that we are so alike that we might start to

take for granted the health of our marriage, as we have, until recently, taken for granted the health of our bodies.

MAY 9

Today I found a Rolodex in a trash can at JFK. I was about to enter the security check when I remembered the half-full water bottle in my bag. I needed to dispose of it before I held up the security line and became the scourge of Terminal B. I found a tall, space-age trash can. Its smoothly rounded mouth resembled a portal. Before throwing the bottle into it, I looked inside. I saw a Rolodex of family photographs. I was in a hurry and didn't have time to wonder *Why is there a Rolodex in the trash can at JFK?* I only knew that the Rolodex made me feel bad to the bone. No matter what I decided to do with the Rolodex (return it to the trash can; keep it), I was in a bind. The statement "The situation demanded something of me" felt extremely applicable. How would I respond to the situation?

Situations have demanded something of me before. Once, in my twenties, when I was studying in France, I was with a group of Americans approached by a con artist looking for money. The con artist, an American who was clearly not a student or a tourist, beseeched us, his fellow countrymen, for help. His wallet had been stolen! Also his father had died! He needed money to catch a train to his plane, which left from Paris tomorrow, and which he had to make so that he could attend his father's funeral! *Thank God I have found some Americans!* He repeatedly said. We all knew the guy was conning us—he wore leather shoes in an era when Americans wore nothing but big white sneakers—but none of us wanted to be the first to call bullshit to his face. The situation demanded a choice. Who did we want to appear to be? To give him money was to appear stupid in front of our friends. To not give him money was to appear heartless. Most people, publicly at least, choose looking stupid over appearing heartless. Or most of the people I know would choose to look stupid.

The Rolodex, like the fake American tourist, was a lose-lose situation that nonetheless demanded a choice. No one was around to publicly shame me, but I am perfectly able to shame myself. And worse—around myself it is not a matter of *appearing to be* stupid or heartless; instead I confirm to myself that I am definitively one or the other.

To keep the Rolodex was to be stupid; to discard it was heartless.

I kept it.

In the security line, I worried. Wasn't I a version of the gullible traveler who acts as an unwitting mule of illegality, i.e., the person who transports, as a kindness, a kilo of heroin hidden in a knitting bag for an innocent-seeming granny? If asked, how would I answer the question, *Did a stranger give you anything to carry?*

The situation gave me a Rolodex. The situation demanded of me that I carry it.

Maybe there was an explosive in the Rolodex. Maybe a suicide bomber suffered a crisis of faith or nerve at the security line and ditched the bomb and went back to Queens. Maybe the photos were acid tabs or coated with cocaine that, following a crafty extraction process, would yield enough to net me a life sentence in an Italian jail. (I was headed to Italy to go to the artist colony.) What if, while going through customs in Rome, a dog smelled the drugs on my Rolodex?

It was already becoming *my Rolodex*.

I made it through security. If the Rolodex contained a bomb, it was a good bomb. Maybe, instead of cocaine, the photos were coated with a bioweapon designed to release at cruising altitude. I called my parents to say good-bye. (I hoped it wasn't *good-bye*.) I told them about the Rolodex. My dad said, "Someone in those photos must have really pissed someone off." I'd also considered this possibility; the cursedness I'd sensed originated from anger or hate directed at a person in the Rolodex photos. Somebody needed to release himself from these bad feelings. He'd thrown the photos away, betting on the psychic exorcism of a landfill burial.

I'd screwed up the process. I'd kept live what should have been dead. Many of the photos had captions. Whoever chose the moments to be memorialized in the Rolodex was obsessed by accidents. There was a photo of a violently shredded white picket fence with the caption "Accident, 1965." There were photos of trees upended in various hurricanes. There was a photo of the Maidstone Club after a fire destroyed the cafeteria. There was a photo of a road hugging a cliff. The caption read, "Dubrovnik, 1971: Accident going down this coast (to Greece)," after which appeared a photo of a man in a hospital bed ("Belgrade—Yugoslavia") reading James Michener's *The Drifters*.

I countered my dad's theory with what was—bombs and drugs and anger aside—the likeliest theory. Many of the photos were taken in nearby Long Island. Probably the owner of the Rolodex had recently died. The children—from the photos, I guessed them to be in their sixties by now—had flown in from wherever they lived to clean out the family museum, long docented by the lone surviving parent. Nobody wanted the Rolodex, but nobody could justify throwing it away. One sibling insisted to another sibling, "You take the Rolodex!" The situation demanded that the sibling not refuse. The sibling who took the Rolodex—it was heavy, and an awkward size, and the photos, in my bag at least, kept sliding out of their plastic jackets—had probably been struggling to find his or her ID to go through security, and the fucking Rolodex was in the way, and it had started to come apart, and in a fit of annoyance the sibling dumped it. He or she had been praying all along for a good excuse to get rid of the Rolodex, just like I'd been praying for an excuse to divorce my ex-husband years ago and was so relieved when he provided me one by spending our savings on the sly. He misbehaved in a way that would hold up in a court of public opinion. It would also hold up in my court of private opinion. I would not appear heartless to the court or to myself by divorcing him. The Rolodex had likewise misbehaved. The sibling was so relieved when it obstructed his basic ability to properly identify himself, find his ticket, and board a plane. He was so relieved to discover it was broken. In all good conscience, the sibling had probably thought to himself: *Finally I am justified in ditching this thing.*

JULY 20

Today we went to a party where the food was very tiny. It is officially halfway through the summer and we are feeling out of scale. We've been drinking too much beer and eating too many jumbo bags of chips. Our shorts don't fit. So my friend threw a miniature food party. We cooked tiny meatballs. Another guest made tiny BLT sandwiches.

Problematically, the drinks were not tiny, and soon we were all really drunk. I talked all night to two women I really like but whom I don't often encounter, even on our small peninsula. One is a doctor who lives in an electricity-free cabin and who is always spectacularly attired. Whenever I see her in the store buying batteries, she looks as though she's just finished a clubbing jag in Marrakech. The other woman is the great-granddaughter of a famous stage actress. She, like me, lives in New York during the year. Despite our geographic synchronicities, we are not close. I think we have mutually agreed—we are just too busy right now to make a good friend from whom we cannot seasonally escape.

The doctor was coming off a hard year. She'd been incessantly sick and stressed. She works so much that she never sees her children. She said she was considering a career change because she wanted to be a more present mother, and also less of a basket case. "My kids are all fucked up," she said.

I entered this conversation at the midpoint. Without the proper context, I probably misunderstood the famous stage actress's great-granddaughter's response. She said of children, "You really have to just *live their lives* if you want to be a part of them." She could do this. She does not have a full-time job. (I arguably also don't have a full-time job; I do have four or five half-time ones.)

My first impulse was to express in my totally polite and agreeable way, *Fuck off.* I said, "You're totally right about that," but any mildly perceptive person would hear that I was really saying, *Fuck off fuck off fuck off.*

But then I realized—my *fuck off* was a trained reaction. I am quick to rage when I think a person is implying that another person cannot be a decent mother if she has a consuming career. Because, in fact, I found that I agreed with the famous stage actress's great-granddaughter. I'd recently come to the same conclusion. In the interests of my family, I'd been so unambitious recently. I'd barely written at all these past few weeks. For my family's sake, I told myself, I'd lost my fire; I just wanted to lie around with my kids if they were home, and if they weren't home I wanted to lie around and read essays written by a poet I'd met last month who I'd found too terrifying in person to befriend, but in print we could just hang out, she and I in my studio, and "chat" about, for example, theme.

Whether or not I was being a better parent because of my ambition failure, I can't say. But I really couldn't disagree with the famous stage actress's great-granddaughter's point about living your children's lives if you want to have any idea of what's happening in them. Until very recently, I felt that I didn't know anything about my children's lives; this spring, my lack of knowledge started to alarm me. I regularly called my husband (when he was out of town, or I was out of town), and left him panicked messages. In hotel rooms, far from the family I no longer seemed to know, my anxiety was even worse. Our family—i.e., our children—became, at a distance, a handful of vaguely familiar people who happened to live in our house. Suddenly the people in our house were lazy and ill-mannered. The people in our house grew holes in their teeth. The people in our house owned no viable pants.

The people in our house were my fault. Our fault, but really, my fault. I'm not being a martyr. I'm speaking realistically, in a manner reflecting the consensus reality of the situation. No men at this party were standing around talking about quitting their jobs so they could be a part of—sorry, *live*—their children's lives. No men listening to these men were thinking defensively to themselves, *Fuck off*, or, after a moment's reflection, *You're so right, actually*. No men would be writing about these conversations tonight in their diaries. My husband would absolutely write about these issues in his diary tonight if he kept one. He worries about and buys all of our children's clothing—the pants, the underwear, the sneakers, the socks. But to the greater world, these pantsless children reflect more poorly on me than they do on him. Women are responsible for the people in the family having pants.

Later, in bed, my husband and I shared party notes. He told me that he'd been speaking to a man, and that this man spoke critically of another couple's child, and that it was clear the man blamed the mother for her child's bad behavior, not the father. The mother traveled for her work. So did the father travel for his work, but this did not seem germane to the matter of the child's failure to be pleasing. I want to say that this man's opinion arises because he's from a different generation, but it's more complicated than just age. He has a very smart wife who, after having children, did not have a full-time job; he also has two smart and well-educated daughters who, after having children, did not have full-time jobs. His opinion supports the decisions made by his wife and his daughters. Sometimes I don't think any of us really believes anything we say; we are just defending our kind.

OCTOBER 14

Today I went drinking with a former student who asked me, "Are you proud of your hands?"

I thought what a good question this was. As a professor, I am always struggling to ask good questions. How can a question be an invitation, not a test? Questions with answers make people scared. If you're an up-rounder, 100 percent of possible responses to questions with answers are incorrect. The odds totally favor wrongness. Good questions can initiate a surprising wend toward an answer that is neither right nor wrong, but can be judged as strong or weak or honest or dishonest on the basis of the steps that brought the answerer there. It is a built thing. Sometimes what it builds is bullshit, but the bullshit can be so well-constructed that it has integrity, a pattern integrity. This can be worth admiring.

I admitted I was proud of my hands, though this hasn't always been the case. I used to hate my hands. Their fingers are short, the nails bitten. When anxious, I unthinkingly chew holes in my hands. Often I do this when I'm teaching or on a stage. I've been on a stage and chewed a bloody hole where once there was a cuticle, and have had to scramble to find a piece of paper with which to blot the flow. Occasionally, while teaching or on stage, I've had to suck on my finger to keep the blood from going everywhere.

In the past I have suffered hand jealousy. Mine are stubby, with fingernails shaped like sideways rectangles. My left hand is visibly smaller than the right. I have one finger on which I can wear normal-sized rings, because the rest of my fingers I jammed playing basketball. I jammed them shorter and fatter. In the case of some rings, they do not make them big enough for my fingers.

It was fortunate, I guess, that the one normal-sized finger I possess is the finger on which wedding rings are meant to go. When I was first married, I was much more interested in wedding-type wedding rings, and those rings tend to be small, especially if you're broke, because you have to buy them used, and so they tend to date back to an age when people and fingers were tinier. My first husband and I bought my wedding ring at a pawnshop. People marveled at our brazenness. "Isn't it bad luck to buy a second-hand wedding ring?" These people assumed the ring had been sold to the pawnshop following a divorce. My first husband preferred to think the woman who'd once owned the ring had died in a sky-diving accident. Years after our divorce, I still own the ring. I keep it in a small box with old business cards and postage stamps of outdated denominations. The box moves around my Maine home, sometimes in this room, sometimes in that. As with many things I don't keep track of or care much about, I never lose it.

JANUARY 11

Today I went to an art museum to see a show. I wanted to escape my head because my head is so stupid these days. I wanted to be inside someone else's head. So I went to a show recommended by a young woman I work with. This young woman is dreamily and predatorially beautiful; she is nervously smart. She dresses to highlight her astonishing legs, and she looks at you as though she is planning to give your face a blow job. This sounds both more disgusting and less complimentary than I mean it to. I am transfixed by the way she looks at me. I find a coy boldness in her to admire. She's giving your face a blow job while talking about Deleuze.

I was interested in the artist this young woman recommended because the artist paints and does video and

sculpts and knits. I figured this artist's head was vora-
cious and energetic and a generally good place for a blue
person to spend the day. This did not turn out to be the
case. Her installation was on the fourth of six very tall
floors. The elevator failed and failed to come. Waiting
for it stretched me to the breaking point. A drink would
have done me, or a drink plus a controlled substance,
or an uncontrolled substance plus a love affair, or all of
these plus a leap from a high window. For some reason I
thought an art show would reroute my defective circuitry. I
thought an art show would keep me from more ridiculous
alternatives.

Once the elevator opened onto the fourth floor, I
exited, I ran. I did a few laps, waiting for my jaggy attention to catch on a photo or a painting so that I could enter
this other person's head. I found no gateway. I slid over
surfaces, uninteresting surfaces. The reviews I'd read
made her work sound so intellectually sensual and object-
driven, but where were the intellectually sensual objects?
The reviews made her sound like a thoughtful hoarder, but
where was the seductive clutter? I found the show so unfo-
cused and completely disconnected and random. I had no
idea who this woman was or what unified her curiosity or
her drive. It might have been a group exhibition. I took the
stairs to the third floor, where the exhibit continued, and
where I turned her failure into my own. I am a jack-of-all-
trades. I edit and teach and at times desire to be a clothing designer or an artist (one who doesn't draw or paint or
sew) and I write everything but poetry and I am a mother
and a social maniac and a misanthrope and a burgeoning
self-help guru and a girl who wants to look pretty and a
girl who wants to look sexy and a girl who wants to look
girly and a woman in her middle forties who wishes not to

look like anything at all, who wishes sometimes to vanish. I thought of what a person said to me once about my short stories—"as a short story writer I just don't know who you *are*." I thought of how I'd screwed up somewhere, that in trying to be so many things and people I'd failed to be even one good thing or one good person. And how now I really, really needed a drink, or I really needed to fall in love with any old human, except that I felt so unattractive today.

I left the museum and went to a clothing store. I thought I might buy a dress to make me feel better. I didn't find that dress. I left the clothing store and went to a bookstore. I thought I might find a book to help me feel better, but I forgot that writers, after they publish books, can rarely enter bookstores and leave happier. Even if you are a writer who never reads her Amazon reviews, the bookstore is a reminder of how not beloved you are. If your books are on the front table, the pile is too tall; clearly nobody has bought any copies. If your books are not on the front table, so much the worse. You're reminded how they might be on the front table if you ever made any sort of effort with booksellers, but you don't, not even the one in your own neighborhood, the one you can practically see from your apartment. You are reminded of how you make a hard situation—surviving as a writer—much harder for yourself by refusing to help yourself, and why? Why do you refuse when you love to meet people, and are so chatty and personable, but usually only with non-bookstore-owning strangers? Why, when you shop at your local bookstore, even on those days when your book *is* on the front table, do you insist on anonymity?

On this day, in this mood, in this bookstore, anonymity was the only option. I did laps. I decided I should read a biography but I couldn't find BIOGRAPHY, and human assistance was out of the question. I didn't know how to ask a question without turning the exchange into something awkward over which I'd self-castigate for the next hour. I looked and I looked. There were people in every nook, hanging out and talking and working on computers. I looked at one person for quite a while before I recognized the young woman who gives blow jobs to faces, the woman who had suggested I see the art show I'd just seen.

We said our surprised hellos. Adding to the tension, which possibly existed only for me, was the fact that the last e-mail exchange we'd had had been of a very personal nature, and I'd failed to follow up. I wrote to her, she wrote to me, I didn't respond. We'd been writing to each other about our respective abortions. I knew of hers because she'd told me about it a few months back. I treated her abortion as an intellectual conceit because she was treating it as an intellectual conceit, and writing an intellectual essay about her choice to terminate a midterm pregnancy. Later I'd done some math; I realized that I'd had my abortion twenty-five years ago and that this woman was as old as the child I didn't have. I don't usually give my aborted child a body or a life; I don't date it or pull it with me through time. I don't really think about it at all. Which is why I was so shocked to contemplate that, had I not aborted this child, it would now be old enough to get its own abortion. Also, this girl's mother had gotten pregnant very young, at about the age that I did. Unlike me, she didn't have an abortion. She had this girl.

So it was awkward in the bookstore because I'd yet to e-mail this woman back about her abortion, or my abortion, or why her mother didn't get an abortion like I did, and why she was born and her baby was not, and my baby was not, and etc. Instead we made small talk about the Oscar nominations, the announcement of which I'd missed. I hadn't seen any of the movies, anyway. Then, somehow eager to make this girl feel that I listened to her, and respected her opinion, even when I failed to write her back about a personal disclosure that I'd, technically, elicited, I said, "I just went to the art show you recommended."

"Oh!" she said. "Was I right or was I right? It was totally amazing, right?"

At times like this, when the stakes are so low and still I cave, I wonder how I can consider myself an honest or a brave or even a good person.

"It was," I said. "That show was totally amazing."

SEPTEMBER 12

Today I received an e-mail from a friend who might introduce me to some people he knows. He and I once spent a summer together in Morocco twenty years ago. I requested these introductions because I want to offer these people some work. I realized, however, that I was not just asking to be introduced; I was asking to be recommended. He and I are both academics and so even innocent introductions have a whiff of *putting one forth* or *putting one up* (tenure language) about them. Character evaluations are required.

My friend said he would introduce/recommend me to the people I wanted to meet. Then he related a story about Paul Bowles, the cultish American writer of *The Sheltering Sky* who lived most of his life in Tangier, and about whom this friend had been writing his dissertation the summer we lived in Morocco. Every weekend he'd take the train from Fez to Tangier to hang out with Bowles.

He wrote, "Did I ever tell you the story of when I asked Paul Bowles to write a letter of introduction for me to William Burroughs?" I told him he had not. He described the encounter.

ME: I mean, I think it would kind of, like, help if you could write a letter of introduction.
PAUL B: Now?
ME: No, like when you had time.

Next day, after about two hours of chitchat.

PAUL B: Oh, I wrote that letter to Bill Burroughs for you.
ME: You did? (Thinking: OMG!! What will it say?)
PAUL B: Yes, it's over there on the table.

I begin searching, on my hands and knees for about an hour. Under Bowles's bed, among the detritus. Nothing. Never found it.

I thought this was such a great story—I laughed about it quite a bit. Then I stopped laughing and wondered: did this mean he *wasn't* going to make the introductions I'd requested? Such is the inconvenience of e-mail. I could not dig beneath his bed for proof of what he maybe had not written.

Today I was searching online for a place to stay in the Bavarian Alps. Ask me where the Bavarian Alps are located (beyond "in Europe") and I could not tell you. A few months ago I might have claimed that "Bavarian" is just a snowier synonym for "German," but I recently had the occasion to learn a little bit, not much, about German states. I'd Googled *frankfurt what german state,* because I was making an e-mail joke to my new agent about posing as my husband's mistress while he was in Frankfurt. My agent is savvy about Europe and presumably also those ancient feudal European subdivisions about which most Americans know nothing. His suits suggest as much. He is a man whose suits say of him, "I know quite a lot about kingdoms." I initially wrote that I was my husband's *Bavarian* mistress, but then I wondered—why was I not his Tyrolian mistress? Or his Thuringian mistress? To claim to be his Bavarian mistress when really I was his Tyrolian or Thuringian mistress (in this joke formulation, at least) might reveal me to be the Old World–ignorant American I totally was and preferred to appear not to be. (Frankfurt, it turns out, is in the state of Hesse, and therefore I was my husband's Hessian mistress. I have begun to fact-check my e-mail jokes, and my e-mails generally, even though I do not use capital letters or proper punctuation. "we write everything lowercase in order to save time," said Herbert Bayer—herbert bayer—of the Bauhaus school. When I discovered this quote I felt so reassured. I'd always worried that I'd naturally defaulted to lowercase letters because I lacked courage or conviction or a healthy sense of self-worth. But in fact it was because I was so busy writing functional and unornamented sentences. I just needed to save time.)

But the Bavarian Alps. Wherever they are, I want to go to them soon. I was trying to find an inexpensive lodge where I might stay; a travel article named a promising sounding place and included a link that led instead to a warning.

PAGE NOT FOUND. This page is unavailable, it might have been deleted or worse: it could never have existed!

I couldn't tell if this warning was sincere or if it was meant to be cheeky. The hotel (to which this unfound page was attached) seemed capable of boutique cheekiness (there was an oversized service bell on the front desk), and, given, the hotel was French—somehow my "Bavarian" search term landed me at a French hotel—and the French are not typically cheeky, well, it would make sense if their cheekiness might unintentionally read, despite their best efforts to loosen up, as philosophical.

Perhaps it was a matter of language. Ideas stated in French sound more dignified than they do in English. I translated. *Page non trouvée. Cette page est indisponible, il aurait été supprimé ou pire: il n'aurait jamais existé!*

French did not clarify matters. The problem was not the language but the punctuation. The exclamation point drained all gravity from the sentiment. It rendered it bouncy and nonthreatening. *It never could have existed! Wheeeeeee!!!!* Once exclamation points were scary and loud; they made you jump. You were in trouble when the exclamation points came out. They were the nun-chucks of punctuation. They were a bark, a scold, a gallows sentence. Not any longer. The exclamation point is lighthearted, even whimsical. If someone responds with an exclamation point you can be sure that you failed to make a lasting impression on her. If your friend says, *I love it!* she means she was temporarily but forgettably energized by the photo you attached or the e-mail observations you so carefully fact-checked before sending. Your contribution to her in-box is the equivalent of a whippet hit. If she says, however, *I love it,* she means she has been soothed by your quotidian display of greatness into a state of contemplation. I wanted to soothingly contemplate the question of whether it was worse never to have existed than it was to be deleted; I love (as in *love,* no exclamation point) an existential reckoning moment with an auto response. But my only possible responses to this auto response (which I understood as a question—*is* it better to never have existed?) seemed to be *Yes!* or *No!* These were not convictions so much as they were hiccups in my attention span. No, I want another whippet, I mean what I meant is—sorry, yes! Please, I want another.

.
.

OCTOBER 2

.
.

Today I was walking to class when I heard a couple fighting on the sidewalk. The other pedestrians and I craned our necks to eyeball the participants, but cautiously, so we wouldn't get busted. Looking is impolite. Space is tight in this city; loved ones have to take it to the streets, sometimes. They deserve a little privacy.

The two fighting people quickly rumbled into view; they resolved themselves into one person fighting with herself. She wore a giant maroon sweatshirt advertising a midwestern college and a sagging pair of chinos. Despite her other-college varsity gear, her rant was about Columbia. "Fuck Columbia University! Fuck Columbia University!" It was her fight song. *If only all cheerleaders suffered from psychotic breaks,* I thought. *They might help their teams to win more games.*

I noticed a few people on the sidewalk, despite themselves, smiling. Columbia University is the gleaming beneficiary but also the occasional victim of its city circumstances. The students and faculty fight like everyone in New York fights for money and for space. Also the university was expanding into a new neighborhood, igniting local protests. Most of the pedestrians on that sidewalk had probably thought at one time, or were thinking right now, *Fuck Columbia University!*

This woman was the voice of the people.

I crossed Broadway. I was far enough away that I could now safely look at her. She was just another anonymous and lumpily dressed outraged person until she wasn't. The body was foreign to me, and so was the voice, but I recognized the face. The face belonged to a student of mine from many years ago, a woman who'd come to my office and was so depressed that when she cried, her tears moved slowly down her face, her whole being enervated to the point where even gravity failed to have an effect on her.

I stood on the street corner. I thought about chasing after her, but she was churning swiftly through the neighborhood—she was already almost a block away—so instead I entered a coffee shop. This is why I was on the street. I was going to a coffee shop, and I was buying a coffee, and then I was walking to class, and then I would teach, and then during office hours I would reassure the students who needed reassuring, and I would be tough on the students who could take it, and if someone cried in my office for reasons unrelated but maybe sort of related to the imperfect short story they'd written, I would tell them that fiction makes you cry, the fiction you read though more often it's the shitty fiction you write that makes you cry, and I would also be thinking, *You poor person, you have no idea what awaits you.* A life awaits you, like a serious fucking life. This is what I would want to say. And then I would go home to my serious fucking life, and it would be so ridiculously unserious; it would involve soup spills and dirty dishes and lengthy logic proofs meant to coerce tired, inarticulate people to bed, and I would think how lucky I was to have this unserious life, i.e., to be forced to do somewhat or even thoroughly banal things every day. Because what awaits you if you don't? What kind of life awaits you then? A life where you don't calmly think, as you're scraping up the crystallized juice rings before showering before getting dressed before buying coffee before teaching class before reassuring people their hard lives would only get harder, *Fuck this whole existence.* You're running down the street and you're screaming at a university to which you no longer belong, you're wearing a sweatshirt not even branded with the insignia of the university on which you blame your breakdown, the university to which you are no longer affiliated, because you are so deeply unaffiliated that you are barely even affiliated with your own face.

JUNE 21

Today I thought I might educate my husband about birth control pills. I said, "You probably don't know how birth control pills work," and he replied, "Actually, I do." By "work"

I didn't mean that I understood how they keep a person from getting pregnant. I had no idea about that. By "work" I meant that every month a person can predict what day she'll get her period. It turned out he knew this much about birth control pills; he knew even more than I did. And yet I had never, until recently, been on the pill during our time together. So this knowledge of his, it predated me, and to predate me meant he'd learned about the pill well over fifteen years ago. What else did he know that I did not know he knew? I thought about how, now that we know each other so well, we rarely talk about the time before we met. Every once in a while we still talk like there is more to discover about each other's past. Often this happens on car rides. When it does, it's so exciting, it makes me feel like we're dating again, and presenting, for inspection to one another, our personal narratives that have been practiced on the lovers that preceded us. I especially want—even now, after hearing it all—to hear again about his ex-girlfriends. Every man I've been involved with, his past girlfriends have played a great part in my falling in love with him. I can't explain it except to say that I have felt with these women a blood connection; these women have parted with a valued possession and now it has fallen to me. I am the beneficiary of a bequeathing. If I'd dated this man before they had, he would not be this man. And so I feel kinship, and gratitude. Also curiosity. I love to meet ex-girlfriends when such meetings are desired and appropriate, and even when they're not. Once, when my husband and I were first dating, I spotted his ex-girlfriend on the train platform. I had already thoroughly interrogated him about her because she, in particular, fascinated me. I had scrutinized pictures of her, I had reclined on pillows she'd sewn, I had admired her artwork, still on his walls. She was a key part of our courtship. And here she was! Standing beside me, waiting for the train! I was still a secret; she had no idea about me. But I knew everything about her. I knew her so well that I was scared to stay in the same car with her for too long. For sure she would *feel* this strange woman knowing her. Yet I half wanted her to notice and wonder about me. I half wanted us to be forced to contend with one another. Right before exiting at the next stop, I half wanted to put a hand on her shoulder and say, one subway stranger to another, *Thank you.*

AUGUST 14

Today I got stuck in an airport due to weather. Formerly, this situation would inspire me to action. I would rent a car. I would drive rather than wait for the fog or rain or snow to clear. Now I have learned the rewards of waiting. I wait.

In my thirties, I did not wait. Once I was stuck in Nashville due to an impending blizzard. The people at the airport were so pessimistic about the chances of us ever leaving. Like *ever*. More than the pessimism of the weather, I could not stand the pessimism of these people. I decided, rather than waiting for their attitudes to improve, that I would to drive to New York.

On the concrete island waiting for any rental car shuttle to appear, a man approached me. Was I on the canceled flight to New York? He asked. I was. He suggested we could do some sightseeing in Nashville together, since we'd probably be stranded here until tomorrow.

"Screw that," I told him. "I'm driving home."

He thought about this.

"Want some company?" he said.

He seemed decent enough, a short-haired man in innocuous clothes. What harm could he really do to me? You can't rape a person while they're driving.

He told me—he sensed I needed swaying—that he was a cop in Staten Island. This meant I was safe from assault and murder but not, as it turned out, dullness or misogyny.

I agreed.

We rented a car. We started driving. *He* drove. I'm bad with maps so instead I hosted. I instilled our car with a party mood. I asked him questions. Eventually it emerged that this man, whose name might have been, or might as well have been, Tom, was not technically a cop. He was a rent-a-cop, and even then hardly ever. Primarily Tom made his living as a stunt diver for movies. Not a diver from the sky, but a diver in the water. He only worked in New York. I didn't imagine there was much movie work for stunt scuba divers in New York, but he reassured me that there was. He'd played a Navy SEAL in a movie I'd never heard of, and an underwater cat burglar in a movie I'd never heard of.

Soon, not too far into the Blue Ridge Mountains, we started to talk about his love life. I asked Tom if he had a girlfriend. He didn't, not really, but he did have an ex-wife about whom he spoke rancorously. She was beautiful, and selfish, and a cheat. In the divorce she "stole" his house, the one he'd bought with his hard-won savings as a stunt diver before he married her. Now he lived in a small apartment and was broke.

Given the depth of his bitterness and his anger toward this woman, I suspected that she was not the first to disappoint him. Maybe I so intuitively arrived at this suspicion because he qualified his ex-wife's every evil move by "that's just what women do" and "she's a bitch like the rest of them." I encouraged him, diver that he was, to do some deep dives into his romantic past. I appointed myself his co–scuba therapist. I quickly identified his problem. He was dating the wrong kind of girl. By his estimation (and using his glossary terms), he exclusively dated "skeezers" and "cheats" and "bitches." No wonder he thought poorly of women.

Tom, however (or this is what I told him, on hour three of our twenty-hour drive), *wanted* to love someone who wasn't a skeezer; he just didn't know how to identify these women. Furthermore, I told him, I was uniquely qualified to give him advice on these matters, because I'd been him once, dating and marrying the wrong men. My current husband, when I'd met him, admittedly "wasn't my type," nor was I his. I'd shown him photos of the even younger me and he'd said, "I never would have dated you."

I made it my project to teach Tom how to reset his erotic compass, as my husband and I had reset ours. I was so confident I'd succeed in turning Tom that I projected into the future. I'd rid the world of misogynists one glum, angry dude at a time. I'd do it surreptitiously, since misogynists wouldn't know that they needed my services. I'd have to trick them into a cure. I'd prowl airports during poor weather and prey on the quietly furious. I'd lock them into lengthy car rides, and then I'd preach my gospel.

And so I made it my project, on this car ride, to teach Tom the glories of certain women. I would act out the prototype. Funny! Self-deprecating! Curious and witty! Not remotely a skeezer yet still worth fucking! What might have been an interminable and hellish trip acquired a purpose. We were having a high time, and I was making lots of gender correction headway.

Until I wasn't. We pulled into a McDonald's after eight hours in the mountains, at which point I discovered my wallet missing. I'd paid for the last round of gas, four hours back. I'd left my wallet at the station. I freaked out. Not because I'd lost my wallet (this was nothing new). I freaked because I now had to rely on this man, this angry man, to get me home. I had to rely on him to *feed* me.

We worked out the terms. He'd keep a running tab of what he spent on me, and I'd send him a check when we got back to the city. But already his attitude had started to sour. I was just another mooching woman. Did I think he was an idiot? Did I think he was so easy to fool *again*?

He went inside the McDonald's and reappeared with hardly any food. I swear he ate virtually no dinner so that he had an excuse to spend no money on mine. In the parking lot, we each consumed a one-patty hamburger and a small container of fries. He paid for another tank of gas. We got back on the highway, neither of us very chatty.

We were still in Tennessee.

We were still in Tennessee when we became too tired to drive. No hotels emerged from the extended darkness until finally one did. Unfortunately this hotel had only one room. I pushed the clerk—was he certain he didn't have another? My experience is that hotels always have more rooms than they're willing to admit.

"Well," the clerk said, "we do have another room, but I wouldn't recommend staying in it." The last resident had stayed there for two weeks with his cat, and the cat had peed everywhere. "We haven't had a chance to replace the carpets yet."

Tom said we'd take the room. Oh gallant Tom! My

heart warmed toward him again. *Sometimes,* I thought, *macho guys are a bonus to have around; they can be counted on to behave chivalrously, and to sleep in the cat piss room.* For all of my gender trailblazing that day, I was conveniently happy to be a female who needed saving.

The desk person showed us to the cat room. It stank from the hallway. It stank so badly that I am smelling that room right now. Fermented animal urine is as sharp as industrial ammonia. The smell made my eyes water. The room was so uninhabitable, I figured that Tom would chicken out, thus forcing us to sleep in the same room.

But Tom stayed strong.

"You can sleep here," he said.

I was so tired I almost started crying in the hallway. I didn't. He was no stereotypical man, and I was no stereotypical woman. I waited until I was lying in the disgusting bed to cry, even though by then I was so pissed I no longer felt like crying. But I forced myself to cry and to keep crying because I figured crying would exhaust me and help me pass out despite the fact that I was basically shut inside a bottle of smelling salts. I lay in that stinking room and hated Tom. What a stingy fucking asshole he was! I understood the story of his marriage quite differently now. No wonder his wife stayed out late with her girlfriends and slept with other men. Tom was not only bitter and angry, he had a charcoal heart. His ex-wife probably took his house in the divorce as compensation for the deprivation she'd endured during their marriage. He'd lorded over her his every act of "generosity." He'd probably loved her parsimoniously, too. He'd given her the barest minimum and then blamed her for taking everything.

I raged myself to sleep. I awoke in a milder mood. I drank bad lobby coffee, I still hated the fuck out of Tom, but as we drove within a hundred miles of New York, and the future of our relationship could be measured in minutes, I found it in my heart to pity him again. In the southern wilds of New Jersey, I made one final attempt to rectify his misapprehensions about women. By the time we arrived at his house at Staten Island, we were buddies once more. As we were saying good-bye, he said, "I've never met anyone like you," probably meaning, "I've never met a woman who, after I made her sleep in a room soaked in cat piss, was so nice to me the next morning." What a miracle I was. He gave me his address so I could mail him the money I owed. I gave him my phone number so we could meet for a drink in the city and revel in our comedy of errors. Among the many ironies of our trip, New York, when we arrived, was snowless.

And then what happened? I sent Tom a check right away. I was no mooch. He left a message to thank me, and asked me to call him back so that we could schedule that drink. I didn't return his call immediately. Would I have ever returned it? I'm not sure. Regardless, he called again. Again I didn't call him back. He called a third time, and a fourth, his messages growing increasingly angry. I understood why. He felt hurt and betrayed. I'd been so nice to him, so responsive and so giving and so concerned about his life. He'd told me, a stranger, his secrets, and now I was blowing him off.

It was true. I *was* blowing him off. I couldn't deal with Tom, or the problem of Tom. He'd ceased to interest me as a project. He was doomed to a life of romantic dissatisfaction. He was a waste of my time. I blew him off knowing that, in doing so, I was confirming his worst beliefs about my gender. I took an inexplicable pleasure in knowing that I'd probably *intensified* his darkest suspicions. I'd given him hope. Find a woman who's smart and funny, rather than one who is obsessed by money and looks, I'd told him, and you'll be so much happier. And then I'd behaved as deceitfully as the skeeziest of skeezers, who, to their credit, were at least up front about their low designs. I'd pitched myself, and my kind, as dependable and caring and forthright. I'd probably proved to be the most deceitful woman of all.

Finally Tom stopped leaving messages. Around this same time, my wallet was returned. The clerk at the gas station in the Blue Ridge Mountains had sent it to the address on my driver's license, no longer my address, and it had been forwarded to my new apartment. I marveled at how strangers are such decent people. I lose my wallet nearly once a month, and always it is returned to me, and always with the money still inside.

NOVEMBER 25

Today we are in Rome because our children, ostensibly in school in Berlin, have nothing but vacations. The weather has turned dour in Germany, and we cannot stay for so many days inside our little house without people going mad. One can play only so many card games and eat so many wet crackers before the collective familial humor flags. This was our thinking when we bought cheap plane tickets and headed to Rome. Better to be in sunny Rome than to be in wet, cold Berlin. Unfortunately Rome was equally wet and cold. Our sightseeing consisted of running from shelter to shelter.

Now it is night. Our shoes are balanced upside down atop the electric heater. Our socks are dry and hard. The

kids are asleep and my husband and I are in bed watching YouTube videos of gurus. We watched Werner Erhard,
founder of est, interviewed on *The Tonight Show* by John
Denver. We marveled at how we were able to do this. Here
we are in Rome in 2013, and we're watching a video of
Werner Erhard and John Denver from 1973! Meanwhile,
the TV in our room doesn't get more than two channels.
All the news is from today. This seemed so limited, suddenly, such a narrow notion of news.

After John Denver we watched a video of a woman
from the Landmark Forum (what I understand to be the
corporate offspring of Erhard's est) pitch her wares on a
national morning talk show.

She said, "It all comes down to these three questions."

Then we watched a video of my best friend's guru, the
one who was enlightened by the sight of a mouse.

The guru said, "It all comes down to these four
questions."

My friend's guru was soft-spoken and spacey; maybe
she was stoned. She stared at her interviewer as though
dopily in love or trying to hypnotize him. She wore what
might have been robes. The interviewer asked her many
more than four questions; she feigned deep thoughtfulness
at each and then replied, as though the answer had never
before occurred to her, *yes*.

I was shocked. As I've said, this guru had really
improved my friend's life. I'd been hoping, when I got
around to it and had the time, that I'd let her improve my
life, too. But this guru, she had no *game*. She was like a
zombie on pain pills. When I someday follow a person, I
want to be impressed by their effortless bullshit passing
and dribbling and slam-dunking; I want them to be a Har-
lem Globetrotter of rhetoric and presentation and spin. I

want them, like that world-famous pickpocket (whose You-Tube videos we watched in order to learn how to avoid being robbed at the Colosseum), to so deeply understand me, and how I perceive the world, that I can be uniquely distracted, fooled, and fleeced. I would happily pay with my wallet (and my watch and my wedding ring) to be understood as deeply as this pickpocket understands his marks.

I'd hoped this guru would understand me like that pick-pocket. But to do this she would have to touch me, fondle me, reach into my front pocket, press her leg against my thigh. Maybe in person she does this. I was not, to be fair, experiencing her *in person*. But in person I could not imagine she would be much different than the human I experienced on my computer screen. We were at an impasse, this guru and I. Maybe I was at an impasse with all gurus. Maybe I was looking to the wrong people for answers and clarity. I turned instead to a guidebook for guidance. A real guidebook. Someone had left it in the common bookshelf of our hotel's dining room. It was called *Getting Along in Italian*. According to *Getting Along in Italian*, one can ably survive a vacation and probably a whole life knowing how to ask and answer a few pages' worth of questions. I narrowed the options down to these essentials:

Are you alone?
Where is my key?
This is a violation.
I have pain in my chest.
There is a mistake in the bill.
Where are the lifeboats?
Did anyone call me?
Did anyone come for me?

I want a felt hat.
I want a novel.
I want a priest.

OCTOBER 4

Today I almost told a woman I barely know that I loved her. This woman is the mother of my son's friend. She and I are also sort of friends. It's hard to make new friends at this stage of life, but she and I are trying. I always want new friends, but I know what it takes to make a good one. It takes years, decades, and back when I was younger I had hours and hours of those days of those years of those decades to dedicate to getting to know a friend. Now I have minutes of hours of days of years of decades. To acquire a new friend under these time restrictions would require three consecutive lives.

To compensate for the time we don't have, this woman and I use the time we do have deeply. We tunnel in. We confess to the hand jobs we gave during our intern years to executives on commuter trains; we confess to coke habits. We talk about anxiety and marital confusion. We know such strange details about each other given the basic details that remain unknown. Are her parents alive? Where did she get married? What is her job?

The commonplace details we do discuss involve child logistics. I will get the boys and bring them here and I will leave them for an hour and then you can pick up yours and bring mine home unless you don't have time to bring mine home in which case my husband can pick mine up and if you can't pick up yours it's no big deal because my husband can take yours home with us and you can pick yours up whenever and we can even feed yours dinner.

These conversations often become extremely confusing. She thinks out her hypotheticals aloud, and I can't tell what is process and what is proposition. Sometimes I stop listening. Sometimes I hold the phone to my ear and make food with the other, or read e-mail, or fold laundry while she is working through the many permutations of tomorrow. Sometimes, when she starts to say good-bye, I have no idea what we've decided.

Today we were having one of these phone conversations. She talked, I emptied the dishwasher; she kept talking, I boiled water. Then she said good-bye. I started to say, "Bye, I love you." The words were half out of my mouth before I stopped them. I hung up, panicked. What would have happened if I hadn't caught myself? So many rules would have been violated. You cannot tell a person you love them too early. You shouldn't tell a person you don't love that you do. More shamefully she'd surmise, after the awkwardness, that I'd stopped listening to her, and that I'd entered that rote response zone, and I'd told her I loved her because I thought she was my husband. She'd know that I don't always listen to my husband when we're on the phone together, and that when I say "I love you," it sometimes means I am too distracted by our home life to listen to him right now, because he's out of town and I am not, and I am doing the work that he is not here to do (and which he does for me when I am not here to do it), and so I am really so busy that I don't have time to hear about his day. I just want to say, "I love you," which I do mean, I do love him, but I need him to be quieter so I can keep our house and family in order. I sometimes say, "I love you," not to open up an emotional vein but to cauterize it, keep it full of blood.

AUGUST 18

Today I rowed back from an island. We'd eaten dinner on this island, my friends and family and I. We'd collectively hauled a thousand pounds of food and gear to this island in order to survive three sunny hours on it. Ours was a motley August crowd—locals with roots that extended back many generations, locals who'd escaped from New York twenty years ago, an editor, an all-but-dissertation philosophy professor, a writer, an artist, two men who run silent meditation retreats in Mallorca and Nepal, three men named Ben, a lot of children. The party extended horizontally along the beach.

The mood was light but also, inevitably, charged. Islands make people competitive, maybe because the subconscious fear of shipwreck and survival permeates even the most casual outing. Who will lead the masses when the weather turns and the food runs out? Who will be sacrificed to feed the starving useful people, the ones who can fish and make fires and sing morale-building sea shanties? I often contemplate my odds of surviving a shipwreck and how to improve them. When I was breast-feeding, I nurtured a lot of shipwreck fantasies. What if I were shipwrecked with my baby and ten adults on an island with a large box of Clark Bars? Wouldn't it be best if I ate the Clark Bars and breast-fed everyone on the island, because my body would transform the worthless sugar into valuable fat and protein? Wouldn't that prove to be the wisest survival strategy, and wouldn't that guarantee I'd never be killed for food?

I was no longer breast-feeding on this particular island trip; I had to prove my indispensability in other ways. So I swam and swam and swam. I could maybe dive for lobsters; I could maybe go for help—that's what my eternal swimming said to the people sitting on the beach. I swam while others drank beer, and slowly realized that they, too, would have to swim, swim or maybe be killed. My individual survival was *clearly* essential to the survival of the group. Was theirs?

I don't think I've ever seen so many people swim on an island trip before. The water is probably fifty-three degrees out there. Then, near hypothermic, we ate the food we'd brought, and not each other. We watched the sun set, and quelled our panic that we'd have to spend the night, because the boat wouldn't start, or possibly it would sink. We loaded the scow with bags and people and transferred them to the lobster boat. I decided to row back to the mainland in a dinghy. I rowed with the artist and his squid-loving son. The son fished and caught a sandbar. His father bit the line loose with his teeth. As the moon rose, and the sun definitively set, and we were in darkness, I told them the true story of Boon Island. Boon Island is a long pile of rocks located six miles off the southern coast of Maine. In December 1710 a ship called the *Nottingham Galley* ran aground on this rock, which measured then and measures now three hundred by seven hundred feet. The fourteen survivors lasted twenty-four days *during the winter.* They did eat one another in order to pull off this astonishing feat.

Boon Island, published in 1956, is a thinly fictionalized account of their endeavor written by Kenneth Roberts. Maine children are (or were in the '80s) assigned to read

Boon Island for English class. Should our own personal hardships overwhelm us, well, we should be thankful our feet weren't turning to translucent sponges in our boots. I guess this was the lesson. Or maybe this is too clichéd an understanding of why we were assigned this book in English class. Buck up, etc. This is so prevalent an attitude in Maine that we didn't need a formal education to learn it. The takeaway horror of *Boon Island* was far more existential. Yes, these men were freezing and eating one another, but the cruelest factor of their island internment was this: they could see smoke rising from the house chimneys ashore. As they suffered, they could watch the cheery proof of people warming themselves by fires and cooking food that wasn't, an hour ago, a friend. That struck me as far worse punishment than simply being shipwrecked on a rock. It seemed an appropriate metaphor for being marooned in Maine as a kid—there was another world out there, you could watch it nightly on TV, but how could you reach it?

On a windless night, without a current, the row from the island back to shore is an easy one. I was no longer proving my indispensability to the group; I simply wanted to take the slow way to shore under the half-moon, because summer is almost over, and these are the quiet, twilight moments that, if properly collected and preserved, help me survive the New York winter. I start amassing these moments during the final weeks of August. I must salt supplies for storage. They must last me until I can return to this place I angled for years to leave.

Today my husband and I decided to rearrange our furniture. Our apartment has never looked right to me; probably we should hire an expert to fix it, but I am too proud. I am too convinced that I am secretly a decorating prodigy and to pay for professional help is beneath me. I understand that, with all of the money in the world, and all of the space, a person would require some help to sort through the infinite options available to her. I don't have such problems. I like what I can afford. I like what fits. Within these narrower choice parameters, I usually choose well.

In this apartment, however, my talents have been stymied. Five years after moving in I've yet to crack the code. The light, as I've noted, is an issue. The light comes from the wrong direction. The rooms are oddly shaped, and the walls are full of doors and windows. My husband tries to discuss with me what to do with the apartment—how we might better sit in it and walk through it—but I often grow testy with him when he broaches home improvement topics. I cannot explain why, save to say that my inability to properly inhabit this apartment feels like a personal failing; I am embarrassed that I need his help. When I disagree with where he wants to put a piece of furniture, I tell myself that he has a terrible sense of space (he doesn't). He cannot eyeball a void, I tell myself, and understand what it is capable of accepting. He'll suggest we put a bed against a wall that is, to me at least, obviously too short. He'll insist, gamely, that we try it. I insist it's pointless to try. I hate that I can't just say, "Sure, let's move that bed," and let the bed be right or wrong. Let the objects in the house fail or succeed to fit in it, not me.

MAY 13

Today I talked with an artist and a poet about luck. The artist (a man) is in his sixties; the poet (a man) is in his twenties. The artist is a cheerful curmudgeon, a man of years; the poet is sweetly irreverent, and still expecting, before he is too much older, his fame day. We started to talk about a book only two of the three of us had read. It soon became clear that the poet, though socially irreverent, was, in his mind and opinions, hard and unforgiving, while the curmudgeon was a man of great compassion. I was speaking in defense of this book, and the poet was speaking against it. He called the book "lucky"—as in, the writer had not been talented or deserving of his success. He'd been fortuitous; he'd stumbled into fame. This assertion made the artist come to the defense of the writer he did not know and the book he'd never read. He spoke sternly to the poet, like a father to his son of whom he is cautiously proud but also a little envious. "That's a cheap shot to call a person lucky," he said. "Everyone relies on luck to succeed."

It was lucky that he said this, because I'd been thinking about luck that day. I'd been writing an essay about my son's birth for an anthology of birth stories. My son was born at home, and the midwife didn't show. This isn't exactly what happened; she showed, I sent her away, she went really far away, and by the time we called her back it was too late. Or almost too late. She arrived with roughly thirty seconds to spare.

Afterward we were told that we were "stupid" and "lucky." Stupid, I agree. But lucky? We weren't lucky. We were really, really, really lucky. I would never claim not to be lucky. I am so fucking lucky that I am terrified of luck. I am terrified it will abandon me. I'm like the women in the Tuscan town where the *Madonna del Parto* is kept. I'm always lying down in the street to keep my luck from leaving. When I was a kid, in elementary school, I would try to divine the day's luck forecast each morning with a yogurt pot. The pot was sealed with foil; if I could remove the foil without tearing it, the day would be a lucky one. If I tore the foil, the opposite awaited me. I'd walk into the day braced against the hex. I still perform witchy meteorology with yogurt tops. It's a habit I can't shake. When the foil top tears I tell myself, *It means nothing.* I don't believe myself for a second. When things are going badly, I scan my life for the cause. Often that cause can be sourced to an object. A material irritant. Once I bought what turned out to be a very bad luck ring in Morocco. Whenever I wore the ring, my paychecks were lost in the mail. My furnace malfunctioned (there's a softly vengeful name for what happens when your furnace covers everything in your house with oily soot—*puffback*). Beyond-my-control bad luck, in other words. Metaphorical puffbacks happened all over the place. I'd put the ring aside and a few months later try again to wear it. Bad luck returned. It wasn't enough to take the ring off my finger; after I returned it to its box, I had a bad luck hangover that lasted a week.

Finally I took the ring to a psychic. I didn't tell her why I wanted her to "read" my ring. I wanted to test her cold.

She said, "I don't like this ring for you." She said it was "associated with an angry man." I'd always assumed the ring had been cursed by whoever had made it, or possibly by the man who sold it to me. But her description sounded a lot like my ex-boyfriend, the one with whom I'd lived in Morocco. He was angry, I guess; in truth I usually attributed his moods—which were never wrathful or violent—to a case of depression. Regardless, I took the advice she gave me. She told me to wrap the ring in black paper and then again in tin foil. I hid it in the back of my closet. Why don't I just throw it away? I don't know why. For the same reason I could not, as a kid, throw away my broken lamp. One thinks a loved object is unique, unique to each human who loves it. But what is really unique is the unloved object. Or rather the unloved object confers uniqueness upon the person who fails time and again to love it and yet who still cannot throw it away.

JULY 22

Today I tried to console my son. He'd gone to sleep and thirty minutes later he'd woken up crying. This happens sometimes—my husband and I think he's down for the night, and then he awakens in a state. I don't think there's anything dangerously wrong with him—tonight he said his ear hurt. Last week he said it was his leg. He sobs and he writhes and he's inconsolable, and we briefly consider calling the doctor, and then we don't.

This time I was resentful when he woke up in inexplicable agony because the day had been too long; there had already been too many phases. There was the cleaning phase, during which I organized lightbulbs and tossed modem cords and tried to put away the folded laundry. Then there was the Enforced Outdoor Fun phase, people dragged unhappily around the harbor on a kayak. Then there was the Local Culture phase, involving a trip to a historical society, which more or less looked like the interior of our barn, itself a historical society spanning many more centuries than the one we visited, because ours included deflated beach floaties and broken plastic sleds. Then there was the eating and drinking and socializing phase. Then there was the putting the kids to bed phase, and then the sitting on the couch and watching bad television phase—the phase of which it can sometimes seem all other phases are in service. Everything we do, we do so we can be sitting on this couch watching *The Bachelorette*.

And then my son woke up.

Soon it became clear that he could not be distracted from his misery fugue state. He would lie awake in his bed and contort and cry for probably an hour, and I would have to rub his back throughout. I tried not to act aggrieved that my final phase had been interrupted. That I was not on the couch watching man after man say, "I'm starting to fall in love with Desiree." That I was not parsing with my husband the phrase *starting to fall*. Isn't the point of falling that it has no prelude or warning, and certainly does not stretch out over the course of many ninety-minute episodes? That it simply *happens*? That you are suddenly on the ground, having already dropped from a higher altitude to a lower one? I thought of *falling* as akin to being tackled by a member of the Boston Women's Rugby Club (this happened to me; I played rugby in college). Women so skilled you didn't feel the transition from running to lying on your back. One second you were sprinting toward the try line;

the next second you were staring at the sky. You were in love with Desiree!

These were the important discussions I was missing while my son sobbed and sobbed. Every situation with a child that irks me, I try not to be irked by thinking: How many more irksome moments like this will I have? My son is four and a half. My hours of rubbing his back while he weeps are numbered. I moved my hand from his shoulder blades to his tailbone, and then I swooped it in reverse. Down up, down up; it was like sharpening a knife, or polishing a bowl. I tried to commit the movement to muscle memory. Whenever I am trapped in a situation, I think of how this entrapment might qualify as work. I am so worried about ever wasting time that I cannot let any small amount of it escape without defining for it a use or a purpose or extracting from it a lasting lesson. I tried to think of how this motion might, in the future, come in handy. I thought, If my son dies, I will sit at the shore, and swoop my hand like this back and forth over a smooth rock that has been warmed in the sun and feels humanlike as a way of remembering him. Then I thought this was melodramatic and gruesome. I thought instead: *Maybe I'll write a story in which a character's son dies, and she could, as a means of coping, go to the shore and do this.* Then I thought this was melodramatic and stupid. I thought instead: I must remember to do this when I am seventy. I must remember to find a rock that feels exactly like my son's four-year-old back. I must remember to close my eyes and imagine that I am me again, a tired mother trying to teach herself how to miss what is not gone.

Today my husband poisoned himself by accident, or this is what we fear. His was an honest mistake. We do not speak enough German to know what we're buying at the market; we've been trusting our ability to identify objects by sight, i.e., without relying on labels and language. At an overpriced health food market, we saw a large bag of reasonably affordable almonds. We bought them.

At home, we remarked on the incredibly almondy taste of these almonds. In Germany, everything tastes like an artificially amped-up version of itself. Raspberries taste strongly of raspberry, tomatoes of tomato, Heineken of Heineken, and so on. It made sense that the almonds would taste measurably more like almonds than the almonds we ate in the States. But these almonds were far tinier than almonds usually are; we became curious. What was up with these almonds? We decided to Google the word on the label: *aprikosenkerne*. The topmost hit was a website introduced by the following text (translated from the original German):

> *Disease is not an accident, not even fate, and*
> *certainly not evil intention of the love of God.*
> *Disease is the result of our own homemade error on*
> *mental and physical level. Only if you are willing*
> *to correct mistakes by yourself, you are also ready to*
> *be healthy again.*

We were willing to correct mistakes! We were ready to be healthy again! We clicked another link that informed us: bitter apricot kernels were what we'd bought. Bitter apricot kernels, we learned from "the official website of vitamin B_{12}" are no plain nut, and maybe not even a food; primarily they are a hotly contested alternative cancer therapy. According to some people, bitter apricot kernels are poisonous. They contain cyanide. Because of this, the recommended daily dosage is one to two nuts. My husband had eaten fourteen.

I reasoned with him. I am committed to reasoning away his illness and his pain (in the same way that I am committed to reasoning him out of the diet beliefs he maintains for the sake of his health). I can expertly talk him out of experiencing what he believes he experiences and maybe even experiences.

Fortunately, illness is almost always illogical. I exploit the holes.

"It says here," I said, reading from another website, "that while the UK believes consuming anything over two to three bitter apricot kernels means you'll die of cyanide poisoning, the Hunzas . . ." Wait. Who were the Hunzas? They sounded like a sci-fi tribe of distant planetary origin whose digestive systems would not resemble our own. I did some quick rewriting in my head. "I mean, the people in, like, Afghanistan who harvest these nuts eat dozens and dozens a day."

This fact did not assuage either of us.

"Look at this bag," I said. I fake almost dropped it. The bag was so heavy! It weighed 500 grams! "If you could eat only two to three nuts a day, this bag would last ten years. Also why would they sell a bag this big without a warning?"

Together we examined the packaging. There were a lot of words on the label, and, granted, we did not know what any of them meant, but, I reminded him, we knew what warnings looked like. There was nothing visually alarmist about the label at all. There was nothing to indicate that this was a bag of death. There were pictures of *blossoms*. Which I suppose could be meant in the funereal sense, the death-and-rebirth sense. I recalled a book about nuclear waste buried in a mountain, and how the waste's deathly potency would outlast the English language. The officials in charge of responsibly protecting the people of the future from the toxic waste did not know how, in the absence of language, to warn these people not to disturb the mountain. They experimented with pictures and symbols. What might constitute a pictorially or symbolically timeless death warning? Maybe blossoms.

"Also," I said, "there's no way the Germans would have *bags of cyanide* on the grocery store shelves." Anything in Germany that might remind a person of WWII has been either eradicated from view or memorialized by a huge stone monument. Hitler killed himself with cyanide. There's no way the Germans would put an unmarked (i.e., unmemorialized) bag of cyanide on the grocery shelves, not least because we'd bought the *aprikosenkerne* at the Kaiser's grocery store that was located less than a kilometer from the Wannsee Conference house.

I'm sorry, but tell me the Germans had not thought about this.

It made me wish, however, that we'd come up with a list of ways we might die in Germany that would permit us to laugh at each other's funerals. I had a boyfriend with dark-humored brothers who generated such lists. When my boyfriend moved to Japan to study the Japanese sword, he gave his brothers permission to laugh at his funeral if he (a) died eating blowfish or (b) accidentally hari-kari-ed himself with his own weapon.

Surely the unintentional cyanide overdose of a half-Jew in Wannsee would qualify as grounds for laughing.

Meanwhile, my husband was upstairs trying to work. I called up the staircase.

"Are you dead yet?"

He said he felt nauseous.

"Me too," I said cheerfully. "I'm so tired right now I'm sick!" It was true. We were still not over our jet lag.

Later he came downstairs for lunch and complained of a headache.

"We haven't been drinking much water," I said. "You're probably dehydrated!"

It's kind of him to tolerate my optimism. Who knows what will happen when we're older, when he's really dying of cancer or something. Or if we're in a car accident. I imagined myself after a car accident reasoning with his decapitated body. *You'll be fine, you're just dehydrated! The Hunzas grow new heads by the dozens!* What it comes down to is this: I just need him to believe me that he's not going to die. I need to win this fight more than any of the others I've won, so that I can prove to us both that I'm right.

SEPTEMBER 1

Today I stopped at an antiques store that I've passed many times but have never visited. A sign outside advertised HAND STICHED QUILTS. Three quilts hung from a clothesline; none of them looked antique. The wooden boat building industry in my town has a name for this new-old crafts pursuit. Boats based on old designs and built with new methods are called "Spirit of Tradition" boats. So maybe these were Spirit of Tradition quilts. In the spirit of tradition—honoring ye olde days—these quilts were "stiched," not stitched.

The quilts should have been a warning sign: this was not my kind of antique store. Flanking the door were architectural ruins—the bases of giant pillars—already repurposed as planters. This store catered to people who pay others to find the promise in junk. I do not think less of these people; I just cannot afford to be one of them. I often buy things because they are cheap and because I hope they will jar my imagination at a later date and become a smart investment. They will prove useful for something. Those cast-iron boot removers, for example, that were once bolted to a barn wall, and into which a farmer once stuck his boot heel and levered out his foot. They've spent ten years on top of my woodstove; their use has not yet revealed itself to me. I trust in time that it will.

I went inside the antiques store. Indeed, the prices were too high. My desires recalibrate in such situations; I am open to liking whatever is simply within my price range. I found a box of old postcards, the long rectangular ones with the twin, side-by-side exposures, usually of national monuments or state parks. When I asked the prices, the man said offhandedly, as though these items were of little consequence to him, "Oh those, I just put those out. I haven't had a chance to price them yet."

But approximately, I asked him. I wanted to know if it would be worth my time to paw.

"Anywhere from $5 to $200, depending on the postcard," he said.

I picked five postcards. The four Maine postcards were too expensive. The fifth—a waterfall in Minnesota, an unremarkable image of a place that meant nothing to me—was five dollars. I bought it.

I gave the man my credit card. He scrutinized my name. "The writer?" he asked. He said he liked my work, but I doubt he'd read any of it. He knew my name because his real trade was people. Antiques interested him because they were the former possessions of people. Our subsequent conversation confirmed my suspicion. I told him I was sad because I was soon returning to New York. He said, "Yes, all of the New Yorkers leave in August." He sounded wistful. Most locals, by the end of a summer tourist season, do not respond wistfully to its conclusion.

The man dropped names of local summer people, some of whom I'd heard of, none of whom I knew. He told me about a thirty-years-dead real estate agent who was, as he put it, "a one-woman zoning committee." (He also described her as a "prissy little woman.") She had ideas about where each type of person (writer, artist, WASP, Irish Catholic) should live. I mentioned a snooty family in our town called the Winfrieds. (I'd been inside their house once because I knew their caretaker.) I told a story about Mrs. Winfried and how she'd snubbed my neighbor, a local woman who'd cleaned Mrs. Winfried's house when she was a teenager.

"Ah," he said. "You mean Mrs. *Winston*."

He talked about how sweetly offensive these people could be without even knowing it. How they assume you're one of them, just because you've made it to the party, so to speak. "They're always talking about 'us white people,' in front of me," he said, "without even realizing that I'm passing."

Was he talking about passing as a summer person? Passing as a straight person? Passing as a straight summer person? Then he mentioned "passing" a second time. He referred to having longer, curlier hair, and much more of a beard. "And even then they didn't know I was passing!" he said.

Now I was really confused. To my eye, this guy was white. I suspected, too, that he wanted me to ask him, "Wait, aren't you white?"

I decided not to ask him.

As I was leaving, I saw a pair of pottery cups and saucers by a now defunct, once influential pottery studio. The old barn and workshop still existed in a town twelve miles from mine; my friend and I had snooped around the property a few weeks ago. The sign remained, and the studio appeared operational, full of dusty wheels and botched pots lining the windowsills, even though the place had been shut down for years. There were rumors (my friend had read somewhere) that you could tour the workshop and the barn. But we found no people and no signs. After trying all the doors, we left.

I told the man at the antiques store that I wanted to buy the two cups and saucers. He said, "They're a very good price."

Compared to the rest of his offerings, this was true.

"Do you know about that pottery?" he said.

I told him that I knew a little bit about it.

"And the woman who founded it," he said, "she really was a remarkable woman."

"She really was," I agreed. I had no idea about this woman. I knew exactly not one thing about her. I'm sure hers was an interesting story, because these stories always are. This stretch of the coast attracts artists, lifestyle eccentrics, self-exilers.

I don't know why I pretended I knew as much as he did when I knew nothing. I don't know why I refused his offer. No doubt he'd met this woman, or knew her son, or could have provided excellent gossip about her odd habits, communicated through her old cleaning lady, whose daughter was now his cleaning lady, or some such connection. But I was late to get home. I figured I'd Google her later and learn for myself what made her so remarkable. I did this. I failed to learn much. Her name was Angelica Baker. The most informative was a piece written by the antiques dealer I'd just been talking to, but the article was more concerned with a modernist pavilion razed by a banker with traditional tastes. I clicked around and discovered that the antiques dealer kept a blog. (He'd written an article called "The Trouble with the Footmen: Servant Problems in Old Bar Harbor.") I realized how much we had in common. He's obsessed with mansions and wealth—his is the adult version of my kid obsession with Greenwich real estate—but he's also struck mute by a simple white cape. I own a simple white cape that's two hundred years old. Antique capes are modernist in their way, two or three cubes and rectangles stuttering across a field. The sight of one relaxes my whole body. On his blog he'd posted a picture of a white cape under a quote from Coco Chanel, "Elegance is refusal." Was it a mark of elegance, my refusal to ask him about his background, my refusal to let him tell me a good story about a potter? Regardless, now I was far more curious about him. I vowed to stop by his antiques store more often next summer. I thought we'd get along.

APRIL 27

Today I went to a Virginia Woolf reading. For some reason this reading was held at a law school. At the front desk

I was asked by an old woman holding a hand-written sign that said VIRGINIA WOOLF, as though she was a chauffeur picking up Virginia Woolf at the airport, if I were going to the Virginia Woolf reading. I confirmed. She said, "I *guessed* that about you." I got offended. Why I didn't know. When I entered the library where the reading was being held I knew. I am of that age now where I am looking for the next age I will be. How will I dress? How will I act? Here were women in their last ages; they wore kimono blouses and ethnic scarves and had buzzed, asymmetrical hair. I felt like I was in a late-80s women's studies class. I'd once admired women who looked like this; what had changed? I said to myself, *They're only dressing for women like themselves.* I often claim that I dress for other women. But this crowd felt more insular and hermetic. There was a formula to belonging.

Since I am older but not yet old, I try not to judge even while, to protect myself, I'm totally judging. So trying not to judge, I surveyed these women and thought: *Maybe when you get older you want to be part of a visually defined group. Maybe it is easier to be recognized and acknowledged as part of a group because to be acknowledged individually becomes harder over time.* I've noticed that I have to look harder at older women in the face to see their faces. I stare and I stare and then suddenly—there they are. I have to look harder at my own face to see myself in it. My face was signifying me so well for a while; now, again, it is failing. When I look in the mirror I literally feel like I'm boring down through a surface that doesn't catch the light, that isn't quickly bouncing back a discernible message. I am starting to fail on the streets to communicate with my face because pedestrians don't have that kind of time. They are in a hurry. Recently I started wearing a bone around my neck. It's a seal vertebra I found on a beach that's for sale;

I hope, if a seal spirit sees fit to deliver unto me a massive windfall, that the beach will someday be mine. The bone makes pedestrians stare, not at me, but at it. This seems a good first step. Who is that woman wearing the bone? Who wears a large bone around her neck? This woman does. Please take the time to look at her.

MAY 17

Today I sat next to an eighty-nine-year-old man at dinner named Mr. Pym. He seems, like Dick Cavett, to have known all of the most interesting human beings of the twentieth century. He was not a name-dropper so much as a man who didn't, by virtue of his lifestyle, know a single unfamous person save his own mother (who was, he thrice repeated in his Georgian accent, "a wonderful woman"; he was haunted, daily, he said, by the unkind words he'd said to her as a boy). When asked by an architect (seated to my other side) if he'd lived his life joyfully or angrily, Mr. Pym replied, "I should have been more angry." He was too nice, he said, and primarily defined himself as an avoider of conflicts. He was too nice, even, to fire people, he said; "I just wait for them to die." But then he confessed that he'd considered hiring a murderer from Russia to kill an employee who was making his life hell. "It would only have cost about $3,000," he said.

For such a conflict-avoiding man, he revealed, through his stories, a fairly consistent aggressive streak. He was, he said, the only person whose advice the writer Mary McCarthy had ever taken. (McCarthy was not a person, apparently, to whom one gave advice.) He'd visited her house in Maine while doing a photo essay on her town and its buildings. (This was the same town with the white house ordinance where Robert Lowell, Jean Stafford, and Elizabeth Hardwick lived.) McCarthy's house was hidden by a pair of trees. He said to her neighbor, "If I had some overalls and a chain saw, I'd take these trees down myself." His remark was reported to McCarthy. "He's right," she apparently said. The trees came down. Later Mr. Pym mentioned going to the theater with the poet Marianne Moore. Over dinner, this man told Moore about his mother's house down south (also, it seemed, his house). He hated this house. He wanted to get rid of his mother's house and move a house from a hundred miles away to the spot her house currently occupied. His own mother would be displaced while this house swapping occurred. He asked Moore what he should do. Live with the terrible house? Or destroy it, make his mother homeless, and truck in, from a distance, the house he desired?

Moore apparently replied, "Mr. Pym, sometimes one must be *ruthless*."

I'm sure Mr. Pym, this too-nice man, was often ruthless. I think a lot of self-defined nice people are ruthless. I do not consider this a cynical stance. I consider it a realistic understanding of the word "nice." If a nice person is famous or successful—and plenty are—that person is not so nice that they are above heeding the logic of status improvement. Right now I am reading a nonfiction book in which a certain poet is portrayed (within the normal range of such things) as ambitious and calculating. I was frankly relieved to discover she was ambitious and calculating because, a few months earlier, I'd read her memoir. She'd presented herself as an angel, a guileless art angel. Her passive approach seemed to implicitly criticize people who had to actually *try* to succeed. She'd just made art alone in her crappy loft. Fame had found her.

But fame hadn't. Fame doesn't. Recently a writer I know expressed irritation with another quite famous writer's claim that she'd just been a mother, and she'd just sat at her kitchen table writing stories while her kids napped, and that she had no ambition at all. "That's bullshit," this irritated writer said. "So an editor decided to randomly phone this housewife and ask her for some stories?"

I'm messily conflating ambition and not-niceness here. To some, to me, I guess, there's a connection. To be ambitious—to exert one's self-interested desires beyond the scope of one's own head—could be seen as impolite. As not nice. I have always been nice; I have been told by others how nice I am. The one person who does not think I'm nice is me. This is because I am ambitious and competitive, and so I must be not nice to someone in order for my otherwise niceness to feel authentic. I am not nice to myself by believing I must pay more than others, and sometimes for others. When I go out to lunch with a person, I must always pay the entire check; splitting isn't allowed, and I will never permit another person to pay for me. I sometimes think my sense that I must pay comes from growing up in Maine. The five purely beautiful summer days per year are mortgaged hard against months and months of mud and ice and damp. The Maine weather instills in one's psyche a seasonal rhythm of payment. Of the cost of joy coming due.

Today I sought advice from the therapist at my daughter's school. My daughter and I are victims of a co-produced play that begins and middles and ends with screaming, tears, accusations of heartlessness and disaffection, faked injuries, faked heartbreak that hides real heartbreak. There's an oxymoronic quality to the unremitting pitch of our relationship; it's a screeching flat line. Finally I could no longer take this relationship. I am not saying that I am not the crazy person here. I am saying I am the adult. I can throw up my hands and claim powerlessness. As the adult, this powerlessness has serious power.

So I contacted the Feelings Doctor. The Feelings Doctor works at my daughter's school. We made an appointment, just the doctor and me. Before our meeting, I mapped out what I planned to say to her. I wanted to be efficient. I wanted to provide an accurate history, but mostly I wanted to get down to business. Establishing background exhausts me. I don't tend to do it. I start talking and the listener can fill in the blanks as he or she chooses. My husband calls me No Context Woman. "'The journey is the goal' is not the goal" is my motto. The goal is the goal. Let's start with the end.

To this end, I had a probably bad idea: I could send the Feelings Doctor an essay I'd written about my daughter and our traumatic history together. I thought the Feelings Doctor might get a very good sense, an arguably more thoughtful and comprehensive sense, of this history by reading an essay.

But then I realized how insane this might make me

appear to be. A mother contacts a Feelings Doctor to speak about her troubled relationship with her small daughter. Instead she sends the doctor her own writing, turning the therapy session into an opportunity for the therapist to respond to her artistic representation of the problem, rather than the problem itself. How could I appear as anything other than a narcissist, or a writer greedy for more readers, or a mother so self-involved that she pretends to care about her daughter when, in fact, she's using the appointment as a sneaky means of gaining an intimate tête-à-tête about her own work with a stranger?

I decided against sending the Feelings Doctor my essay; I regret now that I didn't. I arrived early for the appointment, and good thing, too. I busted the Feelings Doctor lacing up her escape sneakers; she'd forgotten we were supposed to meet. (I seem to have this effect on therapists.) She asked me some questions and didn't really listen to the answers. She said, "Children these days have so much attention paid to them that they can't handle a moment of neglect." I corrected her; in fact, our situation was slightly more complicated. To state it uncomplicatedly, and thus probably inaccurately, I resented my daughter's need of me and thus punished her by neglecting her.

Then the Feelings Doctor told me everything I already knew about my daughter, everything I'd already written about her. I wished I'd given the Feelings Doctor my essay. Not because we would have wasted less time. Not because we would have reached a solution faster. I think I understand, for the time being, at least, that therapy is unable to tell me anything new about myself or my loved ones. But therapy could tell me many interesting things about a stranger. About a person I hope I'm not. It could tell me something about a woman, for example, who makes an appointment with her daughter's therapist as an excuse to talk about her writing. What might a therapist be able to tell me about *that* woman? I wanted to know more about her.

Today I swam out to sea with a stranger. Since my usual swimming partner had left town, I'd put the word out—Swimmer Too Scared to Swim Alone Needs Swim Partner. I am scared to swim alone not because I might drown but because I might be attacked by a shark. Mine is an unwarranted phobia (shared by basically every person in my generation, i.e., those of us who grew up with *Jaws*); companionship is an illogical cure. To date, there have been no shark attacks in our harbor. Should a shark, against all statistics, appear, a friend (unless he or she is swimming with a machine gun) will be unable to save me from it. But I feel safe in knowing—before I am pulled underwater to my death by an animal, I can share a final *what the fuck?* moment with a sympathetic human.

This is the only protection I require.

A friend invited me to swim off her property with her sister, a woman who sees ghosts. The sister and I swam to a motorboat, then to a buoy, then to a lobster boat. We talked about the real estate coincidence that binds us. My husband and I looked at her mother's house to buy, but instead we bought ours. Her mother looked at our house to buy, but instead she bought hers. I told the woman who was sensitive to ghosts that the reason we hadn't bought her mother's house was because it had—and I hoped I wasn't insulting her by saying this—bad energy. Even my mother, not a woman who's ever anxious about energy save the kind that can, via the cord on your coffeemaker, maybe burn your house down, agreed with me. "I think I'd kill myself if I lived in this house," my mother said when the real estate agent was out of earshot.

The woman with whom I was swimming, however, said she hadn't experienced any bad vibes in that house, which was strange given she was so sensitive to spiritual entities. She told me about the ghost she'd seen when she was a child, a man in an overcoat walking up the stairs in her house who was "definitely malicious." She'd seen other ghosts as well. As we rounded the lobster boat we talked about the lodge that was for sale right in front of us. Twenty-one bedrooms for under a million dollars. Why was it such a steal? Maybe it was haunted? We fantasized about tearing down the haunted parts, like amputating a cancerous limb. Would this work? It didn't always work with actual cancer. It hadn't worked with the bamboo in our backyard. Our soil was poisoned by mutant cells. No matter if we killed the plants, their undead genetic material lurked underground and reappeared in strange places, like halfway up the outside wall of our barn.

We emerged from the sea and I thanked her for swimming with me and for distracting me with talk of ghosts. "Better than talking about sharks!" I said. I'd (mostly) stopped worrying about sharks this summer, which was such a massive accomplishment that I considered listing it on my CV. "Ugh!" the sister said. "Please don't mention that!" She told me that sharks were moving northward because the water had become so warm. There'd been a shark sighting not too far from where we'd been swimming, just beyond the protective barrier of the islands.

"What kind of shark?" I asked.

"The bad kind," she said. Then she told me who'd supposedly seen this shark, and I relaxed a little. The shark-spotter is a famed alarmist. Once she'd told us that our elm tree was sick—the little tendrils sprouting from the trunk were, according to her, signs of its imminent expiration—and that it would cost $5,000 to remove it, and that we had to do so immediately, because the next big wind would blow it over and it would crush our house. In a panic, we called a tree expert. The tree expert laughed at us. "Those tendrils mean it's healthy," he said. The alarmist also whipped us into a panic froth about firewood—"You'll never get dry firewood at this time of year; the only firewood you can buy is green, and if you burn it in your stove the creosote will clog your chimney and cause a fire"—and about drinking alcohol while pregnant—"Even one sip of one drink will diminish your child's intelligence and abilities." I pointed out that her mother, as she'd bragged at one point, drank a martini every night while pregnant with her.

"*Exactly,*" she said. "Who knows what I might have been? I might have been an Olympian."

So the fact that the alarmist had reported the bad kind of shark sighting meant that (a) she'd mistaken a porpoise for a shark, or (b) she had seen a shark but had no idea what kind of shark it was, and likely, given she was right about practically nothing, this shark was not a bad shark.

Still, I worried about this supposed shark sighting for the rest of the day. I loved swimming so much! Part of what I loved about swimming was that I was no longer scared while doing it, so every minute I was in the ocean was another pat on my back. Way to go! You are no longer such a huge scaredy-cat! I teach for the same reason. I used to be as scared of public speaking as I was of sharks. Every time I teach I get an endorphin high off the fact that I did not have a panic attack. I teach and swim in order to measure my improvement as a human. I am no longer terrified of quite so many things.

I considered how to stanch this renewed shark fear before it grew so large that I could no longer swim. I considered Googling *great white shark spottings recent maine*. Even if one shark had been spotted, or two, this could reassure me that the shark situation was not unusual; i.e., this new sighting was not proof of an imminent invasion I might wisely seek to evade by keeping to the land.

Also, it's not like there had *never* been great white spottings off the coast of Maine. When I was a kid I used to visit a seal who lived in Rockport Harbor. I have his biography—*A Seal Called Andre,* piquantly described in the jacket copy as "the true story of a unique human/animal relationship"—in which there are a number of pictures, including one of a young girl in 1960s houndstooth pedal pushers beside a dead great white. The caption reads, "Beauty and the beast: Carol poses uneasily with the monstrous great white shark that devoured Basil." Basil was the other seal with which the author of the book, Harry Goodridge, had a unique human/animal relationship. Harry made friends with lots of harbor seals; his semi-related hobby was harpooning great whites in order to prove the marine biologists, all of whom insisted great whites seldom swam farther north than Cape Cod, wrong. Maine was considered by these biologists no more than the "casual range" of the great white, to which Harry riposted, "I'd harpooned a dozen or more in Penobscot Bay in the course of several summers and had sighted many more. It struck me that the presence of that many man-eaters constituted more than a 'casual' population." Harry's point being that I *should* have been scared of sharks when I was a kid. His point probably also being that I should still be scared. However, no one to my knowledge has ever been attacked by a great white shark in Maine, and since Harry saw great whites in the 1960s, meaning they'd lived in these water for *decades,* these were clearly some lazy-ass sharks. I was less scared to know that there were sharks than that there weren't. The evil was among us, but it was fine, it was all fine. We were not awaiting some future species clash, the initial trials of which might involve me.

And yet I still felt tempted to Google the sharks. Maybe a human *had* been attacked by a shark in Maine recently. I was not very up on the news. I barely knew who the Republican presidential candidate was. Maybe there were so many sharks now that the biologists had revised their casual range projections. I began to feel like my friend who suspected her husband of having an affair, and who had the power to satisfy her curiosity if she just dared to read his e-mail. I just had to Google *great white shark spottings recent maine.* But what good would our sleuthing do either of us? She probably wouldn't leave her husband. I probably wouldn't stop swimming. Why bother knowing? I saw no point.

OCTOBER 8

Today I heard a terrible noise. I was in my office and I was talking to a student. She'd written a story about a semi-neurotic woman trying to buy salmon at a fish shop. We were both, this student and I, cognizant of the fact that we are somewhat like this character. We are subtextual, and sub-subtextual, and sub-sub-subtextual readers of the world.

Suddenly, in the middle of our conversation, we heard the terrible noise. From somewhere on the quad, where there is always a landscape maintenance crew performing destructive acts of beautification, a vibration jostled the air. Not just the air, the buildings. The sound it produced was of a very low frequency, and nearly inaudible. It registered in my molars.

I covered my ears until it stopped.

"Wow," I said.

"Wow," she said.

"That was crazy," I said.

"Yeah," she agreed.

"What *was* that?" I said.

"What?" she said.

"That noise," I said.

"What noise?" she said.

"Didn't you hear that noise?" I said.

"No," she said.

"You really didn't hear that noise?" I said.

She hadn't. We continued talking about her short story, but now I was distracted. How had she failed to hear that noise? At a different point in my life, I might have congratulated myself for hearing what she did not hear. I was so sensitive I might qualify for extrasensory perception status. I detected what no one else detected. But I am no longer at that point. Now when I see or hear something that no one else sees or hears, I worry that a part of me is failing. I am not extra-anything, I am less-something.

I am reminded of my less-somethingness when I cannot find pleasurable a book or TV show that everyone else finds pleasurable, even brilliant. Am I the only person who can't perceive the genius of this book or that TV show? I used to believe my failure was proof of a refined intellect; that I refused to see genius where lesser people, with lower genius standards, found gobs of genius. But now my failure to find the genius makes me worry that I'm missing something, not receiving something. What do all of these people understand that I don't?

Regardless: the noise. The student suggested that maybe I had something wrong with my inner ear. This seemed plausible. I have children who yell and who cause me to yell. Who knew what frequency contusions the invisible chambers of my ear had suffered.

I made an appointment with an ear doctor. Just the act of making the appointment reassured me: something was failing, but that something could be fixed. I should have seen a doctor when I could not understand how anyone found that multi-prize-winning novel remotely good. My inner ear, it must have been my inner ear.

Then I told my husband about the terrible noise, and how I'd made an appointment with the doctor to discover why I'd heard it and my student had not.

"Interesting," he said. "So there really was a noise?"

"What do you mean?" I said.

"The noise you heard actually existed?"

"Yes," I said. "It actually existed."

"You didn't just hear it in your head?" he said.

What noise don't you hear in your head? I wanted to ask. But his question freaked me out. I heard a noise, but had there been a *noise*? How many people have to hear a noise before it becomes a *noise*?

I promised him: there was a *noise*. It existed. I really did hear it, and my student really did not.

August 23

Today I visited antiques shops. I'd invited my daughter and her friend along as my shopping enablers. They did not fulfill their mandate. I found a poster I liked of a pregnant Girl Scout, circa 1969, smiling beside the slogan: Be prepared. She wore patent leather Mary Janes and kneesocks. She was kind of like Piero della Francesca's pregnant *Madonna*. (I just looked up *mary how old annunciation*. Internet estimates put her between twelve and sixteen years old, meaning she could have been a Girl Scout Cadette or a Girl Scout Senior.) My daughter and her friend counseled me not to buy the poster. I tried to sell them on selling me on buying it. "Why do you like it?" they asked. "Because it's so funny!" I said. They scrutinized the poster. "Why is it funny?" they asked. I didn't know why it was funny. Because teenage pregnancy is hilarious? I bought it because I didn't fully get the joke, and because I wasn't certain there was meant to be a joke at all. But I liked that the Girl Scout appears to have no idea that she's pregnant, I liked that "Be prepared" might simply refer to her stylishness and her psychotic smiling gameness, both of which, it seemed to me, were classic Girl Scout traits. And isn't being prepared to be unprepared the best form of preparedness? If you think you're ready for anything, you're probably not ready at all.

Today I read the letters exchanged between a young boy and his mother in 1930. These letters are not published. They are not public domain. These letters were in an old suitcase discovered in the corner of a rental house occupied by my friends. I had no business reading these letters, is what I'm saying. I read them anyway. I read them using the same logic I use in cemeteries, when my children climb on the tombstones or stick their fingers into the engraved dates or delight over the strange names or dismantle the spooky implications of "Lost at Sea." *These people are dead and in many cases forgotten, but now they are receiving some welcome attention.* As a dead person, I would very much appreciate a child climbing on my gravestone, so long as they were respectful and interested, and I can promise that my children are exactly these children. If they were terrible children who topple cracked gravestones and yell and cannot be respectful even to the living, I would probably, as a dead person, be frustrated by my inability to discipline them, but I'm assuming the dead have their ways of expressing outrage, especially on their home turf. I could drop a rock on a toe, or trip a small criminal with those wires that hold fake flower arrangements together. Regardless. I feel when I visit a cemetery as I might feel if I were ever to visit a retirement home. These are the forgotten people, and they have stories, and they just want someone to listen to them.

Such was my rationale when I read the letters I found in the suitcase. That I generated a rationale in the first place was because the people in these letters, though I'd met neither of them, did not qualify as complete strangers. They are the relatives of my good friend (it is through his family connection that my other friends are renting the house). The mother in the letters is my friend's great-grandmother; the son is his grandfather. The suitcase in which the letters were found was already open when I discovered it in the laundry room. The letters were already spilling out of it. They were already free of their envelopes. They were already unfolding. Still, I hesitated. I had heard about the grandfather and the great-grandmother from my friend, because he often uses his family as a medium by which to practice his considerable storytelling gifts. I thought of e-mailing him to ask his permission to read these letters that described, more or less, events he'd already told me about (in his way), but this struck me as a request he'd probably agree to without my needing to ask. What became creepy was me asking in the first place. Asking would cast suspicion over my mostly innocent curiosity.

I did not e-mail him to ask his permission. Obviously I did read the letters. They were heartrending, or maybe I was just in a mood to have my heart heaved up by letters sent to and by a boy who is dead because he would be over one hundred years old now if he were not. The boy had been sent to boarding school and was, I gathered from his mother's letters to him, miserable. His mother tried to convince him that being sent away from home was the best and most adoring thing she could do, that it would toughen him up and that in general he had to learn to be much tougher because he was not tough and, as a result, he was a bit of a disappointment. She wrote for pages exhorting him to be tougher and tougher and tougher and then she would slip into the third person and write, "Boo still loves his mummy, doesn't he?"

Later that day I took my son to the cemetery. He is in a phase where he wears no clothing. He is small enough that, in a cemetery, he might be mistaken for a marble cherub sprung to life, i.e., his nakedness seemed less disrespectful than it did a fanciful extension of the graveyard aesthetic. He stood, naked, in front of the grave of the man who had been the little boy whose letters I'd just been reading (He died at age ninety-three) and who'd once been so lonely at boarding school. I took a picture of my naked son in front of the man's grave to e-mail to his grandson, my friend. I thought he might find it touching, or funny, or I don't know what. Like the earlier e-mail asking his permission to read his family letters, this, too, I did not send.

APRIL 21

Today I walked across the Brooklyn Bridge with my daughter and her friend. They are both nearing nine but seem much older. These are my last years to be interesting to them. Knowing this, I try to be so exceedingly interesting that I might hold their attention longer than my natural expiration date allows. I told them, as we walked across the bridge, educational anecdotes about developing from a girl into a woman, featuring me as the protagonist. (This was my more utilitarian attempt at *la tendresse Américaine*.) After twenty years in this city, it seems that at nearly every Manhattan corner or monument there is an instructive girl-into-woman story I can tell. This bridge is the setting for a number of stories. I told my daughter and her friend about cross-country skiing across this bridge in a blizzard; how I was the only person, aside from a few people in cars, on this bridge. How it was so quiet, and all I could hear was the wind and the metal tips of my poles hitting the walkway under the snow. How the lesson of this story was that even when you're in your twenties, and adrenaline-crazed, and living in a loft with lots of other adrenaline-crazy striving people, there is something edifying about being cold and alone in the city version of nature.

Then I told them a story about a very stupid thing I did with my first husband. We'd just started dating; we'd been drinking gin. We decided to run home. Literally, to run. Through Tribeca and over the Brooklyn Bridge. This was not exercise; this was not "running" as in marathons. This was the kind of running people did in *The Sound of Music,* over fields and singing. We were a third of the way across the bridge—to the first stone arch—when my first husband bent down and opened a trapdoor in the middle of the wooden walkway.

It sounded so implausible—a trapdoor? In the bridge? But indeed there was a trapdoor, and for some reason it wasn't locked. It led to a rung staircase and then a spindly catwalk suspended under the bridge's roadway. Beneath this catwalk was air and then water. There was nothing to catch us if we fell. The cars drove a few feet over our heads. It was so loud above us, so quiet below. We chased each other. Back and forth, back and forth. The catwalk was metal and responded jerkily to running; it was constructed of welded rungs with a few inches of space between each one. When we ran we could see the far-down water strobing under our feet. Then, as I was being chased, i.e., my first husband was chasing me, I felt a violent vibration behind me. I turned. My first husband had run headfirst into a low-lying girder. He'd been knocked out.

I then told my daughter and her friend, because I'd

forgotten this crucial detail, that although the catwalk had a thin metal railing for your hands, by your feet there was nothing; if you were lying on the catwalk, for example, and knocked unconscious, you might tilt right off into the river.

My first husband was tilting.

But I saved him. I saved him so he could go on to be married to me and then divorced from me.

My first husband and I climbed back through the trapdoor. We ran the rest of the way across the bridge. We walked down some steps that led to a deserted underpass. Suddenly, a car pulled up. In this car was one of my first husband's best friends and his girlfriend. (An ancillary point of interest: this girlfriend would grow up to host a reality TV show that my current husband and daughter and I watch.) They gave us a ride to our apartment. That night, I lay in bed and could not sleep. I was traumatized by what might have been. *I might have lost the love of my life to a tragic and stupid accident.* He would have been the love of my life had I lost him. I did not, and he was not.

After I told this story to my daughter and her friend, I became embarrassed, not least because they liked this story, and clearly held me in higher regard because of my stupidity and daring, which is of course why I told them the story in the first place. Even once my daughter no longer found me interesting, which would be soon, she couldn't completely reject me; I'd run under bridges; I'd saved a man from death. To my face she'd scorn me, but to her friends she might proudly tell this story, because she'd heard it before she understood why I was telling it. It would be lodged in her brain before that brain could skeptically wonder, *Why on earth is she telling me this inappropriate story?*

But what really made me pathetic was that I hadn't

told the whole story. In telling only the dramatic parts, I'd failed to tell the truth; i.e., I'd failed to shape from these events an educational story that little girls getting older and eventually leaving home need to hear. The truth about the skiing story is this: I skied across the Brooklyn Bridge because I was losing the thread. I felt disconnected from the person who once trekked alone through blizzards, the person who was from Maine and didn't give a shit about parties and fame. The stone used to make the bridge's arches was quarried in Maine, and taken from a hole in the ground that had since filled up with water and in which I'd once gone swimming. Both of these stories are about my first few years of what would become two decades in a city that didn't immediately feel like home and still sometimes doesn't. It so didn't feel like home that I married a man I knew I should not because his mother lived in a house that, because of its windows and its molding and its old plaster smell, reminded me of Maine; New York so didn't feel like home that I would often walk across the bridge to lean my forehead against the stone arches and touch the ground from which I'd come. If they could persist here, these stones, and retain their shape, then so could I.

AUGUST 31

Today I was so relieved to get a migraine. For the past thirty-plus years I've gotten migraines regularly; they were part of the weather that happened within and without. I would get a migraine after a manic jag. I would get a migraine before a blizzard. Now I rarely get them. I don't want to say that I miss being in pain, but I do miss the excuse to not give a shit about all the big and small things I often care too much about and that a migraine eradicates. When I have a migraine I do not grieve the shirt that was put in the dryer by accident and its texture forever ruined; I do not feel undermined by the passive-aggressive person at my workplace; I do not blame myself for failing to be in better touch with my grandmother. My body used to have the good sense to give itself a regular break from my mind. It is no longer so sensible.

I welcomed a migraine today because it permitted me to forget that it is the end of summer and we are about to leave until basically next summer, and I feel guilty for abandoning my house. I turned out the lights and sat in the dim living room. I thought, *This is what it's like in this house for the other nine months of the year.* Lightless and empty. I tried to put myself in the house's position. I tried to feel what the house feels because this house is a people house. I worry, without people, what might become of it. When I was a teenager, my mother, who hated cats, agreed to buy a Maine coon cat because it was a people cat. It was a dog in cat form. I soon left for college, and then so did my brother, and my parents did not come home from work until late. A people cat without people proved a bad combination. Its personality changed. It opened the cupboards and pulled out the food. After months of daily solitude, it stationed itself at the top of the stairs one night and would not let my mother pass. It took angry swipes at her with a claw whenever she approached it. We realized our mistake. We are not people-cat people. We gave it to people who are.

So I worry about this house being alone for most of the year because it is a people house. We bought this house because, after we'd seen it with a snobby real estate agent (who said of it, "it is not an important address"), we'd driven by it again to see if our good hunch held. We slowed as we drove past. Every window was lit; the then-owners were having a party. The house looked like the movie cliché of a house on Thanksgiving or something, aglow with human joy and coziness. Then we almost hit a large animal. I remember it as a stag, though I've never since seen a stag, nor do I really know what a stag is. A mythically large deer-type creature, that's what I remember seeing. It appeared from the darkness on the north side of the house and leapt across the road. I took it as a sign. *We should buy this house.* (My husband remembers the stag as a moose. I didn't learn until ten years later that he differently remembered this trenchant—to me—moment in our co-history. Of the two of us, I'm the only one who believes that the sudden appearance of a large animal means we should invest in real estate.)

Despite my migraine, we went to our neighbor's house for cocktails. Our neighbors serve me margaritas in challenging times. They made me margaritas twenty hours after I'd spent twenty-seven hours in labor. This evening I applied a vise to my temples with my two hands. Every once in a while I'd free a hand to take a drink. A second couple arrived and asked if they smelled like skunk, because their dog had been sprayed that morning. The husband had driven up to the general store at five a.m. to buy de-skunking supplies—baking soda, vinegar, other household items that our store reliably carries (it also reliably carries white bread, celery, rubber gloves, and tonic). The husband said he ran into a lobsterman who, when he learned of the skunking, said, "You know what you want there, you want some of that ladies' douche." The husband recounted this with a perfect Maine accent. I was in such pain, and I was fighting the end-of-summer sadness, but

I said a small thank-you to the stag, or the moose, or the migraine, or whatever was responsible for my sitting on a stool across the street from our people house, my head in my hands, so that I could be hearing that sentence.

OCTOBER 12

Today my friends and I gossiped hard. We gossiped athletically. It was as if we'd met for a run, but we hadn't. We'd met in heavy coats and mittens to sit on a bench and talk. My friends and I, we are pixilated conversationalists. There are no lines of thought. Together we amass data points, and only later, while in bed and thinking back over the words I'd uttered and absorbed, does the day's big picture come into focus, if even then. In truth I no longer crave the day's big picture. More and more I crave the day's quick tagline. A useful takeaway like, *Buy cheap '70s East German ceramics on eBay* or *Never assume you are the love of anyone's life.*

My friends and I warmed up on real estate. Then we moved indoors and got out the knives and made the soup. We started talking about people. We talked about the man who left his wife for another woman, and had, out of pity, agreed to go on a last vacation with the wife (even though their marriage, in his opinion, because he was very much in love with the other woman, was over), and by accident while on this vacation he'd impregnated the wife while having "what is as close to platonic sex as you can possibly imagine," and still he refuses to return home to the wife, now pregnant with his child, and their preexisting kids.

We talked about the man whose wife left him for

another man (also married at the time), and how the wife was impregnated by the new man, or so everyone thought, until a paternity test revealed that what she thought was her boyfriend's child was actually her husband's.

We talked about the beautiful woman who was inexplicably marrying the man from Kansas City who wore cravats and resembled a turtle.

We talked about the woman who reconnected with her med school boyfriend over Facebook, and who, out of guilt, included her husband in their online flirtation, and who arranged for them to meet and have a three-way in Paris—though in fact this was just an excuse for her and the med school boyfriend to have husband-sanctioned sex with each other—and when the husband figured this out, she "opened the door" for his betrayal and defection, and her husband has since fallen in love with the woman's work colleague, and is probably going to leave her.

The men showed up for dinner. The men were enthusiastic gossip participants but not so useful because they couldn't remember specifics. They could only recall the haze of a scandal, and the haze is not what's important. It's the hard data that's important; it's the motivations and the causality. What makes what happen? What's connected to what? It's the equivalent of disassembling a car engine before putting it back together. Every plug and cable is important. So the men participated by saying stuff like, "What was it about that guy who had the secret second family?" and then the women would tell the story.

This man, he'd been dumped by a rich woman who later found out she was pregnant with his son but refused to get back together with him, which was fine because the man had met another woman whom he married and with whom he had two children, but he never told his wife about his biological son with this ex-girlfriend. Tr. ex-girlfriend—this was an important detail—was boundlessly wealthy and as such was never emotionally involved with anyone very deeply. On a whim, the rich ex-girlfriend decided she wanted this man back, and he returned to her, at which point his wife found out about his secret son, and she was so upset that she had him legally removed from the business they'd formed together, and so when the rich ex-girlfriend dumped the guy anew because she didn't like his parenting style—the son was "feral" and told every adult who disciplined him, "My mother is going to fire you!" and the man tried to discipline his son and so was basically fired—he had no job, and no money, and no family, and now nobody knows where he is.

Another woman talked about her sister who left her husband for an "asshole" who was famous in the theatre and thus somewhat excused for being an asshole, and who she'd been with for three years when she found his diary detailing the many affairs he'd been having with other women during the same three years he'd been with her. Another man, we were told, kept his diary on his family's home computer, where his wife read about the women he'd slept with in the darkroom she'd had built for him, because she was a successful surgeon. (At this point I tried to initiate the term "guy-ary," defined as "a diary written by a husband detailing his extramarital affairs and kept in a place where a wife could easily find it.")

A man said, "We're so horrible, talking about these people!" But he said it insincerely, and besides, we weren't saying anything mean. Thomas Mann, in *Buddenbrooks*, wrote of a marriage that everyone in town found "queer": "To get behind it even a little, to look beneath the scanty outward facts to the bottom of this relation, this seemed

ut certainly a stimulating task." We were
stimulating task! But we were also speaking
were trying to figure out the rules to a game
ing yet (or were naive enough to think we
ng yet) because we were still in love.

We had no reason to feel confident. Sitting in our midst was a man whose wife had, a year earlier, slept with his best friend. His wife had believed he'd never leave her, no matter how she misbehaved, but her sleeping with his best friend was the last straw, and he'd left her, and now she was alone, and now he had a new girlfriend and was very happy.

But we already knew his story; nobody needed to tell it again tonight. His presence was reminder enough. The day's tagline was a simple one. One of three things would happen to us: we would stay married, or we would leave, or we would be left. We are in our forties, and this is what our futures have winnowed down to, these three possibilities. The stimulating task in which we were engaged would help us figure out how to deal with this clarified future. How, as one man put it, to "best maneuver through the situation."

I don't maneuver. I distill. I distill from the many possible anxieties a primary one. I can imagine that point in time, if my husband and I stay together, and I believe we will, where our future will function like this: every night we'll go to bed wondering who won't be alive in the morning. When we kiss good night, it won't be as we kiss now in our forties. I won't be worrying whether or not I should be more passionate more regularly because if I'm not he might leave me for another woman. I'll be kissing him wondering if we'll never kiss again. I'll be wondering if this is not good night but good-bye. I can imagine, too, that this anxiety is somewhat purifying, because it is so simple, so unavoidable. You believe you can prevent your husband or wife from leaving you for another person—this is one reason we gossip in our forties. But someday we will leave or be left, and it won't be anyone's fault or anyone's choice. There is no available gossip to teach us how to avoid this fate.

MAY 5

Today I met for lunch a famous German artist, the one who violates the homes of others with her personal possessions. She arrived in New York a few days ago to install a show in a church. She was violating the house of God now.

I professed to her my adoration when, a month earlier, I'd interviewed her over Skype. She'd suggested, or maybe I'd suggested it: when she was next in town, we should have lunch.

The artist agreed to meet me at Café Sabarsky. I arrived first. I was worried we'd lose our chance at a table, so I lied to the hostess and told her the artist was in the restroom. When I called the artist to check on her whereabouts, she was still many blocks away. I confessed to the hostess, "I was mistaken about the artist's location. Would you like your table back?"

Ten minutes later, the artist arrived. Though German she smelled of certain powerfully feminine moisturizers and shampoos I associate with the French. We sat. She wondered about the size of the small Wiener Schnitzel. "But will it be small enough?" she mused. I ordered a beer. We discussed female sexiness. I mentioned my ten-year-old daughter who was, in my opinion, very sexy. She'd been sexy since birth. One of the first things I remember noticing about her body, at thirty seconds of age, were her sexy and muscular arms. (I equivocated to the artist: probably every woman thinks her baby is sexy.)

Not long after I mentioned my daughter, the artist announced that she did not often befriend people with children. The artist does not have children. She said that if a person with a child uses the child as an excuse to explain why she cannot go out with the artist—to a restaurant or a movie—the artist stops calling the person. She waits twenty years until the person's children are gone to call her again.

After lunch we walked to the church to see the show the German artist was installing. It was hard to tell where the church stopped and the art began. People were praying and crying in the pews; others were scrambling to see the artist's show, not yet open to the public. A Brazilian woman succeeded in pleading her case (she was flying home that night) and was admitted. The Brazilian and I wandered the church together while the artist asked our opinions about lighting. There was something so relaxed and easygoing about the artist. She seemed happy just having people around, even if she didn't speak or interact with us much. Maybe she made friends this way, by fast-forwarding to the point where no one needed to perform, when not every second required that someone behave like a genius worth getting to know better.

"Do you want to go to MoMA?" the artist asked me.

We took a cab to MoMA. En route we passed some police installing crowd rails along Fifth Avenue. We quickly deduced: these were preparations for a fancy ball that night. In prior years I would have spun meaning from this confluence of the German artist and me passing a red carpet event in a cab. I would have spun a message from the universe: someday I would be famous like the artist and I would be invited to a ball. When I was twenty and visiting Florence and not yet a writer, I had received such a message. I'd planned to eat at a restaurant where all the renowned Florentine writers ate (ask me to name a Florentine writer). One day of each year (I read in my guidebook) the restaurant was closed for a literary awards ceremony. The day I tried to go to the restaurant was the day it was closed for the literary awards ceremony. I couldn't have been more thrilled. The universe was telling me: I was going to be an award-winning writer!

Today I received no such message about my future.

The German artist and I arrived at MoMA. We wandered around the show of another German artist, Sigmar Polke. I owned a book by Sigmar Polke, though to be honest I wasn't sure if Sigmar Polke was a woman or a man. I study so much, I read so much, yet there seems no avoiding these moments when the basics escape me.

In MoMA it was unclear how much space the German artist wanted or did not want when looking at art, whether or not she wanted to be alone. I stayed close but tried not to hover. The German artist, unsurprisingly, knew a lot of people in the museum. She stopped to say hello to this person and that. I'd wander off and reconnect with her when she was by herself again.

"He should be dead," she said of one man with whom she'd just been speaking.

This man was also an artist. Last she'd heard, she said, he'd been terribly sick. His appearance in this gallery, she seemed to imply, nearly qualified as a resurrection. Fittingly he'd been brought back to life not in a church but in a museum. Or maybe not so fittingly. Most artists I know hate MoMA.

We stopped in front of a painting of socks. I proclaimed Polke to have a good sense of humor.

"That man," she said of the man who should be dead, "he told me that, in person, Polke wasn't funny." With the artist I could not tell: was she delivering a plain piece of information, or was she schooling me?

We hurried through the rest of the show because MoMA was closing. The guards funneled us through a hallway where we re-encountered the man who should be dead.

I asked the man who should be dead about Polke's supposed lack of funniness. I wondered if maybe he wasn't funny in the manner of certain Germans. As Primo Levi said of Germans, "They love order, systems, bureaucracy; even more, although rough and irascible blockheads, they cherish an infantile delight in glittering, many-colored objects."

The man who should be dead conceded—maybe, in that sense, Polke might be considered funny. He knew a lot of famous people, this man, because his family had run a hotel in the Alps; Picasso had stayed there, too.

The German artist asked, Was Picasso funny?

No, said the man, Picasso was a ladies' man. He was not funny.

We mused for a while on the topic of "Were They Funny?" Shakespeare, was he funny in person? Was Manet? Was Rilke? All of these dead people, were they funny or not? You couldn't tell by their work what it would have been like to hang out with them in person. I couldn't tell by the German artist's work what it would be like to hang out with her in person. It was different than I'd expected for sure, and all day long I'd been managing the shortfall.

After a stop in the MoMA design s⁺
the German artist asked to see a Scan
I liked, and which she clearly didn't, we ex⸜
street. On the corner of Fifty-third and Sixth, ⸜
ways. Our good-bye was unceremonious, as thoug⸜
see each other in three days or never again. At this sᴀ
intersection is a Hilton Hotel where, when I was twenty-
three, I used to cash the paychecks I received from my
temp job as a secretary. This corner signifies a time when
I was young and I was broke and I was using a hotel as a
bank, and yet I felt certain that my line was true. Now I no
longer have strong gut feelings about rightness or wrongness. I lack quick conviction. I can no longer process the
messages the universe is sending me, if it is sending me
messages at all. I don't even know whether or not today I
made a friend.

AUGUST 30

Today we climbed Blue Hill. Tonight we went to the
Blue Hill Fair. The Blue Hill Fair is the fair E. B. White
writes about in *Charlotte's Web*. A blue moon rose over the
animal barns. I've been told more than once what it means
for a moon to be blue. A friend told me a moon is blue
when it is the second full moon in less than a month. An
excess of brightness is a blueness. All day I was blue. The
weather is too beautiful. The summer was too beautiful. In
two days we return to New York where, when the weather
is beautiful, I become frustrated. What to do with this
weather in the city? There is no good use for it.

At the top of the Ferris wheel you can see the ocean

as though from a plane that is flying away from it. Usually my daughter and I ride in the same carriage, and we say good-bye to the ocean together. But now my daughter is eight. She wants to ride the Ferris wheel with her friends. My husband lobbied for us to ride as a family. I fought for her to be apart. I said, "She wants to ride with her friends."

We rode the Ferris wheel separately. I didn't say to her, "Be sure to say good-bye to the ocean!" I didn't need a cohort. I could say good-bye to the ocean alone, and probably that would be for the best. Come the end of August, I grow pathetic. In the air I experienced the accumulation of time traumas as we spin around and around. I am twelve years old at the top of that Ferris wheel and I am equally ninety.

A few cars behind me, my daughter laughed and feigned terror with her friends. I am the only ridiculous person left in my family now, I realized. I am the only one crying on a carnival ride.

We disembarked. We stood in the dust and contemplated our next snack. My daughter walked with me to the cotton candy. "Did you say good-bye to the ocean?" she asked. I tried not to hug her. I told her that I did say good-bye to it. She told me she did too. I was so thrilled that she was laughing with her friends while remaining true to her blueness. We are bright and we are blue, my daughter and I. We are excessive and we hide it. We are too often full.

JUNE 8

Today I flew home from Italy after living for a month with a ghost. This Italian ghost and I had a not-so-great relationship, though arguably I got along with her better than did the others at the art colony. One man, the father of four children who famously, and to the presumed irritation of his wife, never had insomnia, the ghost woke up every night at four a.m. A woman fell down a flight of stone stairs and landed on her face. Another woman was beset by a monthlong headache. Another had a nightmare in which the ghost sat on the edge of her bed and unfolded a letter containing bad news about her kids. Another was sent to the hospital for a week with a hemorrhage (she'd been trying for years to have a baby).

If pressed to say a little bit about this ghost and her issues, I'd wager she had a problem with children. Maybe her objections were aesthetic, i.e., maybe she felt toward them as the German artist did—she simply disliked them and found boring people who had them.

Or maybe (given she was a ghost, clearly an unhappy one) her children had died before she did and she still, understandably, hundreds of years later, wasn't over it. I honestly couldn't tell if she was malicious or just incapable of keeping her emotions to herself. Like a few alive people I know, she unwittingly contaminated everyone who entered her radius. Regardless of her motives, the energy she generated and dispersed made me, for the month I was living in proximity to her, afraid for my children. Every moment I spent in this castle, I did not consciously believe but on some less conscious level totally believed, would increase the likelihood that they would die while I was gone.

A few weeks into my stay, I woke up in the middle of the night (I did not check the time) to see the ghost—a woman, black and opaque and wearing a long dress—floating horizontal above me, as if the poor thing were wondering what it might be like to lie down and go to sleep. She looked at me. I looked at her. I should have been scared, I guess, but instead I was calm. She and I shared a silent moment of interspecies respect. We wordlessly agreed, as I have agreed with bears I've come upon in the woods, not to mess with each other. Then she disappeared.

After our encounter I was no longer so worried about my children. But I remained (though living in the hills of Italy and being fed two incredible Italian meals a day with unlimited access to a very fine Italian espresso machine) exhausted. I suffered from a low-grade, unspecified malaise. Was it emotional? Was it physical? The symptoms were impossible to sort. They felt barometric in nature. My mind/body had become a gadget obliged to record the heaviness of the atmosphere. I felt put-upon, overtaxed. I did not hemorrhage like the other woman, but my female problem, the muscle down there, dormant for two years, tightened up. I stopped reading books. My personality, as it had when I'd last had that pain, went into hiding. But it wasn't just the pain that oppressed me. Emotionally, I was a muffled version of myself. I was a jam jar inside an aquarium. Between me and the world were many thick panes of glass.

Finally, it was time to leave. I rode a van to the nearest town. I boarded a train. My friend from London, who'd joined me for my last night at the castle, scrolled through the photos she'd taken. I'd shown her the bedroom where the woman had dreamt of the ghost reading the letter containing bad news about her children. In this place, laughingly (because neither of us wanted to admit that we believed in the ghost), my London friend had snapped a photo of me. On the train we looked at this photo and could not believe what we saw. My body was in focus and so was the room. But my head, the right side of it, was a pixilated mess. It looked as though a snake were exploding out of my skull.

My London friend and I freaked out. We freaked out all the way to Rome. We wondered if I were possessed. Among other things, this presented certain legal problems. Would I have to declare my "possession" on my customs form? I'd considered smuggling truffles back in my suitcase, but then I'd heard the fine could be $10,000 for transporting meat or produce into the United States. Did a ghost count as a vegetable or meat? What kind of fee would my government exact from me for running over its borders a ghost?

I soon stopped worrying. In Rome my personality reengaged with a vengeance, suggesting the ghost had chosen not to emigrate. I endorphin-surfed like a person who'd escaped death, because I had. I'd been hanging out with a really blue dead lady who'd maybe lost her children, and over the long term, what a drag that had been. Now I was back among the living. I felt synaptically dangerous; after all of these weeks with my hubs blunted, I was extra-sensitive, like all I needed to do was desire a connection and it would happen. I chatted with our waiter at dinner and learned that he and I shared a birthday. I'd planned, while in Rome, to find the apartment of a dead French actress I wanted to write a book about, but now it seemed certain that she would find me. Every vintage store I entered, I expected to find photos of her or old movie posters with her on them or old clothing with her name tag sewed into the laundry. (This didn't happen.) I thought of the landscape architect I'd met in Rome a few months earlier—she was literally the only person I knew in the city—and felt confident, even amidst the millions of summer tourists, that we would cross paths. We didn't, but the next day on the airplane back to New York, I sat in front of a chatty American man. His seatmate was also American and chatty. I listened to them get to know each other. He mentioned, at one point, the landscape architect. He'd just visited her studio in Rome; he said, kind of bitchily, "She's from a competing firm" (he was also a landscape architect) and that her most recent project was "basically just maps on a wall." Then his seatmate, who turned out to be a novelist, told him about studying with a woman I'd just been living with for the past month in the castle.

If I'd failed to get along with the ghost, I'd really failed to get along with this woman. I have no idea why. She was brilliant and lovely but something between us grated. We never had our bear-in-the-woods moment. We never silently agreed to tolerate each other. In her erudite presence I talked only about reality TV and trashy novels and the Amanda Knox case. Whenever we spoke about the most benign topic—the pleasure of small rooms, for example—it seemed that we were, in fact, engaging in a not-so-veiled battle. Even though I am a professionally certified conflict avoider, with her I was unable not to take the dangled bait (and unable to see her plain conversation as anything *but* bait). I left our encounters mystified. I was willing to accept that maybe I just rubbed her the wrong way, and she me. Later I would write to this woman, feeling bad about how I'd behaved toward her at the castle. I apologized for being so sensitive and demented, and blamed it on the crazy semester I'd had, the deadlines and the intense barometric pressure of my regular life. She wrote back an incredibly gracious note and confessed to having had a similar experience a few years earlier. "The exhaustion made me very vulnerable to people around me, who, I'm sure, meant no harm, but everywhere I saw insults and infamy!"

Maybe this was also true of the Italian ghost. She

meant me no harm. Possibly she didn't even exist. I'd mistaken my exhaustion for a long-dead woman who'd lost her children. To be melancholy is to be self-haunted, and among the many reasons this is an unsatisfactory explanation for living inside a jam jar inside an aquarium, foremost among them is that there are no good stories to tell of your bleak time in a beautiful place, and no specter to blame for the fact that happiness, though it should have been inescapable, evaded you.

AUGUST 16

Today I browsed for skirt suits online. During the summer this qualifies as an unusual event, sort of like not cracking a beer at 3:55 p.m. My studio is located just beyond the winds of our house's Wi-Fi signal. The occasional gust will blacken my signal delta, and my e-mail will ping into my in-box, but this is rare, an accident of weather. Even at their strongest the signal's bands are adverse to multitasking. If someone is sending an e-mail, another someone cannot shop for wool jumpers on eBay. A week after arriving, I come to understand the Internet as I understand my well water. You cannot bathe and do laundry. You cannot stream and shop. Resources get taxed beyond the limits of recovery. By sundown, the pumps are sucking air.

Each June, when we arrive in the Internet-challenged wilderness, I adjust to my new deprivation pretty seamlessly, much as I adjust to showering once every five days. The first week in my studio I was miffed that I couldn't search for the nautical flag alphabet while writing a piece that had nothing to do with nautical flags. I almost needed to know so badly that I unplugged my computer and walked it around to the north side of the porch, and crouched under the Bee Tree (a tree filled with so many bees that it hums like a cavity drill), and Googled *nautical flags*. I struggled with my desire. *How badly did I need to know this?* Not that badly, I decided. Within a few minutes, I'd lost the urgency. I remain curious about nautical flags—like, right now, I'm curious again—but it's been seven weeks since it first occurred to me to be curious, and here I am, still not knowing.

This makes me sad. It worries me. I want to want to know things (or at least those things that don't involve shark sightings in Maine). I want to want the urgency. I am always wanting urgency. The best part of being pregnant is how urgent your desires become. You need to eat *right now.* Not thirty seconds from right now. Thirty seconds from now will not do. My husband didn't immediately understand this. Once I picked a stupid fight with him while I was trying to feed myself. He was talking to me and wanting me to talk back (really! He expected me to talk to him!) while I was trying to push a knife through a loaf of locally crafted spelt bread. My thirty seconds expired. I pitched the spelt loaf at him. I hit his hand. Spelt loaves in these parts are no joke. They weigh as much as cement blocks. I drew blood. I was unapologetic. *You do not mess with my need.* I am usually so flexible. I am usually so quick to sublimate my desires. Here was a desire my mind could not override. Politeness and conflict avoidance were no longer compelling end goals. I found this fascinating and full of future potential (except that my husband threatened, after I threw the bread at him, to divorce me). My future identity, I momentarily thought, might operate on an entirely different premise. Not *How can*

I be selflessly of service to you, the people of the world? but
Fuck you all, this is what I need.

Internet curiosity is an area of my life where my needs
can always come first. These needs often come at the
expense of other needs (the need to do my work), but I can,
and I do, become more and more impetuous and insane as
a form of luxurious desire fulfillment. I rewatched *Fatal
Attraction* and thought *I must search for Anne Klein '80s
wool overcoats.* This type of search usually nets me a random object—a pair of vintage silver knife rests shaped like
foxes—regardless, my intense need to search and find,
even if I locate something I didn't know I was looking for,
this is a satisfaction in and of itself. This is proof that I am
giving myself what I need, when I need it. This is proof
that I experience need in the first place.

When I have been off the Internet for a while, however,
I forget how to need. I forget how to be urgently curious.
Today I took my computer to a friend's house so I could
work while the kids swam. The wireless at this house is
abundant. I felt it on my skin, in my hair. I realized I could
go online and my bandwidth consumption wouldn't even
register. Theirs was a Korean bathhouse of bandwidth.
I opened my browser. And then I didn't know where to
go. I didn't have a hankering for anything. I thought maybe
I might replace some of my grandmother's Buttercup
Spode dinner plates, one of which is unfixably cracked,
but my heart wasn't in the hunt. What about gossip? What
about celebrities, what about politics? I skidded through
the usual websites, but my clicking was obligatory.

I recalled being a kid and my mom taking me to a
plant nursery called Skillins. I hated Skillins. As a child I
was gifted at finding objects to desire. To take me to basically any store was to court my begging for items I had no

business wanting. It was desire for the sake of desire. The plant nursery, however, confounded my meta-desire mechanism. I tried and I tried, but I could never find a single thing to desire at Skillins, not even in the room with the ceramic frog planters. I didn't want anything, and because I didn't want anything, Skillins made me anxious. In Skillins I experienced what it was to desperately want to want something, and to find nothing to want. Even as a kid, this struck me as the worst possible way to feel. I sometimes think this is why I became a writer. Here was a way to regularly exercise my desire. I could desire to do this thing that no one does perfectly, and by doing it and doing it I could learn how to desire more, and better. Here was an activity that would always leave me wanting. When I want something—that to me is not youth exactly, but the opposite of death. That to me is a way to always feel like I am nowhere near the end.

JULY 4

Today we were in the Fourth of July parade again. Probably we wouldn't have gotten our asses in gear were it not for the vengeful motivator of last year's loss. Or rather our *Second Place Tie* distinction that was, yes, so much more insulting than a total failure to be recognized. From the moment we tied for second place—literally minutes after we were bestowed with this dodgy honor, and handed a twenty-dollar bill—we'd enlisted the children in a small-fry smear campaign against the judge. I taught them about village politics and corruption; I taught them how to read between the lines of a local Xeroxed newspaper reported and written by a single home-schooled eleven-year-old boy, in which it was stated that, "the crowd cheered most enthusiastically for the Dolphin Rescue float, involving children in doctor coats rescuing a sick dolphin. First place was awarded to the Farmers Market float." Could they *hear* the unspoken allegations of corruption?

The kids dutifully took up the cause. Their whispered accusations apparently made it back to the judge, who (because the job is so politically thorny) tried not to be the judge this year, but no one else would take his place. Again on the morning of the Fourth, riding a mountain bike and wearing an American flag button-down shirt, he corralled the Model Ts and fire trucks and motley acts into line by the Odd Fellows Hall.

Our float this year was Maine-themed, involving tourists and black flies. We got a standing ovation by the general store (or the standing ovation equivalent of already-standing people). After us came another float. A bunch of lobsters in bathing suits boiled tourists in big pots while reading *Cooks Illustrated*. My friend said, "Shit, that's really good." We knew we'd never beat this float, but we didn't really care. They deserved the win. We wanted the deserving to win! That was the important takeaway for the kids. *Let the deserving win even if those people, this year, are not us.*

But the deserving didn't win. We won. We beat the better float. Which was confusing at first, because it was explained to us, when we worried to a stranger about the goodness of the really good float, that we weren't a float, we were a "walking act," and so we would be judged in a different category.

Then we won first prize in the float category.

A bit of on-the-spot research revealed—the judge gave

the "walking act" first prize to the color guard, a crew of octogenarians in uniform, because one of the color guard members suffered a small cardiac event while waiting for the parade to start. When you cheat death, was the judge's thinking, you deserve a prize.

I had no issues with this.

But the poor judge, still bruised by the bad chatter we'd initiated via the kids over the past year, and not wanting to endure another winter of child-fueled rumors about his fraudulence, decided to reclassify us as a float so that we could win, and so that we would leave him the fuck alone. And so we won. And so the other float, the really much better float, didn't win.

The children, meanwhile, were jubilant; they felt the cosmos have been righted. I don't know how to explain that sometimes, in the righting of things, there are occasionally more wrongings. Last year I was all about lessons. This year, I'm all about silence. I don't even know what the lesson is this year. That unfairness is actually fairness in disguise, or fairness is unfairness in disguise? That the squeaky wheel gets the grease? None of this is news to me. But I want these lessons, for a little bit longer, to remain news to them.

MAY 16

Today I examined the Rolodex I found at JFK. I flipped it around and around. The photos tumble over themselves like the individual letters and numbers of train departure signs at Penn Station. Blink, blink, blink. The Rolodex is a clock that runs forward and backward. There's an order but there's no predetermined point of entry. I can enter at the car accident or the marriage of the daughter or the party in Palm Beach or the marriage of the parents or the club fire or the motel pool or John as a baby or John as an adult or John as a hippie driving to California. I can enter at the midpoint and work my way back around. The Rolodex resets at whatever point I decide—this is where it all begins.

I might start reading books this way.

As of yet I have not Googled this Rolodex family. I know their last name. If my last name were more WASPy it might sound like theirs. Maybe they removed their *its* in the night. Maybe they are Turkish apples and related to me. I haven't Googled them because I'm enjoying what I don't know as my means of knowing them. I'm trying not to miss the photos that slipped out of the Rolodex in the trash can, meaning there exist a few captions (on the white paper backgrounds) with no photo to accompany. What image belongs to "Four Generations of Men" or "Front of Inkpot, Apaquogue Rd"? What image belongs to "Home from Belgrade after Op. in June"? I can see the shape of the image—the browned outline of the square it once occupied—but inside the frame it is blank. Maybe I will meditate upon that space, as I am meant to meditate upon the face of the *Madonna del Parto* should I wish to change my outcome.

(By the way, I am certain it was John who threw away the Rolodex. John was the sibling who took the Rolodex to the airport and tossed it in the rubbish bin. John, goateed and wearing a poncho on the Pacific Coast Highway. John, a baby in a snowsuit, petting a lamb.)

I am missing my grandmother right now. The family in the Rolodex spent winters in the same small Florida town as my grandmother, and during the same decades. Since my grandmother knew everyone, I am certain she would have known these Rolodex people. She suffered from accuracy. If she pronounced a person "dreadful," you could bet they were, and in ways invisible to most eyes.

I am also missing a person I know only from a book. The book has ended. I finished it. Based on this new way of reading, I thought perhaps I could rescue the book, a diary, and its author, from finitude. The diary was written during World War II by a Russian émigré named Maria "Missie" Vassiltchikov. Missie was such a sensible person; she reminded me of my grandmother. She persevered with normal life even when nothing was normal. She remained clear-eyed; she spoke the plain truth. ("I saw that the lorry was loaded with loosely tied sacks. From the one nearest to me a woman's legs protruded. They still had their shoes on but, I noticed, one heel was missing.")

Missie rationed her food and I rationed her. I read one diary entry a day so that Missie and I could hang out for longer. When the diary was over, I was so sad to say good-bye to her. She'd been my compatriot and tour guide throughout the four months I lived in Berlin. But I, too, was leaving. I was returning home. Missie's diary ended in the manner of a Victorian novel.

MONDAY, 17 SEPTEMBER 1945

Drove back to Johannisberg via Bad Schwalbach through the beautiful forests of the Taunus. The silence is total there, the sense of quiet and peace pervasive. . . .

Here my diary ends.

(About this time, I met my future husband, Peter Harnden.)

During our last days in Berlin, I'd look up at twilight and see jet trails. Tons and tons of jet trails. They were sky paths pointing to elsewhere. I always notice jet trails when I am about to leave a place. My imminent departure is marked for me overhead. I see jet trails toward the end of each summer when we're soon to leave Maine; I saw jet trails at the end of my first marriage. Once I saw clouds that looked like jet trails. I'd been in Boston attending a therapy session with my best friend (this was before she switched to the guru). She was trying to forgive me and I was trying to forgive her. My friend told the therapist that I was cheating on my first husband, and the therapist, knowing my less-than-happy marital situation, replied, *Good for you.* Her approval made me feel so much worse. It was not good for me to lie every day. I was stressed; I'd surprised myself by turning out to be a different person than I'd thought I was. It was measurably not good for me to be having an affair. But apparently she knew something I did not. I left the therapy session and got into my car to drive an hour south to cheat on my first husband with my future husband. Through the windshield I noticed the jet trail clouds leading me south. I had no idea at the time that I would one day marry this man. But I do remember thinking, *I am driving home.*

JANUARY 17

Today I went to the Grand Central Oyster Bar at midday. I was feeling lost and this bar is like a church. The ceiling is a series of arched brick vaults; at the entrance to the bar is a whispering gallery like the one in St. Paul's cathedral in London (or so I've read; I have never been). I've spent many winter days standing in front of this entrance when it is too cold to be outside but you must go somewhere or lose your mind. Because we can get to this underground church by barely touching the outside air, i.e., we can practically take our elevator to the subway beneath our building that, with one change, leads us here, this is where we come. Often on a January afternoon you will find me whispering into one stone corner while my children push their heads into the opposite stone corner and whisper back. We never have much to say to one another except *Hello* and *Can you hear me?* But this is mostly what is whispered in churches, too.

No children accompanied me today. They were in school; it was lunchtime for them. It was whatever time for me. I sat at the bar and ordered a drink and thought that this bar in fact less resembled a church than it did a crypt. I eavesdropped on my neighbors, a pair of businessmen. The one with the British accent said, "It's brilliant how they've put those monitors in the subway that tell you when the next train will arrive," to which the one with the American accent replied, "What does it matter? The train comes when it comes."

After a drink I felt much better. I walked down Park Avenue and decided that I was on a spiritual quest. Since I'd failed to find a guru to follow, maybe I needed a god. I entered a church, an actual church, but I couldn't seem to get past the gift shop. I considered buying an academic book on spirituality, then I considered buying a pop culture book on spirituality, then I noticed, across the street from the gift shop a restaurant called Le Relais de Venise. I'd never seen this restaurant before, though I've lived twenty years in this city. Just the sight of this restaurant made me afraid. It took me back to that semester in France, which was also my first time out of the country. I'd been dreaming, as I've said, of going to France for years, in fact I'd pestered my parents (neither of whom had been to Europe) so regularly that my mother, when she put me on the plane, said, with pride and sadness, "I always thought I'd get to Europe before you did." She didn't, which was why I felt so terribly that I'd had no fun. I'd found Paris typified by these Le Relais de Venise–type brasseries, the lamps polished to a cornea-stabbing sheen and the red pleather upholstery and the wryly indifferent vibe, like maybe Sartre was the manager. I remember drinking vanilla tea in these brasseries and everything stunk of old tobacco smoke and there was never a sun in the sky, only a horizon-wide tarp that lifted slightly to allow the light in at noon and then lowered again at three p.m., returning the city to gloom. This wasn't happening now—until suddenly, again, it was. The Relais de Venise, this catalyst of remembered Parisian despair, started to infect New York. I imagined Lexington Avenue as a street in Paris, and this formerly familiar point of geography unpinned itself from the familiar and suddenly I was standing in the middle of a strange city, with no idea what came after this street, where it led, and how it connected to the bridge that connected to the highway that connected to the street where I'd grown up. How much of my daily life in New York, even now, is made possible by the fact that I have, in my head, a clear map to take me back?

And yet. An innocence is lost when the path becomes too clear. I still remember the first time I ever came to New York. I'd wanted so long to escape from Maine and finally, for the length of an April vacation, I did. I rode into town on a Greyhound bus, alone. I was eleven. The bus pierced the outmost rim of the city, it seemed, an hour before we reached Port Authority. By the time we unloaded at the gate, I felt I'd been wound downward into the gears of a sooty clock. I would never find my way out. I felt spooked and happy at the thought of being so lost. Now I am never lost in New York. Whatever mastery I feel is instantly undone by the suspicion that I have ruined my capacity for awe.

Speaking of awe. A few days ago—I am spinning time now (it is ten months later than "today")—I was in Rome with my family for the children's school vacation. I had not been to Rome in twenty-five and a half years. The last and only time I'd been to Rome had been in the spring of 1988, after my semester in France. I'd been reunited with the boyfriend whom I'd imagined dying every night before I fell asleep. It was spring, and we'd lain on a grassy hill near the Piazza del Popolo, and watched dogs chasing one another, and we felt the thrilling expansiveness, or at least I did, of our futures.

This was my expansive future. I was in it. My boyfriend was not. My children by a different man, though soaked and cold, were uncomplaining as we walked past this same grassy hill. Our family, though we ought to have been cursing the wet skies, was happy. I should have felt mastery over the weather and also the many fates and also over myself, but instead I felt nothing. I experienced, as I passed that same slope, not a single trace of that girl. She was no longer—because it was cold and wet and almost three decades later—lying in the grass. I wanted to show myself and say to her, "This will be you someday!" She might have been relieved to know—it all worked out. But we could not connect. It felt like losing a child. Not to death but to adulthood. I suppose this is more or less what happened to her. She lost herself to me.

Speaking of lost. I seem to have lost "today." Now it is six months earlier than it was when I started this entry. I am in Maine, and it is a year since I began this book, and I am trying to finish it. I have just spent the weekend with my parents. I am convinced that it is impossible to temporarily visit people with whom you used to permanently live. We cannot tap back into the old ease of cohabitation. We try and we try, and I don't want to call these attempts futile, because for every million misses there exists a single success. I had a success five days ago. I rowed to an island with my father and my son. My son ignored us—he set mussel shells afloat and then sunk them with a raining hellfire of pebbles. My father and I, meanwhile, admired the rocks balanced atop other rocks. In Maine, on islands, rock manipulation is a form of tagging. *We were here.* The rock manipulation feats of our predecessors were daunting, almost spooky. They were supernatural acts of object levitation. A tall, thin rock balanced on its narrowest point, like a saltshaker on a pile of salt. I thought we could never practice this variety of beach sorcery, but we tried and we did. We were either extremely skilled or what we were attempting was not, despite appearances, very hard. Regardless, the activity consumed us. My father and I, we walked along the shoreline and searched for rocks. We tried to find the right combination of hollow here and jag there. Though we'd never before performed such precarious and optically illusory balancing acts, the activity felt familiar to us both. I had spent many summer days as a kid trying to lose myself to fun on islands. My father had spent many summer days—and winter days, and fall and spring days—trying to lose himself to fun with me. We were at the mall. We were spinning tops. We were drilling downward. The disappearance of the invisible but present object—time—is how we fall back into love with people we never, according to language at least, stopped loving. E. B. White once wrote, "The whole problem is to establish communication with one's self." Sometimes the self I return to loving belongs to me.

But to return to "today." The today when I was in Manhattan. I walked back to the church gift shop. I almost bought the academic book on spirituality, but then I realized I would never read it, and that I would feel bad both for wasting money and for failing to pursue what others pursue so passionately and with such discipline. I stood on the subway platform and wondered, when would I become a regularly, rather than erratically, spiritual person? Probably never. One cannot orchestrate an aperture. One cannot plan a feeling. One can plan for other things, however. One can plan for trains.

The best I could manage, on this day, was to plan to plan for the unplannable. I had to have faith that someday I'd be doing rock tricks on beaches with my father and my son. I did not know at that time that I'd be doing this in exactly 166 days. Such math was not available to me on that platform and likely never will be available, but who can say anymore what we'll someday easily know. Instead of reading the spirituality book I didn't buy, I watched the countdown on the monitor. Like the British guy in the Oyster Bar, I found this improvement brilliant. I had no uncertainties about time this time. I knew exactly when my train was coming.

THE USES OF ENCHANTMENT

One autumn day in 1985, sixteen-year-old Mary Veal vanishes from her Massachusetts prep school. A few weeks
later she reappears unharmed and with little memory of
what happened to her—or at least little that she is willing to
share. Was Mary abducted, or did she fake her disappearance? This question haunts Mary's family, her psychologist,
even Mary herself. Weaving together three narratives, *The
Uses of Enchantment* conjures a spell in which the halluci-
natory power of a young woman's sexuality, and her desire
to wield it, has devastating consequences for all involved.

Fiction

THE VANISHERS

Julia Severn is a talented student at an elite institute for psychics. When Julia's mentor grows jealous of her protégée's
talents, she subjects Julia to the painful humiliation of reliv-
ing her mother's suicide. But Julia's gifts, though a threat to
her teacher, prove an asset to others. Soon she's recruited to
track down a missing person who might have a connection
to her mother. As Julia sifts through ghosts and astral clues,
everything she thought she knew about her mother is called
into question, and she discovers that her ability to know the
minds of others—including her own—goes far deeper than
she ever imagined.

Fiction